THE FOUNDATIONS OF CITIZENSHIP

THE FOUNDATIONS OF CITIZENSHIP

DAWN OLIVER AND DEREK HEATER

 HARVESTER
WHEATSHEAF

New York   London   Toronto   Sydney   Tokyo   Singapore

First published 1994 by
Harvester Wheatsheaf
Campus 400, Maylands Avenue
Hemel Hempstead
Hertfordshire, HP2 7EZ
A division of
Simon & Schuster International Group

Typeset in 10/12 pt Ehrhardt
by Columns Design & Production Services Ltd, Reading

Printed and bound in Great Britain by
Biddles Ltd, Guildford and King's Lynn

British Library Cataloguing in Publication Data

A catalogue record for this book is available from the British Library

ISBN 0-7450-1421-6 (pbk)

---

1 2 3 4 5 98 97 96 95 94

For
THE CITIZENSHIP FOUNDATION

CONTENTS

List of cases   xi
Preface   xiii
Introduction   1

1 **Historical Outline**   10
The classical tradition – The Liberal tradition – Social
citizenship – National identity – Multiple citizenship –
Education for citizenship

2 **The Contemporary Debate**   31
The search for a modern meaning – Marshall and his
commentators – Ideological arguments – Feminists
and minority groups – Demands, proposals and
policies in Britain

3 **States and Their Citizens**   52
International law and citizenship – Acquisition of
British nationality – Citizenship and subjecthood in the
United Kingdom – Subjects, sovereigns and the rule
of law – Emancipation, autonomy and citizenship –
From emancipation to citizenship?

4 **Civil and Political Rights and Duties**   70
The rights of citizens: first generation rights – People
excluded from full citizenship rights – Rights in the

United Kingdom – Free speech in the United
Kingdom – The right to vote – Civic duties – The rule
of law and the duties of the state to its citizens –
Conclusions

5 **Social, Economic and Environmental Rights**   92
The nature of second and third generation rights –
Rationales for social and economic rights – Legal
provisions for social and economic rights – The 'right'
to health services: a case study – Empowerment and
citizenship – Choice in education: the Cleveland
School case – Social and economic rights and the
Citizen's Charter – Environmental rights –
Conclusions

6 **'Civic Virtue' and 'Active Citizenship'**   114
The good citizen – Republican civic virtue – Liberal
virtue – Active citizenship – Comparisons and
problems

7 **The European Dimensions of Citizenship**   133
Civil and political rights and European citizenship –
Citizenship and the European Community – The
European Community, citizenship and the nation-state
– Whither Community citizenship? – Conclusions

8 **Citizenship in Schools**   147
Background – Should citizenship be taught at all? –
Schools and syllabuses – Before the National
Curriculum – The National Curriculum

9 **Improving the Legal Foundations of Citizenship**   170
Subjects and sovereignty – The monarchy and the
Christian religion – Citizens as rights-bearing
individuals? – How could the legal foundations of
citizenship be strengthened? – The entrenchment of
civil and political rights – The protection of social and
economic rights – Environmental rights – Conclusions

10 Current Perspectives **195**
The problem of diverse views – Multiple citizenship
– World citizenship – Some models

References 213
Index 217

LIST OF CASES

Attorney-General v. *Guardian Newspapers (No. 2)* [1990]
1 AC 109   80
Beresford-Hope v. *Lady Sandhurst* (1889) 23 QB 79   73
Bolam v. *Friern Barnet Hospital Management Committee*
[1957] 1 WLR 582   103
Case of Prohibitions (1607) 12 Co. Rep. 63   61
Chorlton v. *Lings* (1868–9) 4 LRCP 374   72
DPP v. *Joyce* [1946] AC 347   58
Ensign Tankers v. *Stokes* [1992] 1 AC 655   87
Entick v. *Carrington*, (1765) 19 St Tr 1030   61, 62, 71, 75
Furniss v. *Dawson* [1984] AC 474   86, 87, 89
Gaskin v. *United Kingdom* [1989] EHRR 36   136
Gillick v. *West Norfolk Area Health Authority and the
Department of Health and Social Security* [1986] AC 112   64, 65
Income Tax Special Purposes Commissioners v. *Pemsel*
[1891] AC 531   97
IRC v. *Duke of Westminster* [1936] AC 1   85
Re J (A minor)(Medical treatment) The Times, 12 June
1992, CA   103
Kenlin v. *Gardiner* [1967] 2 QB 510   82
Malone v. *United Kingdom* [1985] 7 EHRR 14, ECHR   135–6
Marbury v. *Madison* (1803) 1 Cranch 103 (US)   185
R. v. *Cleveland County Council, ex parte Commission for
Racial Equality The Times*, 28 October 1991   106–9

R. v. *Ethical Committee of St. Mary's Hospital*
(Manchester), ex parte H [1988] FLR 512   103
Reg. v. *R.* [1991] 3 WLR 767   64
R. v. *Secretary of State, ex parte Rose Theatre Trust* [1990]
1 All ER 754   178
Rice v. *Connolly* [1966] 2 QB 414   83
In re S (Adult: refusal of treatment) [1992] 3 WLR 806   68
In re T (Adult: refusal of treatment) [1992] 3 WLR 782   68
Van Gend en Loos v. *Nederlandse Administratie der*
Belastingen [1963] ECR 1   145
In re Walker's Application The Times, 21 November 1987   102
In re W (A minor)(Medical treatment: court's jurisdiction)
[1992] 3 WLR 758   67, 68
Woolwich Equitable Building Society v. *Inland Revenue*
Commissioners [1992] 3 WLR 366, HL   88–9

PREFACE

We have written this book for those who are interested in citizenship, whether they be university undergraduates, sixth formers or the generally interested citizen. In writing it we have brought together material and ideas from a range of academic disciplines: philosophy, political science, history and law. As teachers, we are conscious of the importance of citizenship, not only as a matter of practice in the community, of individual legal rights and duties, and of state duties and responsibilities, but also as something that needs to be taught and experienced in schools and universities.

This is an important point: citizenship has to be experienced. True, effective citizens need knowledge about how the system works and what their rights and duties are. Merely 'drumming in' to pupils and others their rights and responsibilities and moral duties will not transform them into citizens. This is only possible if people have the opportunity to participate in the decisions taken within the organizations with which they are involved at public and private levels. They thus acquire political and social skills, and an understanding of political and social processes and the responsibilities that are involved in them.

We consider citizenship to be an important subject within each of our disciplines. We trust that this book will serve to provide material and ideas, and to encourage discussion of issues among students of philosophy, politics, history and law, as well as among the general public.

Dawn Oliver
Derek Heater
September 1993

INTRODUCTION

In the last decade or so a vigorous debate has arisen about the constitution of the United Kingdom. The Liberal Democrats have been advocating the adoption of a Bill of Rights and proportional representation. Other pressure groups – Charter 88, Liberty (the National Council for Civil Liberties), the Institute for Public Policy Research – have advocated Bills of Rights and other reforms to the system of government that would enhance the position of the individual. In the late 1980s ministers in the Conservative Government began to talk about 'active citizenship'. In 1991 the Prime Minister introduced his plans for a 'Citizen's Charter'. However, until recently very little has been published about citizenship as such. This is our reason for writing this book.

Before 1950 or so there was lively literature and debate about what form of citizenship was being, or ought to be, practised in the United Kingdom. It is not clear why this stream of debate dried up: perhaps it was because the introduction of the welfare state in the aftermath of the Second World War strengthened, and at the same time reflected, a strong sense of community and made it possible for all individuals to feel that they were fully respected members of society. Citizenship could be taken for granted – it was not problematic. At that period, too, there was broad satisfaction with the system of government in the country, especially the relationship between the individual and the state, and there were very few calls for the introduction of a Bill of Rights, electoral reform, freedom of information, decentralization and many of the other topics which have returned to the political agenda since the mid-1980s.

Why is it that interest in the constitution and citizenship has now revived? There are a number of interrelated factors. Since 1952 the United Kingdom has been a party to the European Convention on Human Rights: a number of cases have been taken to the European Court of Human Rights at Strasbourg in which the UK legal system has been found to fall short of the standards required by the Convention. This has inevitably raised the issue as to whether the Convention ought not to become part of UK law, or whether our law ought in some other way to improve its protection of civil and political rights.

In the 1980s there was increasing concern about authoritarianism on the part of Government and local authorities, and of partisanship in those quarters: this again generated interest in constitutional reform. The crime rate has been rising inexorably for many years, and public opinion has come to the view that a lack of a sense of communal values and community may be partly responsible for that. For various reasons, local community ties have weakened in the last twenty or thirty years – the move of people out of the inner cities and into suburban areas, job mobility, slum clearance and redevelopment. These and other factors have meant that well-established communities and extended families have been dispersed and the controls that they imposed informally on their members have disappeared.

It is felt by many people that the emphasis on individualism in the 1980s discouraged a sense of community responsibility. This trend was not helped by the opinion expressed by the Prime Minister at the time that 'there is no such thing as society'.

Anglo-Saxon cultural domination provided homogeneity, but this has come to be increasingly resented by the Catholic population in Northern Ireland, the Scots and the Welsh, and regarded as inappropriate for ethnic minorities with different cultural backgrounds.

Our increasing involvement with other member states in the European Community has meant that many people in the United Kingdom have become familiar with other constitutional systems, which include Bills of Rights, proportional representation and decentralized government: inevitably this raises questions as to which is the better approach to the regulation of state power and the relationship between the individual and state institutions. For these, and no doubt for other reasons, citizenship in Britain has come to be regarded as problematic, and the promotion of 'good citizenship' is seen as a possible solution to many of the ills of society. So it is the purpose of this book to explore a range of conceptions of citizenship and how it is or could be embodied in laws and in institutions of the state and civil society, and taught.

The first two chapters lay the foundations for our examination of theories, laws and practices relating to citizenship. We start in Chapter 1 with discussion from a historical perspective of developments in the theory and practice of citizenship. We identify six strands or themes in debates about citizenship, which will be interwoven in the following chapters in the book. Much of our discussion will be devoted to the exposition and exploration of these themes and the relationship between them.

The first theme draws on citizenship theory as it emerged in the Graeco-Roman world which developed concepts of 'civic virtue', and the 'good' citizen. This strand was later revived in Renaissance Italy and eighteenth-century America and France.

The second theme is the liberal view of citizenship which was particularly powerful in the nineteenth century. The liberal style stresses the importance of legal and political rights. This was soon complemented by the third theme, the idea of social citizenship, which is concerned with issues to do with property and emphasizes the right of the individual as citizen to enjoy a certain minimum level of welfare.

Since the nineteenth century the political identity of individuals and the prime call upon their loyalty has often been the sense of nationality. This aspect of citizenship theory forms the fourth theme in our consideration of the subject.

In the Roman Empire it was possible to have 'dual citizenship', and now in federations such as the United States, individuals are both citizens of their particular state as well as of the federation. Since classical Greek times the belief in 'world citizenship' as a possibility has often been advocated in various forms. These theories of 'multiple citizenship' form the fifth theme in the discussions.

Being a truly good and active citizen involves knowing about public life. Attempts have been made at many periods in history to educate pupils in the schools for this role. This sixth theme will be explored briefly in Chapter 5 and at some length in Chapter 8.

In the second chapter we continue laying foundations by focusing on the dominant elements in the contemporary debate about citizenship. This debate has often been conducted in ideological terms – the Right emphasizing duties (reflecting aspects of the first theme in our discussions); the Left emphasizing entitlements (influenced by the second and third strands).

Recent interest was revived through the work of T. H. Marshall: he established a threefold analysis of citizenship as a set of entitlements – civil, political and social (the second and third themes, woven together). These rights are considered further in Chapters 4 and 5.

Another issue discussed in Chapter 2 is the relationship of citizenship theory with the economic ordering of society. Central to this issue is the perceived incompatibility between the right to property – an important part of strands two and three – and the undermining of that right by taxation to finance the welfare state that is central to strand three. There are, we shall see, tensions within and between our themes. The relationship of citizenship and market forces has been highlighted by the success of capitalism compared with command economies. The citizenship principles of liberty and equality implicit in themes two and three come into conflict when market forces are uninhibited. The Left has generated a considerable literature that emphasizes the primacy of the citizen's social and economic rights. Others stress the need for constitutional reform to give enhanced legal protections to rights and promote the liberal citizenship ideal. There are important groups in society, especially women and racial minorities, who feel that they are treated as second-class citizens and demand changes to improve that condition – reflecting the influence of themes one, two and three. The contents of the 'citizen's charters' produced by the three major political parties illustrate the continuing ideological differences in the interpretations of the concept.

In Chapter 3 we turn from historical and philosophical aspects of citizenship and embark on our examination of the general legal framework for the relationship between states and their citizens, with particular reference to the United Kingdom position. We lay the foundations for the legal side of the discussion by examining a hotchpotch of issues which affect the themes of citizenship theory. This hotchpotch should resolve as we reach our conclusions. First, we pick up on the place of 'nationality' – theme four – in law. We establish that, although it has complex rules controlling immigration, the law in Britain makes relatively little distinction between citizens in the international law sense and other individuals lawfully resident in the country. As far as the law is concerned an individual's political identity and loyalty are not defined or fostered to any great extent by special privileges which are denied to 'non-nationals'. Next in Chapter 3 we turn to the conceptual basis of the legal relationship between the individual in the United Kingdom and the state. This is influenced by the old idea of the relationship as one between sovereign and subject – the reverse of the liberal ideal in theme two. Nowadays the sovereign–subject relationship is only residual in the legal system. A process of legal emancipation of individuals from subjection has taken place through the development of the rule of law. This substitution of autonomy for subjecthood represents the ascendancy of a liberal conception of the relationship between the individual and the state.

In the next two chapters we focus more closely on the rights and duties of individuals in their relationship with the state. Rights may be divided into first, second and third generation rights. We shall concentrate on the first generation, civil and political rights (part of the second, 'liberal' strand identified in Chapter 1) and on legal duties of good citizenship (associated with strand one) in Chapter 4.

In Chapter 5 we turn from first generation rights to those of the second and third generations: social and economic rights forming part of the third strand of citizenship theory, and environmental rights. The former enable individuals to participate in the life of the community and in politics, and thus further the values of classical and liberal theory. Giving legal effect to such rights raises difficult issues of resource allocation which make their legal protection more complex than that of civil and political rights. However, there are non-legal methods of protecting them. Some of these are to do with 'empowerment' of individuals – a relatively recent development in citizenship theory. The question arises as to whether 'empowerment' in this context is consistent with any of our established notions of citizenship – whether, for example, it is to do with the autonomy of individuals or whether it adds a new dimension, that of the economic actor, to the status of citizenship.

Environmental rights, the 'third generation' of rights, have come on to the political agenda as a result of the increasing pollution of the environment in the late twentieth century. Their protection commonly requires international cooperation, since pollution will often cross the boundaries of nation states; they involve, therefore, ideas of multiple or even world citizenship – theme five. They also require senses of responsibility to the community – theme one. In Chapter 6 we move away from the law to consider 'active citizenship' and 'civic virtue' in the United Kingdom. We suggest that citizenship, in the fullest sense of the word, means not just a status which can be protected by the law in the ways explored in Chapters 3, 4 and 5, but an attitude or set of attitudes. Citizens ought to want to act so as to benefit their community – in short, be good citizens. However, there is much disagreement about what is meant by 'good' in this context. It is sometimes suggested that the liberal view of citizenship gives such a high priority to the rights of the individual that there is little room for civic virtue, i.e. themes one and two cannot be reconciled or resolved. This is something we start to discuss in Chapter 3. We suggest in Chapter 6 that this is not necessarily the case. Liberal qualities such as tolerance and respect for others, a desire to defend freedom and impartial justice can mark out the good citizen in this tradition.

In Chapter 7 we return to the legal aspects of citizenship and widen our horizons to the increasingly important European dimensions of the status – an aspect of strand five, multiple citizenship, or even the creation of a new 'nationality'. This development flows partly from the United Kingdom's membership of the Council of Europe, and the jurisdiction of the European Commission and Court of Human Rights at Strasbourg to deal with complaints that British law does not conform to the European Convention on Human Rights; and partly from Britain's membership of the European Community (or, since the Treaty of Maastricht of 1993, the European Union).

Originally the Community was primarily concerned with market matters and not with the political and civil rights of nationals of Member States. The conception of 'European Community citizenship' has been primarily of individuals as economic actors rather than political ones – reflecting, in part, aspects of liberal theory, but without the political rights that it generally involves. Under the Treaty of Union (the Maastricht Treaty) citizens of Member States will be 'Citizens of the Union', and this will involve some new political rights. For example, individuals will be entitled to vote in local government and European Parliament elections in the state in which they reside, even if it is not the state of which they are nationals. However, the European Community conception of citizenship is exclusive: it does not benefit the many people of nationalities outside the Community but who reside within it – in some senses, then, it is nationality based, reflecting theme four.

In our last three chapters we begin to draw the threads of our discussions together. In Chapter 8 we turn away from legal issues for a while to return to the subject of education for citizenship, the sixth theme mentioned in Chapter 1. Education is clearly one way in which the foundations for citizenship may be laid and laid better. We shall concentrate on schools, though education in schools is but one aspect of the many ways in which individuals may gain the knowledge, experience and understanding necessary to enable them to be true citizens.

In Chapter 9 we turn to explore ways in which the legal foundations for citizenship might be improved. Remnants of the status of subjecthood, and institutionalized exclusion from the sense of belonging to the community (for example, some aspects of the monarchy, and the establishment of the Church of England) could be reformed. Popular sovereignty could replace the sovereignty of 'The Queen in Parliament'. Citizens' ability to hold government to account and participate in politics could be enhanced. Civil and political rights could be improved in various ways. Social and economic rights could be enhanced by specific statutory provisions. Such reforms, we suggest, ought not to take a form that precludes acceptance of the idea that individuals owe obligations and responsibilities to their community.

Finally, in Chapter 10 we draw some conclusions from our exploration of citizenship. The association of citizenship with nationality seems increasingly inappropriate in modern conditions, multiple citizenship has become an attractive alternative approach to resolving the conflict between these themes. This accepts that an individual may have more than one civic identity, psychologically and in law. Multiple citizenship can be successful and effective only in a healthy civil society which will promote senses of civic virtue. At the state level it is helpful to distinguish between 'nationality citizenship' and 'new citizenship'. The latter recognizes the existence of human rights outside the context of the nation state. The idea of world citizenship cannot yet be said to have any firm legal or political reality, but it is a concept which many find useful for a spectrum of programmes from reform of the United Nations to federal world government.

Owing to the complexity, even subjectivity of the citizenship idea, no universally accepted definition or description has been produced. However, we conclude by outlining four models which attempt the task in different ways.

This book is a text rather than a monograph: we set out to explore, expound and analyse rather than to press a particular theory of citizenship. However, we do share a vision of citizenship. It is broadly as follows. First is a picture of the sort of people citizens should be: individuals should have respect for others and be tolerant of diversity. They need a sense of their own worth. They should value and respect those with whom they deal, especially those who are less fortunate or powerful than themselves. They should be, and feel that they are, valued and valuable members of the many communities that they belong to, both public and private, and they ought to feel a sense of commitment to their communities. They should have the skills and understanding to enable them to contribute to communal activity effectively – abilities to negotiate, compromise, persuade, protect their own interests. However, they should realize that their own interests may have to yield to those of others or the public good.

Second, the law should treat, and promote the treatment of, all those who are *de facto* members of society equally, regardless of their nationality, class, sex, race, ethnicity or any other irrelevant differences between individuals. It should protect and promote the dignity, autonomy and respect of individuals, by providing legal redress for infringements of civil and political rights, and securing the availability of social and economic provision. It should enable individuals to participate effectively in decisions that affect their lives, and in the political and decision-making processes in the communities they belong to. It should in all ways possible promote the formation of the sort of citizen we described above.

We consider, in other words, that it is possible and desirable for citizenship to be a synthesis and drawing together of the six strands we identify. Individuals are citizens when they practise civic virtue and good citizenship, enjoy but do not exploit their civil and political rights, contribute to and receive social and economic benefits, do not allow any sense of national identity to justify discrimination or stereotyping of others, experience senses of non-exclusive multiple citizenship, and by their example, teach citizenship to others.

Yet such people are not born; each individual has to learn to be a citizen in these senses. The educational system, as well as the law and institutional arrangements in civil society – at work, in the family, in clubs and churches, and so on – and in state activities ought all to promote the learning of this form of citizenship.

1

HISTORICAL OUTLINE

SUMMARY

This historical chapter does not tell the story of the theory and practice of citizenship in strictly chronological order. We have chosen, rather, to analyse the historical evidence under six main headings, though there is a very rough chronological sequence to the order of the first four sections. Citizenship emerged in the classical Graeco-Roman world. The idea of 'civic virtue', of being a 'good' citizen, which was one of the features of the classical ideal, was revived especially in Renaissance Italy and eighteenth-century America and France. The second strand is the liberal view of citizenship which was particularly powerful in the nineteenth century. The liberal tradition emphasizes the importance of legal and political rights. This was soon complemented by the notion of social citizenship, which stresses the right of the citizen to enjoy a certain minimum level of welfare.

However, citizenship is more than duties and rights. It also gives an individual a political identity and a focus for loyalty. Since the nineteenth century, therefore, citizenship has become associated with nationality. On the other hand, an individual need not be restricted to being a citizen of just one state. In the ancient Roman Empire it was possible to have 'dual citizenship'; and in federations such as the United States individuals are simultaneously citizens of their particular state as well as of the federation as a whole. Moreover, since classical Greek times the belief that one can be a 'world citizen' has often been argued. Finally, because being a truly good and active citizen involves learning much about public life, throughout history numerous attempts have been made to prepare the younger generation in the schools for this adult role.

THE CLASSICAL TRADITION

Mankind has experimented with many socio-political relationships: chieftain and tribe, king and subjects, lord and vassals. Even the tiny city-states of Greece in the times described by Homer had kings. So too did Rome at about the same time. As the monarchies decayed or were overthrown so the idea developed that at least some portion of the inhabitants of these city-states should participate in the processes of law and government. Those who were eligible for such participation were clearly defined, as were the duties they were required to perform and the rights they could expect to enjoy. The concept and practice of citizenship had been born.

Even so, there were wide variations in the ways that the states evolved in these early times. In Greece Sparta became a byword for exacting a highly disciplined militaristic loyalty from its citizenry. In contrast, Athens experimented with greater freedom, evolving a form of democracy. The very word 'democracy' derives from two Greek words meaning 'government by the people'. However, the 'people', that is, the citizens, who shared in the formulation of policy and the making and administration of laws, were a small proportion of the total population: children, women, slaves and resident aliens were not citizens.

Aristotle provides us with three clues concerning the nature of Greek citizenship.

1. First, reflecting its diverse expressions, he declared 'The nature of citizenship . . . is a question which is often disputed: there is no general agreement on a single definition' (Aristotle, 1948, 1274b).
2. Secondly, citizens are '*all* who share in the civic life of ruling and being ruled in turn' (Aristotle, 1948, 1283b).
3. And thirdly, this rotating system presupposes a state small enough for the citizens to 'know one another's characters' (Aristotle, 1948, 1326b).

It is clear that the Greek style of citizenship presupposed, by today's standards, a small, tightly-knit community.

Box 1.1

One of the most famous Athenians, Pericles, delivered a funeral oration for some of those who fell in the Peloponnesian War (in the fifth century BC). In this speech he gave a, no doubt idealized, picture of citizenship as practised in his city; and he claims that no other city-state had developed the practice of citizenship to such a sophisticated degree.

Here each individual is interested not only in his own affairs but in the affairs of the state as well: even those who are mostly occupied with their own business are extremely well-informed on general politics – this is a peculiarity of ours: we do not say that a man who takes no interest in politics is a man who minds his own business; we say that he has no business at all. We Athenians, in our own persons, take our decisions on policy or submit them to proper discussions: for we do not think that there is an incompatability between words and deeds; the worst thing is to rush into action before the consequences have been properly debated. . . .

And I declare that in my opinion each single one of our citizens, in all the manifold aspects of life, is able to show himself the rightful lord and owner of his own person, and to do this, moreover, with exceptional grace and exceptional versatility. (Thucydides, 1954, pp. 118–19)

About the time Aristotle was born (384 BC) the Romans were extending their sway over the territories and peoples of central Italy. The status of citizenship required adaptation to these new circumstances of a rapidly expanding state. The Romans devised two new facets to the basic idea. These new elements, which in many ways were contradictions of the Greek concept, rendered citizenship much more highly flexible. They were:

(a) the extension of the status to the non-Roman peoples whom they conquered;
(b) the division of the status by introducing the second-class category of *civitas sine suffragio* (citizenship without the franchise, i.e. legal but not political rights).

By the first century BC (that is, during the last decades of the Republic), many men in the several lands of the Mediterranean basin enjoyed the status of Roman citizenship. Moreover, the idea now came to be held that the citizen should behave in a manner suited to his status – echoing in rather less stark and brutal manner the Spartan practices. The politicians Cato and Cicero and the historian Livy were most famously insistent that the citizen should cultivate the quality of 'civic virtue'.

This term is a rough translation of the Latin word *virtus*. It was a word with many overtones. It meant manliness, especially in the form of a readiness to perform military service and to fight with valour. It meant patriotism; and it meant an unswerving devotion to duty and the law.

This Roman vision or ideal of 'virtue', often called 'civic republicanism', exerted a powerful influence in Italy at the time of the Renaissance. It remained a significant thread in the history of citizenship to the nineteenth century. It was a model, an image of the perfect life to be lived by a man in his capacity as a citizen. Perhaps the more one was conscious of the imperfections of men and states, the more one felt the urge to present the unattainable ideal as a measure of the need to strive to narrow the gap. Thus it was that the Florentine statesman and political theorist Machiavelli came to write his praise of ancient Roman qualities, *Discourses on the First Ten Books of Titus Livius*.

Machiavelli glumly surveyed the parlous condition of the Italian political scene of his time. Few of the numerous states of the peninsula displayed the qualities of a *republica* and few men the qualities of *virtù*. It must be remembered that the modern constitutional distinction between monarchy and republic did not obtain in the sixteenth century. By 'republic' Machiavelli meant a form of government in which there is some share of power to prevent autocratic and arbitrary rule. He uses the Italian word *virtù* as having similar meanings to the Latin *virtus*.

Machiavelli recorded that in his own age there were

fewer republics than there used to be of old, and that, consequently, in peoples we do not find the same love of liberty as there was. (Machiavelli, 1970, II, ii)

For him, therefore, a love of freedom, especially from foreign oppression, was a valuable component of civic virtue. Furthermore, people become apathetic if prevented from performing their citizenly role. For he believed that men had to be kept constantly up to scratch in the performance of their civic obligations. Men must be made into citizens and kept true to that status and function by means of education, religion and a healthy fear of the consequences of any dereliction of citizenly duty.

A second quickening of interest in the politics of the classical world occurred in the eighteenth century. Many of the thinkers of the Enlightenment looked back, just as Machiavelli had, to an idealized Roman Republic as their exemplar. Most notable of these was the French lawyer Montesquieu. In *The Spirit of the Laws* he argued that a state based upon popular participation, as distinct from other forms of government, depends for its stability on the civic virtue of its citizens.

Sparta was also popular in the eighteenth century as an exemplification of civic virtue. Of all the political thinkers of the age Jean-Jacques Rousseau was the most influential. By praising the Spartans' selfless concern for their city-state, he was able to highlight what he considered to be the selfish social behaviour of his own age (see Box 1.2). The size of the Greek city-state also appealed to him. Like Aristotle he believed that true citizenship depended on the intimacy of a small-scale political community.

While Rousseau idealized Sparta, a regime of rigid discipline, what of freedom? For freedom is surely a condition which helps to distinguish the citizen from the slave, the vassal or the subject? The problem of freedom worried Rousseau a great deal.

Box 1.2

One of Rousseau's books, entitled *Émile*, is a treatise on education. In this book he relates an anecdote which illustrates his understanding of the classical ideal of civic virtue:

A Spartan mother had five sons with the army. A Helot arrived; trembling she asked his news. 'Your five sons are slain.' 'Vile slave, was that what I asked thee?' 'We have won the victory.' She hastened to the temple to render thanks to the gods. That was a citizen. (Rousseau, 1911, p. 8)

The sons sacrificed themselves for the state; the mother put her feelings for the state above those for her sons.

He believed most passionately that true freedom involves people unselfishly governing themselves. In other words, freedom requires both civic virtue and participation. In another important book, *The Social Contract*, he wrote:

> Those who are associated in [the body politic] take collectively the name of a *people*, and call themselves *citizens*, in so far as they share in the sovereign power. (Rousseau, 1968, I, vii)

Rousseau had a mental picture of all citizens contributing without thought of personal advantage to political decisions. He called this the General Will. If all citizens behave in this honest way, all would benefit overall and would not experience the oppression suffered under governments where there was no true citizenship.

Twenty years after the death of Montesquieu the American War of Independence started; and we may date the start of the French Revolution ten years after the death of Rousseau. Montesquieu's ideas had particular influence in America, Rousseau's in France.

In both revolutions (for the American events are often considered to be a revolution) the political reformers were particularly worried by the problem of corruption. By corruption they meant the pursuit of luxury at the expense of civic duty. In America, Alexander Hamilton warned that a policy of commercial expansion would breed an attitude of selfishness. In France, Maximilien Robespierre, known as 'The Incorruptible', was willing during the period of the Terror to shed blood to ensure the triumph of virtue. In a speech a few months before he was himself guillotined, he spoke of

> virtue without which terror is disastrous, and terror without which virtue is powerless.

France had to be cleansed of the enemies of the new republic in order that civic virtue should prevail.

The men of the Renaissance, the Enlightenment and the American and French Revolutions who were interested in citizenship looked at the problem through the eyes of classical antiquity. The writers of the nineteenth century who thought in the civic republican tradition focused their attention more realistically on the modern industrialized nation-state. Hegel in Germany and T. H. Green in

England are the most important of these writers. They emphasized the need to make citizens aware of what their role is in the modern state.

By the nineteenth century, however, the classical tradition of citizenship was giving way to new, liberal ideas. Where civic republicanism stressed a stern adherence to the citizen's duties, the liberal style stressed the citizen's entitlement to justice and rights.

THE LIBERAL TRADITION

To understand the origins of this alternative emphasis we must retrace our steps in time to the seventeenth century. This was the age when Englishmen (including the American colonists) claimed rights which they declared could not legitimately be overridden by the monarch or the royal Government. The idea grew up that Government and people should act as if there was a kind of legal contract between them: the people would be obedient to the Government, but, in its turn, the Government is never justified in depriving the people of certain basic rights.

Although the word 'citizen' was rarely used at the time of the English Civil War, it was this conflict and its aftermath which brought the matter of rights to the surface. The demands were twofold, legal and political; equal access to a just law and a wider franchise. These have been the two cardinal features of the liberal version of citizenship.

In the 1670s the legal (or civil) rights of English people were improved – by confirming the independence of juries and the passing of the law of habeas corpus. On the issue of voting rights opinion was split. Some persisted with the view that the right should be restricted to those who owned property; others argued for virtually full democratic rights for men. The most famous expression of this second attitude was a speech by Colonel Rainborough in 1647. He declared,

> I do think that the poorest man in England is not at all bound in a strict sense to that government that he has not had a voice to put himself under.

The struggle to establish effective civil and political citizenship has continued since the seventeenth century and has extended beyond England and her North American colonies to the rest of the world. The French Revolution gave the idea and practice a particular boost. In its most radical phase, aristocratic titles were abolished: all were addressed by the equal title of 'Citizen' or 'Citizeness'. However, the Revolution went deeper than mere symbolism. The Declaration of the Rights of Man and the Citizen provided an impressive list of civil and political rights, while the Constitution of 1791 to which it acted as preface, gave the right of voting to a reasonable proportion of the male population.

Throughout the nineteenth century there was constant pressure in all states for the liberalization of civil and political systems. In Britain, four Reform Acts from 1832 to 1918 successively extended the franchise. The arguments centring on the liberal concept of citizenship were clearly expounded by the British philosopher, John Stuart Mill. He believed passionately in freedom in all its aspects. Though to his mind, the freedom to participate in political affairs is crucial. He argued that moral maturity is impossible unless the individual involves him- or herself in some form of collective activity with or on behalf of fellow citizens. Furthermore, citizenly vigilance in public affairs is an essential safeguard against the abuse of their authority by 'faceless' bureaucrats.

Even so, Mill was uncertain whether, on the matter of voting rights, some citizens should not be more equal than others. He was very keen, for example, that women should have the same rights as men. In his essay *Considerations on Representative Government* he wrote:

> All human beings have the same interest in good government.... If there be any difference, women require it more than men, since, being physically weaker, they are more dependent on law and society for protection. (Mill, 1910, p. 290)

On the other hand, he was fearful of allowing ignorant people of either sex to wield any political influence: giving uneducated people the franchise, he argued, would not lead to wise government.

The pressure to extend the franchise has, of course, been inexorable in most states in the twentieth century. Restrictions by reasons of wealth, sex and age have all collapsed before the logic of the democratic case and popular pressure. The achievement of legal

---

Box 1.3

A famous example of a nineteenth-century attempt to extend political citizenship was the People's Charter and the Chartist Movement in Britain from 1837 to 1848. The Charter contained six points:

1. *A VOTE for every man twenty one years of age, of sound mind, and not undergoing punishment for crime.*
2. *THE BALLOT – to protect the elector in the exercise of his vote.*
3. *NO PROPERTY QUALIFICATION for Members of Parliament – thus enabling the constituencies to return the man of their first choice, be he rich or poor.*
4. *PAYMENT OF MEMBERS, thus enabling an honest tradesman, working man, or other person, to serve a constituency, when taken from his business to attend to the interests of the country.*
5. *EQUAL CONSTITUENCIES, securing the same amount of representation for the same number of electors – instead of allowing small constituencies to swamp the votes of the larger ones.*
6. *ANNUAL PARLIAMENTS, thus presenting the most effectual check to bribery and intimidation, since . . . no purse could buy a constituency . . . in each ensuing twelvemonth, and since members, when elected for a year only, would not be able to defy and betray their constituents as now.*

---

universal suffrage has not, however, brought the debate over political citizenship to an end.

Both scholarly investigation and practical experience have led to the raising of two particularly awkward questions. One derived from the success with which unscrupulous demagogues have been able to manipulate a credulous citizenry. The other is raised by the realization that, in the modern state of disciplined political parties and pervasive bureaucracy, citizens, for all their legal rights, are virtually impotent as a political force. What price citizenship when so many citizens in Germany in the 1930s shouted for Hitler? What price citizenship when the election results in most constituencies in Great Britain are usually predictable?

These two sets of observations have led to quite opposite conclusions. Fear of rabble-rousing dictators has led to the suggestion that ordinary citizens should not be allowed too much political power. The best citizen is the passive and apathetic citizen. Only a wise and dedicated élite should be allowed any real political influence. Yet, in contrast, the evidence that most citizens are politically impotent in any case has led to a search for alternative means of exercising power – for 'empowerment', to use the jargon word. Various forms of local community involvement and demands for the devolution of power from central government have been popular, especially since the 1960s.

If the bulk of people are to be encouraged and given the opportunity to be civically conscious and active, it is often argued that their interests will lie not so much in the fields of high politics as in their own working conditions and welfare. Citizenship is not only embodied in civil and political rights; it also has a social form.

SOCIAL CITIZENSHIP

The relationship between the ideal of citizenship and the creation, acquisition and ownership of wealth has generated much debate over the centuries. Is the possession of a certain level of wealth essential for the proper discharge of one's functions as a citizen?

Aristotle was convinced that this was the case:

> The *citizens* of our state must have a supply of property [in order to have leisure for goodness and political activities]; and it is these persons who are citizens – they, and they only. (Aristotle, 1948, 1329a)

The argument is two-pronged. One is the view that the possession of wealth gives an individual a stake in the community; the poor have no incentive to take an interest in public affairs. The other is the belief that participation in civic life requires time to study the issues and attend meetings. Those whose economic condition forces them to labour for most of their waking hours do not have the leisure to be citizens in any proper sense.

The contrary case has also been expressed by two main arguments. The first is that the very process of acquiring wealth is a selfish activity and inevitably diverts the individual's mind from that altruistic, community spirit which is the hallmark of true citizenship. The second argument is that the denial of the status of citizenship to those lacking the qualifying wealth is itself a denial of that very principle of equality which should lie at the heart of the citizenship ideal. The whole point of citizenship is that it provides a preferable alternative to the social and political divisions which are the characteristics of monarchical, feudal and despotic regimes. The possibility of advancing two quite contradictory sets of arguments concerning the relationship of citizenship and wealth is reflected in the work of Karl Marx on the relationship between citizenship and capitalism. On the one hand, capitalism destroyed the social divisions of feudalism; on the other, it created the oppression of the working class by the bourgeoisie. In its first function, capitalism created the conditions in the modern state for citizenship to develop; in its second, it allowed the supposed equality of the citizenly status to mask the true social and economic divisions which kept the bulk of so-called citizens in proletarian subjection. The destruction of feudalism, Marx asserted, led to modern man's schizophrenic condition: part liberated, selfish individual, part moral citizen.

Communists have seen citizenship as a temporary phenomenon to be replaced by true comradeship once the state has withered away. Social democrats, in contrast, have wished to strengthen citizenship by affording everyone equal civic rights and opportunities through the provision of social welfare.

It is important to distinguish between the motives which have sometimes led governments to make state welfare provision. These include fear of discontent, electoral bribe and philanthropic charity. These considerations may produce the desired reforms, but are utterly unrelated to citizenship. The social dimension to citizenship involves the acceptance that the state owes certain services to the citizen as a right in return for the loyalty and services rendered by the citizen. It is part of the reciprocal relationship between the individual and the state which is central to the concept of citizenship. Furthermore, the levelling-up process of social welfare support is necessary in order to realize the egalitarianism and dignity involved in the citizenship ideal. Finally state-provided education is essential since an ignorant citizen is tantamount to a contradiction in terms.

As we shall see in the next chapter, the English sociologist T. H. Marshall, in a book published in 1950, put forward the idea that citizenship may be divided into three elements – civil, political and social. Moreover, he believed that the rights associated with these three facets developed in that order. He wrote:

the modern drive towards social equality is, I believe, the latest phase of an evolution of citizenship which has been in continuous progress for some 250 years. (Marshall, p. 7)

The concept of social citizenship appeared explicitly in France earlier than in Britain. The Jacobin version of the Declaration of the Rights of Man and the Citizen, drawn up in 1793, was particularly forthright:

Public assistance is a sacred duty. Society owes its unfortunate citizens subsistence, either by providing them with work, or by ensuring the means of existence for those who have no work. (Thompson, 1948, Article 21)

In Britain, early welfare-state legislation, in both its pre-First World War and post-Second World War phases, owed a great debt to the teachings on citizenship of the philosopher T. H. Green and his followers. William Beveridge, architect of the reforms of the late 1940s, had been influenced by this school of thought in his earlier years in Oxford.

In the 1980s, as we shall see in the next chapter, the idea of social

---

Box 1.4

Marshall believed that the principle of social citizenship really 'took off' in England in the late nineteenth century:

A new period opened at the end of the nineteenth century, conveniently marked by Booth's survey of Life and Labour of the Poor in London and the Royal Commission on the Aged Poor. It was the first big advance in social rights, and this involved significant changes in the egalitarian principles expressed in citizenship. But there were other forces at work as well [narrowing wealth gaps]. . . . All this profoundly altered the setting in which the progress of citizenship took place. Social integration spread from the sphere of sentiment and patriotism into that of material enjoyment. . . . The diminution of inequality strengthened the demand for its abolition, at least with regard to the essentials of social welfare.

These aspirations have in part been met by incorporating social rights in the status of citizenship and thus creating a universal right to real income which is not proportionate to the market value of the claimant. (Marshall and Bottomore, 1992, p. 28)

welfare as an entitlement owed by the state to the citizen came under attack. This was particularly so among the New Right thinkers and politicians in the United States and Britain. For them citizenship meant not so much rights as patriotism.

NATIONAL IDENTITY

The civil, political and social rights and duties associated with citizenship have varied considerably over the centuries. They have also been and still are often subject to varying interpretations. However, whether a person is legally a citizen of a given state and feels a sense of loyalty to that state is usually much more clear cut.

Both the legal status (see Chapter 3) and the feeling of belonging have become associated with the nation-state. Whatever the form of the state, the matter of the individual's political identity in this dual sense has always been a feature of citizenship. The Romans established explicit laws about who had the status of citizen; and it came to be a title worn with pride. Cicero's famous declaration '*Civis Romanus sum*' was both a statement of legal fact and an expression of self-respect.

In the age of the nation-state, especially since the eighteenth century, constitutions and laws have been drafted to define exactly who qualified for the status of citizen. The state also adopted symbols such as flags and national anthems so that its citizens could the more easily identify with the state and focus their loyalty on it. For example, the emphasis on citizenship in the French Revolution was reinforced by the use of the tricolore and the 'Marseillaise'.

Two different criteria have been used by states for conferring the legal status of citizenship. One is *jus sanguinis*, that is, descent from an individual of that nationality. The other is *jus soli*, that is, the fact of birth within the state's territory. A survey conducted in 1935 revealed that *jus sanguinis* was the more common. Some states have developed laws which are a combination of the two.

The creation of European overseas empires complicated the matter of citizenship. The imperial powers treated their colonial peoples in different ways. Let us take three brief examples. The Portuguese pursued a policy of few admissions to the status and even then of denying any real rights. The French tried to juggle with the

---

Box 1.5

The French Constitution of 1791 listed in great detail everyone considered to have the status of French citizen.

II. Those who were born in France of a French father;
Those who, born in France of a foreign father, have fixed their residence in the kingdom;
Those who, born in a foreign country of a French father, have returned to establish themselves in France and have taken the civic oath;
Finally those who, born in a foreign country, and a descendant to some degree from a Frenchman or Frenchwoman who fled the country for religious reasons, come to live in France and take the civic oath.
III. Those who, born outside the kingdom of foreign parents, reside in France, become French citizens after five years of domicile . . . and take the civic oath.
IV. The legislative power can, for important considerations, confer naturalisation on a foreigner. . . .
V. The civic oath is: I swear to be faithful to the nation, to the law and to the king, and to maintain with all my power the constitution of the kingdom decreed by the National Constituent Assembly. . . . (Thompson, 1948)

---

principle that all inhabitants of French territories were citizens while admitting only a limited number of Africans and West Indians to rights comparable with those enjoyed in France itself. The British have never developed an explicit definition of citizenship for themselves. It is not surprising, therefore, that they never attempted to devise a coherent policy for their colonial peoples.

However, whatever the policies of the imperial powers had been, the process of decolonization raised two difficult general problems. One was the need of the newly independent states to create their own rules and sense of citizenship. The other was the question of defining the rights of the inhabitants of the former colonies *vis-à-vis* their former mother country.

If citizenship is defined and thought of in terms of nationality, the concept takes on cultural overtones – because nationality is a cultural concept. However, most of the successor states to the European empires were, and still are, culturally very mixed. They inherited and, in large measure, retained the borders drawn by the imperial powers in utter disregard of the ethnic composition of the lands they seized.

It has been extraordinarily difficult to build a feeling of national identity and common citizenship in states where linguistic, 'tribal' and religious divisions tug powerfully towards a sense of separateness. Bitter civil conflict has even ensued in, for example, Nigeria and Sri Lanka.

The second problem, that of defining the rights of former colonial people to citizenship of the former imperial state, has been complicated by the magnetic effects of employment opportunities and consequent immigration and settlement, hence the people of African, West Indian and Asian origin in Britain, France and the Netherlands particularly. In Britain, various Nationality and Immigration Acts from 1948 to 1981 attempted to tackle the issue. The 1981 Act, by creating separate categories of 'citizens' and in effect 'sub-citizens', emerged, in the view of one authority, with 'many of its provisions . . . so obscurely drafted that they are unfit to be in the statute book' (A. Lester, quoted in Commission on Citizenship, 1990, p. 76).

The idea of combining citizenship with nationality was an obvious device in the era of nation-states and nationalism. On the other hand, it has in fact led to new and often intractable complications (see Chapter 10). A possible way out of these difficulties is to place a much greater emphasis on the concept and practice of multiple citizenship.

MULTIPLE CITIZENSHIP

As early as the times of the Greek and Roman city-states it was possible for a man to be simultaneously a citizen of his original home city and of another. By the time of Augustus, the principle of dual citizenship – of Rome and of another city – was firmly established in Roman law. A famous example of this system at work concerns Paul, one of the founders of Christianity. Although a citizen of Tarsus, in Asia Minor, when he was arrested he was able to claim certain privileges by virtue of being, also, a citizen of Rome.

In the modern world, federally-structured states need to make provision for their inhabitants to hold both state and federal citizenships. The founding fathers of the United States wrestled with this problem before arriving at the succinct formula in Article IV.2 of the Constitution: 'The citizens of each State shall be entitled to all privileges and immunities of citizens in the several States.' This did not, however, cope with the question of which level of citizenship had priority when the laws of and loyalty to the state clashed with those of the overarching federation. The matter was complicated in the United States by the ambiguous position of slaves. It took a civil war to resolve these queries. The subsequent Fourteenth Amendment to the Constitution was quite plain:

> All persons born or naturalized in the United States, and subject to the jurisdiction thereof, are citizens of the States wherein they reside. No State shall make or enforce any law which shall abridge the privileges or immunities of citizens of the United States.

If we turn now to contemporary history, we have the unique example of an evolving European Community. In some senses citizens of the Member States have been acquiring the characteristics of 'European' or 'Community' citizens also. Rights, duties and a sense of identity have been growing at the Community level, albeit in a piecemeal way. Community passports have been made available; direct elections to the European Parliament have taken place since 1979; a European flag has been adopted; a Social Charter has been accepted by all Member States except Britain. Moreover, there has been considerable concern in both the Commission and the Parliament to transform a 'Technocrats' Europe' into a 'People's Europe' – or, in the more telling French term, 'Europe des Citoyens'. At the same time, much store has been put on the principle of subsidiarity. This is the rule-of-thumb that decisions should be reached at the lowest possible level in the province–nation– state–Community pyramid. This may be taken as a guideline concerning the priority which individuals should give to the different levels at which they behave and act as citizens in a multiple sense. The desire further to enhance the status of citizenship of the European Community was greatly emphasized in the 1992 Treaty of Maastricht (see Chapter 7).

It is not, therefore, difficult to discover historical examples of individuals being able, even required, in law to hold at least dual citizenship. There is, in addition, another, greater, though less tangible, sense in which the term 'multiple citizenship' may be used. This is the notion that there is or can be a world citizenship which can be held and honoured alongside a state citizenship.

The Greek word *polis* is usually translated as 'city-state'.

Cosmopolis is therefore the 'city of the world' or the universe conceived as a city. The idea that there is a cosmopolis, governed by natural law, as distinct from manifold *poleis*, governed by man-made laws, emerged in Greece in the fifth century BC. Its most distinguished theoretical exponents were the Greek and Roman philosophers known as Stoics: Zeno, Chrysippus, Seneca and Marcus Aurelius.

The idea of world citizenship was attractive two thousand years later to the thinkers of the Enlightenment. The French writer Voltaire took the philosopher–Emperor Marcus Aurelius as his model. The English radical Thomas Paine declared, 'My country is the world'. The German playwright Schiller asserted, 'I write as a citizen of the world'.

In reaction to the perverted nationalist and racialist ideologies which psychologically triggered and intensified the two world wars of our own century, the ideas of world citizenship blossomed once again. Only to fade before the accusations of impracticability levelled by the cynic or realist (depending on your point of view). Even so, in more recent years, the ideal has been revived in the belief that ecological disasters will overwhelm our planet unless a sense of global loyalty and responsibility, that is, world citizenship, is strongly cultivated.

Throughout the intermittent history of the idea of world citizenship two major problems have inhibited its widespread acceptance. First, there has never been a world state; nor would its creation necessarily be desirable. However, citizenship is, fundamentally, a relationship of an individual with a state. It obviously follows that world citizenship has never existed in any legal or political sense – only in belief or as behaviour. The second difficulty is whether world citizenship, even in its weak sense of a commitment to universal values and concerns, can be held in association with state citizenship. For it is evident that many self-proclaimed 'world citizens' have wished to deny their allegiance to the state in favour of their adherence to what they believe to be a higher responsibility.

Yet, many others have not; and have sought the realization of a multiple citizenship, rendering unto the state that loyalty which is properly the state's and rendering unto the world that loyalty which is properly the world's. Socrates, perhaps the most famous of all philosophers, is said to have declared, 'I am not an Athenian or a Corinthian, but a citizen of the universe'. Yet when condemned to death, he chose to drink the cup of hemlock in obedience to the laws of Athens, of which he acknowledged that he was in legal fact a citizen.

EDUCATION FOR CITIZENSHIP

Except in terms of legal nationality, one is not born a citizen. Citizenship involves enjoying rights, performing duties and behaving with due loyalty and responsibility. All these aspects of citizenship must be learned and cultivated. No one, therefore, can be a citizen in the proper and full meaning of the term without being educated for the role.

In the ancient world, young men were taught the prime civic skill of rhetoric: the practice of law and politics required the oral capacity to present a case logically and persuasively. It is no accident that the most influential Roman educational theorist was Quintilian, whose widely-used book was *Education of an Orator*.

We have seen, however, that the classical view of citizenship emphasized civic virtue. Educational theorists from ancient Greece

---

Box 1.6

It is interesting to compare the following two excerpts. They both express the belief that basic, state citizenship needs to be complemented by a higher form of citizenship.

Every man's interest consists in following the lead of his own constitution and nature. Now my nature is a rational and civic nature; my city and my country, so far as I am [Marcus Aurelius] Antoninus, is Rome; but so far as I am a man, it is the universe. Whatever therefore is to the advantage of these two cities, and that only, is good for me.

The Union shall set itself the following objectives: ... to strengthen the protection of the rights and interests of the nationals of its Member States through the introduction of a citizenship of the Union.

The first extract is taken from the *Meditations* of the Roman philosopher–emperor Marcus Aurelius, dating from the late second century (reprinted in Barker, 1956, p. 320). The second is from the Treaty of Maastricht for consolidating the European Community, 1992 (Title I, Article B).

onwards often advocated developing in the young a responsible public spirit. The Greek philosopher, Plato, wrote 'what we have in mind is education from childhood in *virtue*, a training which produces a keen desire to become a perfect citizen' (Plato, 1970, p. 73). Aristotle also advocated general civic training despite his comment quoted in Box 8.2.

The classical tradition of education for citizenship tended to emphasize skills such as presenting an argument and making the young person want to behave as a good citizen. In contrast, the liberal style has placed greater stress on rational, clear thinking and factual learning. The English, American and French revolutions of the seventeenth and eighteenth centuries all prompted recommendations along these lines.

However, it was not until the nineteenth century, with the steady

---

Box 1.7

It was in eighteenth-century France that serious proposals were first made for a truly national system of education. During the Revolution, in 1793, Condorcet drew up a *Report on Public Education*. One of its notable features was its emphasis on civic education. Owing to a change of government, the report was not put into practice. Nevertheless, it is an interesting indication of what some influential people were thinking at the time. Here are a few extracts.

You owe it to the French nation to provide an education in accord with the spirit of the eighteenth century, of its philosophy. . . . It is from this very philosophy that we have considered the moral and political sciences as an essential part of general education. . . .

In the primary schools each individual is to be taught what is necessary to be self-reliant and to enjoy his rights to the full. This education will even adequately include lessons designed for men to fit them for the simplest public offices, to which it is good that every citizen should be able to be nominated, such as those of jury-service and municipal officer.

Condorcet (1982) presents the need for life-long education for citizenship. Therefore,

Each Sunday, the teacher will start a public lecture, which will be attended by citizens of all ages. . . . Here . . . that part of the national laws, ignorance of which would prevent a citizen from knowing and exercising his rights, will be expanded upon.

expansion of the franchise in the states of North America and western Europe, that politicians took much effective action to encourage citizenship education. By the 1880s 'civics' textbooks were in common use in the United States, Britain and France. In Britain even the term 'citizenship' appeared in the titles of school books from the 1880s to the 1950s. By the 1970s teaching about constitutional and political affairs was virtually universal, in one form or another. The American educational philosopher, John Dewey, was influential in the early years of the twentieth century, in teaching that democracy is inconceivable without an appropriate, supporting education.

Nineteenth-century socialists, notably in Britain, France and Germany, strove to introduce the younger generation to their political and social views. Governments became nervous of what they considered to be indoctrination. A similar nervousness can be detected in the liberal–capitalist democracies in the period since the 1960s concerning any teaching which seemed to smack of a left-wing challenge to the Establishment.

In contrast, education to promote patriotism and a feeling of national cohesion has been supported by governments for the past two centuries. A Prussian document of 1818 declared that 'the most sacred duty of all schoolmasters and schoolmistresses' was to make every school 'a nursery of blameless patriotism'. New nations, from the United States in the late eighteenth century to the independent states of Africa in the 1960s and 1970s have recognized the central function of schools in the process of nation-building.

Finally, teaching the principles of world citizenship has been persistently advocated for the past century. The educational case has been supported by different concerns and hopes at different times: first, the disarmament movement prior to the First World War; then the foundation of the League of Nations after that conflict; and the United Nations after the Second World War; and most recently global environmental consciousness. Since the Second World War UNESCO (United Nations Educational, Scientific and Cultural Organization) has promoted school progammes in global studies under the capacious if cumbersome heading of 'education for international understanding, cooperation and peace and education relating to human rights and fundamental freedoms'.

Brief as this historical summary has been, we hope that it has given some indication of the rich tradition of citizenship and the complex meaning of the term. Although the words 'citizen' and 'citizenship' are both often used in slightly different ways, it is as well always to keep in mind their full breadth of meaning. A true understanding of citizenship depends on some appreciation of its long and varied history.

Given the complexity and importance of the topic, it is not surprising that discussion concerning the nature of citizenship has persisted. Indeed, during the past few decades the matter has been the subject of quite penetrating analysis. This contemporary work requires a separate chapter for its treatment.

Note

An earlier version of this chapter appeared in the University of Hull journal *Curriculum*. We are grateful to the editor for permission to reproduce this in a revised form here.

FURTHER READING

Barbalet, J. M. (1988) *Citizenship* (Milton Keynes: Open University Press) ch. 3.

Heater, D. (1990) *Citizenship: The Civic Ideal in World History, Politics and Education* Part I (London: Longman).

Howe, S. (1991) 'Citizenship in the New Europe: A last chance for the Enlightenment?' in G. Andrews (ed.) *Citizenship* (Milton Keynes: Open University Press) ch. 3.

2

THE CONTEMPORARY DEBATE

SUMMARY

After a long and variable history citizenship has again in recent years become the subject of considerable interest and discussion. Much of this debate has been couched in ideological terms – the Right emphasizing duties, the Left entitlements. The starting point of recent interest was the work of T. H. Marshall, which established a threefold analysis of citizenship – civil, political and social. It has also been the subject of much critical commentary.

The major reason for the intensity of disagreements concerning the *nature* of citizenship as distinct from the details of its practice is its relationship with the economic ordering of society. One aspect that has been particularly emphasized is the perceived incompatibility between the right to property and the undermining of that right by taxation to fund the right to social welfare.

The recent relative success of capitalism compared with command economies has highlighted the matter of the relationship of citizenship and market forces. The citizenship principles of liberty and equality are seen to come into conflict when market forces are given free rein.

The Left has generated a considerable literature to emphasize the desired primacy of the citizen's social and economic rights. Others emphasize the need for constitutional reform to protect rights by law and invigorate the citizenship ideal. Many groups in society, especially women and racial minorities, feel that they are second-class citizens and demand changes to improve that condition. All three major political parties in Britain have produced 'citizen's charters'. Their contents reveal the continuing ideological differences in the interpretations of the concept.

THE SEARCH FOR A MODERN MEANING

Interest in citizenship has fluctuated considerably during the past two-and-a-half thousand years. Fourth-century Athens, Renaissance Florence and Revolutionary France were times when the matter was especially prominent.

In recent decades the topic has again given rise to a great deal of discussion. The deeper the investigators have probed into the meaning of citizenship, the more problems they have uncovered. They have increasingly revealed its complexity and engaged in disagreements about the priorities that should be accorded to its various facets.

The thesis propounded in 1950 by the British sociologist, T. H. Marshall, may be taken as the starting point of this modern revival of interest. Sociologists from his day onward have been very interested in the relationship between citizenship and capitalism, a theme which has bred a copious literature. The general philosophy which has underlain the status of citizenship in liberal democratic states has been the principle of individual rights. That concept has, however, appeared too permissive for those who wish to place a greater emphasis on the community – the communitarians who have striven to revive the classical belief in civic virtue. In addition to these strands various groups have complained of 'second-class citizen' status. Much of the debate has been conducted in academic language, sometimes in philosophical and sociological terms difficult for the lay person to understand. However, politicians, notably in Britain, have attempted to popularize the concept in several of its guises.

This chapter examines some of the major threads in these recent debates. Some other questions which have featured in these discussions are dealt with separately in other chapters. The issues of civic virtue, the idea of the good citizen and the attempted revival of the classical 'civic republican' tradition are treated in Chapter 6.

European citizenship is handled in Chapter 7, and the idea of multiple citizenship appears in Chapter 10.

As a result of all this analysis and argument, many commentators believe that it is quite impossible to reach a general agreement on what citizenship should be today. Apart from the complexity of the subject, it has become bound up in mutually incompatible ideological positions. The purpose of the present chapter is to present this complexity. The possible ways of reconciling these positions must wait until Chapter 10.

MARSHALL AND HIS COMMENTATORS

In 1949 T. H. Marshall gave a series of lectures in Cambridge, which were published the following year: the title was *Citizenship and Social Class*. This work has been the subject of considerable interest and debate in the United States as well as in Britain, especially since the late 1970s. We may note three main reasons for this response:

1. Until quite recently few people in Britain have given much thought to the topic of citizenship. Marshall provided a lucid and succinct survey of the topic.
2. He also analysed the concept into three distinct components – civil, political and social: a fairly novel interpretation at the time.
3. By linking the topics of social class and citizenship, he entered controversial territory concerning the relationship between capitalism and the citizenly status.

It is convenient therefore to start this chapter about aspects of recent discussions on the nature of citizenship with Marshall. We shall first of all provide a synopsis of his lectures, then present some of the major commentary and criticism which they have provoked.

Marshall's basic concern was to show that citizenship evolved in Britain in alliance with the social forces of capitalism; but, as it became evident that civil and political rights were of little value without social rights, so citizenship demands became a threat to the class and market features of the capitalist system. It must be remembered that Marshall developed his thesis as Britain's post-war welfare state was being constructed.

Marshall argued that citizenship basically involves the enjoyment of three sets of rights which can only develop through the creation of appropriate institutions. Civil citizenship, which in England is associated roughly with the eighteenth century, relates to personal freedom and justice ensured by the courts and the jury system. Political citizenship relates to the franchise and opportunities to participate in politics and communal decision-making, extended in England particularly in the nineteenth century. Social citizenship – adequate standard of life assured by education and social and welfare services – has been the characteristic contribution to the ideal of the twentieth century.

According to Marshall capitalism benefited from the consolidation of civil rights because freedom embraced economic freedom. However, the demand for social rights could be satisfied only by increased taxation. It was a policy which involved an attack by the state on the property and profits which capitalism holds as sacrosanct. In a famous phrase Marshall declared that:

> in the twentieth century, citizenship and the capitalist system have been at war. (Marshall and Bottomore, 1992, p. 18)

The picture which Marshall painted, therefore, is of the principles and practices of social class and citizenship interacting. The process of securing rights eroded class differences and enhanced the egalitarianism implicit in citizenship. At the same time, paradoxically, this threat to class privileges prompted a reaction in their defence: in a later book, *The Right to Welfare and Other Essays* (1981) Marshall wrote of the 'hyphenated society' in which the economically dominant class defends its position against the extension of social rights.

Marshall's explanation of citizenship has been subject to considerable criticism of varying degrees of justification. Some interpretations have even been mutually contradictory (see Box 2.1).

Let us outline a few of the main criticisms of Marshall's analysis. First, his tripartite description of citizenship is said to give the false impression that the three elements are similar in kind. In truth, however, social citizenship is distinct from the civil and political dimensions because of its threat to capitalism and because the rights enjoyed in that category involve the redistribution of money by taxation. Second, Marshall has been accused of being too complacent. By failing to emphasize sufficiently the element of struggle in the acquisition of rights, he gave the impression that the achieve-

---

Box 2.1

The most famous and influential English work on citizenship is *Citizenship and Social Class* by T. H. Marshall. Yet his influence has not been straightforward. Different commentators have interpreted his thesis in different ways.

The earlier interpreters of Marshall took him to be indicating a necessary integration of the working class into capitalist society through the development of citizenship and a subsequent decline of class and class conflict. . . . More recently, . . . the idea that the systems of class and citizenship exist in tension with each other, and that the quest for citizenship might promote rather than reduce conflict, has been emphasised. . . .

The strength of Marshall's theory is partly in its complexity, in its ability to proffer almost opposite possibilities without being contradictory. (J. M. Barbalet, 1988, p. 11)

---

ments were irreversible. The contrary case has been made that constant vigilance and struggle are necessary to protect these past achievements, let alone to extend them. The third perceived weakness of Marshall's work is its lack of general applicability. His conception of citizenship derived from his vantage point, namely, welfare-state England. He mentions neither the tensions between England and her Celtic neighbours in the United Kingdom nor the existence of different traditions of citizenship in other ages and other states.

For all its great value, therefore, in its own right and for the commentary it has generated, *Citizenship and Social Class* has limitations as a universal explanation and theory of citizenship. There are two reasons for this. In the first place, it is clear that Marshall had set himself a more limited task, namely, to show how in Britain (or England more properly) 'the drive towards social equality is . . . the latest phase of an evolution of citizenship which has been in continuous progress for some 250 years' (Marshall and Bottomore, 1992, p. 7). Second, even within his own narrow terms, it might be reasonable to excuse him for failing to foresee recent events which undermine the simplicity of his scheme. Immigration and other social developments have rendered England a more pluralistic, less culturally homogeneous society; and New Right Thatcherite policies have weakened the welfare state.

Broader historical and geographical perspectives, new social and political conditions, and a range of ideological questioning about the nature and validity of citizenship have rendered the study of the topic far richer and more complex than Marshall could have conceived.

IDEOLOGICAL ARGUMENTS

Many a distinguished writer on citizenship has argued that agreement concerning its nature is utterly impossible. The reason for this contention is that the concept and status are inextricably bound up with the relationship of the individual to the state and economic and class structures. Since disagreements on these matters can never be resolved, so agreement on citizenship is impossible. Some of the arguments are of long standing; in recent times, differences on the topic reflect the ideological conflicts across the Socialist–Social Democratic–New Right political spectrum.

Part of the controversy focuses on the relative merits of the civic republican and the liberal traditions. However, as this bears particularly upon the concept of civic virtue, we shall deal with this separately in Chapter 6. Here we shall concentrate on the economic arguments which have so intensified recent discussions.

Let us start with the perceived relationship of citizenship with the ownership of property. There is a firm tradition from Aristotle onwards that the ownership of property is necessary for an individual to be a 'solid citizen', to be a stabilizing, responsible influence. This view was, of course, expressed in modern terms by the restriction of the suffrage and membership of legislative assemblies to those men of certain defined economic standing.

In recent decades, however, it is the right to property which has been recruited to the citizenship debate by the New Right. If the language of political liberation uses the vocabulary of political freedom and rights, then the language of economic liberalism uses the vocabulary of economic freedom and rights. The commentators of the New Right therefore hold that the citizen's right to property is of prime importance. The corollary of this attitude is that the state should not undermine this right too severely by high taxation. Two kinds of citizen's rights now come into collision. The right of the wealthy citizen to maintain his or her property relatively inviolate is incompatible with the social right of the less advantaged citizen to welfare state benefits.

Naturally, the interpreters of citizenship on the left of the political spectrum give a higher priority to welfare than the sanctity of property. There is a further and very basic objection to equating citizenship with property ownership. The argument is that wealth is unevenly distributed; wealth is very useful in exerting political influence and gaining access to law; therefore the ownership of property undermines the egalitarian principle central to the citizenship concept. Critics on the left also make the distinction between *owning* and *making* wealth. The stress on the ownership of property undermines the ability of the state to provide welfare; emphasis on the process of accumulating property undermines a sense of civic harmony and community. Individual creators of wealth may well not be very good citizens: their pursuit of riches may breed a selfish, even greedy mentality; and egotism is the antithesis of citizenship. In the words of Michael Walzer, 'autonomy in the marketplace provides no support for social solidarity' (Mouffe, 1992, p. 95). (See also the distinction between autonomy and citizenship in Chapter 3.)

This brings us to the related matter of citizenship in the context of market forces. It is a question, moreover, which has been given increased significance with the sudden collapse of the rival command economies of the twentieth-century Communist states. If the free-market principles of capitalist economies are now to be universally applied, then they will shape a world-wide understanding of the nature of citizenship. The problem is in many ways a reflection of the familiar tension between the ideals of freedom and equality.

Part of the strength of the West's case against Communism in the Cold War was its claim that political and economic freedoms were mutually dependent. Despite the existence of many authoritarian capitalist regimes throughout the world, the simultaneous demand for political and economic liberalization in eastern Europe and the Soviet Union in 1989–91 appeared to be a triumphant confirmation of the thesis. However, if, in defence of freedom, the state does not interfere in the operation of market forces, then the marked divergence in the fortunes of individuals, which the principle of social citizenship is designed to abate, will increase. Indeed, in Reaganite America and Thatcherite Britain it did so.

There is an inherent tension between citizenship and capitalism. Barry Hindess has expressed it succinctly:

Box 2.2

The relationship between citizenship and capitalism has been of considerable interest to sociologists. Professor Bryan Turner has provided the following summary:

Citizenship is not simply about the abatement of class struggle in capitalism; it provides a major criterion for what it is to be a modern society based upon some notion of universalism and justice in opposition to local, particular and hierarchical attitudes and institutions. The societies of western industrial capitalism are essentially contradictory and there is an ongoing dynamic relationship between citizenship and the inequalities of the market place. The dynamic feature of capitalism is precisely the contradiction between politics and economics as fought out in the sphere of social citizenship. (Turner, 1986, p. 12)

Citizenship poses a problem for a market economy as a result of the contrast between the principled equality of rights in the political sphere and the unprincipled inequalities of the market. (Hindess, 1987, p. 60)

During the 1970s and 1980s the ideologically right-wing made implied or overt attacks on the concept of entitlement to social citizenship rights. These attacks suffered little sustained counter-*argument* (as opposed to shocked protest) from the Left. The left-wing tradition, derived from Marx, was that citizenship is not a useful concept; it is the practical, social and economic subordination of the disadvantaged that must be rectified. Recent left-of-centre writing and commentary on citizenship can, in fact, be very roughly divided into three points of view.

In the first place, and developing the Marxist interpretation, is the argument that historically the lower orders have been cheated. They struggled to achieve the concession of citizen rights; but the governing classes ensured that their own crucial social and economic privileges and essentially dominant position were not impaired in the process. Civil and political rights of citizenship are superficial trappings of equality. The working class remain essentially subjects rather than citizens (see Chapter 3).

This interpretation leads to the second left-of-centre approach to the matter: that is, that what is missing from citizenship is a fourth dimension, variously called economic or industrial citizenship. If the so-called citizens have no control *as a right* over the way they work, then the concept of citizenship has little value for working-class people. The exclusion of this area of life from the notion of citizenship has been part of the historical process of its evolution. This point is made vigorously by Anthony Giddens:

> The separation of the economic from the political meant that, in the early years of capitalist development, the worker who walked in through the factory gates sacrificed all formal, and much actual, control over the work process. (Giddens, 1985, p. 208)

On the other hand, and thirdly, there are left-of-centre writers on citizenship who see the interconnections across all dimensions of the status. Political citizenship is not irrelevant to the acquisition or strengthening of social and economic forms of citizenship. Citizens must be more alert to their rights and more active in demanding them. Constitutional and administrative reforms are essential to help these processes. In short, to use the vogue word, the emphasis must be placed on the 'empowerment' of the citizen. In Britain, organizations like Charter 88 have been campaigning for such a reform programme. Citizens must be able to know what is happening (a Freedom of Information Act); must be able to defend clearly defined rights (a Bill of Rights); have greater real opportunities for political participation (constitutional reform); and have easier access to welfare benefits (bureaucratic simplification). This modern left-of-centre case, therefore, is that citizenship need not be a fraud – if only it were fully and fairly implemented.

Although the ideological quarrels relate to live present-day problems, the differences between the right- and left-wing interpretations are also grounded in variant readings of the history of citizenship. The right-wing view is that citizenship rights have been gradually extended – both in kind and in the numbers enjoying them – by a generous and democratically minded governing class. The left-wing view is that, on the contrary, the rights have been extracted from a reluctant governing class by a process of relentless struggle. Two contrasted questions now arise. One, from the Right, is whether the process of extension has gone too far, so that the principle of citizenship is in danger of undermining the advantages of capitalist wealth creation and rising standards of living. The other, from the Left, asks whether the heart has gone out of the struggle, so that the gains of past generations and the needs of the future will be lost in the right-wing counter-attack.

FEMINISTS AND MINORITY GROUPS

A significant distinguishing feature of citizenship is its egalitarianism. In ancient Greece, women, aliens and slaves were discriminated against in various ways; but, then, they were not citizens. Adult men who were citizens, were equal in political and legal terms. In modern history citizenship has eroded class distinctions and has thus been an equalizing force.

In practice, however, many groups in most states feel that they are 'second-class citizens'. This was a term popularized by the American politician Wendell Wilkie during the Second World War. He was referring to American Blacks. Today many groups, both ethnically identified and not, feel that they suffer from being treated in an inferior way compared with 'full' or 'proper' citizens. Whatever the law might decree, in reality these citizens can show that they are not treated on a par with those who enjoy the full panoply of citizens' rights and the citizenly status.

In some cases the complaint derives from the other side. In these circumstances, the 'proper' citizens complain that a given group behaves as if it does not wish to display its loyalty and perform its duties in the ways expected of those enjoying citizenship status.

The largest of all these 'second-class citizen' groups is women. Others are cultural, ethnic or religious minorities. Another group is homosexuals. Finally, there is the 'underclass' of people suffering extreme poverty, whose condition mocks the egalitarian principle of citizenship, even if that is primarily of a legal and political kind (this is one of Marshall's main messages, see pp. 33–4). The more that citizenship is emphasized as the crucial feature of the modern state–individual relationship, the more these groups resent and/or display their inferiority or distinctiveness.

Let us examine the various strands of the feminist argument first. Indeed, the very notion of citizenship was invented by men for men. It was not until the nineteenth century that women even started to enjoy civic rights in a few states. A strong case can be made that parity has still not been achieved. If half the population of any given state are not fully citizens, then the whole status and concept are seriously weakened. However, feminist writers are not agreed among themselves about the diagnosis and treatment for this felt disorder of the body politic.

The basis of the feminist complaint is generally agreed. It is that modern societies have evolved from heavily male-dominated, or 'patriarchal', traditions and that many of the relative male privileges have not yet been sloughed off. To take just two examples from British history: not until 1882 could married women be the legal owners of property; and not until 1928 were women over 21 allowed to vote in parliamentary elections. Another example: in 1992, in half the Member States of the European Community (including Britain) only 10 per cent or less of the body of members in the national parliaments were women.

Since citizenship is primarily a political concept and status, it might be thought that the struggle of women for equal access to political rights and power has been of central importance for achieving the feminists' objectives. Some do indeed argue that it is vital to continue a kind of suffragette campaigning to strengthen the

---

Box 2.3

Feminists have put forward several different political demands which have a bearing upon the nature of citizenship. The following passage from an American academic offers a very straightforward agenda.

... for a vision of citizenship, feminists should [show] ... a willingness to perceive politics in a way neither liberals nor maternalists do: as a human activity that is not necessarily or historically reducible to representative government or 'the arrogant, male, public realm'. By accepting such judgements, the feminist stands in danger of missing a valuable alternative conception of politics that is historically concrete and very much a part of women's lives. That conception is perhaps best called the democratic one, and it takes politics to be the collective and participatory engagement of citizens in the determination of the affairs of their community. The community may be the neighbourhood, the city, the state, the region or the nation itself. What counts is that all matters relating to the community are undertaken as 'the people's affair'. (M. Dietz in Mouffe, 1992, p. 75)

citizenship of women: for more women members of Parliament (MPs) and ministers; for constitutional reform so that more opportunities would be opened up for women's participation in devolved government.

However, some take the opposite point of view, namely, that the very institution of citizenship is damaging to women's interests. By emphasizing the individual's *public* role, it degrades the *private*, domestic role which is of such cardinal importance to women. Similarly, by giving a blanket identity to all, citizenship smothers particular interests:

> In a society where some groups are privileged while others are oppressed, insisting that as citizens persons should leave behind their particular affiliations and experiences to adopt a general point of view serves only to reinforce that privilege. (Iris Young, quoted in Andrews, 1991, p. 83)

It is a text for the whole of the present section of this chapter. In the context of feminism, the message is clear: citizenship reinforces patriarchism.

In the plethora of feminist writing, the American political scientist, Mary Dietz, has identified two main strands: Marxist and maternalist (Mouffe, 1992, pp. 69–74).

1. Marxists perceive male oppression in the division of labour between the two sexes. They believe that this condition is supported by the bourgeois state, which reinforces the power of the dominant, male ruling class. Citizenship is merely one method of exercising this dominance. Revolution is the only means of liberation; the liberal path of extending citizenship rights more fully to women is a sham.
2. The maternalists have a positive view of citizenship. They base their argument on the belief that male and female personalities are very different. Since citizenship has been constructed on male principles, this form should be dismantled and replaced by a new-style citizenship based on female characteristics. These are identified as the moral values of love and protection associated with motherhood and the family. In the process, the distinction between the male/public and female/private facets of life would be dissolved.

The second most important category for whom citizenship is a problem is the group of people who are distinct by virtue of culture, race or religion from the majority of the population. Problems arise for three reasons:

1. The group is or has been subject to discriminatory laws. The most extreme example of this first category were the American Blacks, who, even for generations after the abolition of slavery, suffered from the aftermath of the servile status. For example, despite the existence of a democratic suffrage, various devices were used in the southern states to prevent Blacks from being eligible.
2. The group is or believes itself to be subject to social prejudice. Not only the Black people of the United States, but racial minorities in most countries are or feel that they are discriminated against, in job opportunities particularly. They also often accuse the police of unfair harassment and the courts of unfair sentencing. These feelings of injustice occasionally burst out into civil disturbance, for example, in Brixton, Britain, in 1981.
3. The group feels and wishes to remain distinct. This may result from the resentment caused by the above problems. It can also be a positive wish to retain their distinct cultural identity and a determination not to be assimilated into the majority culture (see also p. 40). The difficulty arises in the context of citizenship because a vital characteristic of that status has traditionally been cultural homogeneity within the citizen body. Islam provides an interesting example of this tendency in the United States, where the 'Black Muslims', of all the movements for Black rights, had a programme for secession.

The heart of the problem has been pithily expressed by a French academic:

> How can citizenship be combined with the coexistence of different cultural groups which only communicate between themselves with the deafness of resentment. (J. Leca, in Mouffe, 1992, p. 30)

So many states are now composed of a patchwork of culturally distinct groups. Post-imperial migration, the lure of employment opportunities, the artificiality of national frontiers, the flight of refugees have all contributed to this condition. We live in an age of plural societies. Cultural homogeneity can no longer be a foundation for citizenship.

The problem, therefore, which has to be faced is how to combine the legal and politically integrative thrust of citizenship identity with the differentiating force of cultural identities. The obvious answer would be to separate the individual's political life from his or her cultural life. Yet this is not easy, for two reasons.

1. Nationalism demands that the cultural/ethnic unit and the political unit shall be one and the same. Nationalism therefore renders multi-ethnic states unstable as we have seen most dramatically in recent years with the disintegration of the Soviet Union and Yugoslavia. A pertinent example from the former USSR is that when Estonia adopted its new constitution, it precluded its Russian inhabitants from the status of Estonian citizenship.
2. If a cultural minority suffers persistent discrimination, they, as a body of citizens, may justifiably wish to seek the support of the state. Laws to ban discriminatory practices, to enforce equal opportunities, even to rectify inequalities by 'positive discrimination' may be necessary. However, if the minority has virtually no access to the country's political and legal institutions, they may attempt, as a cultural entity, to remedy this. The need for civic, political justice reinforces the feeling of group cultural distinctiveness.

Complaints of second-class citizenly status have proliferated; so many groups are conscious of their grievances. Two possibilities exist. One is that the multiplication of self-conscious groups will undermine attempts to strengthen the unifying bond of citizenship. The other is that the idea of citizenship will be able to adapt itself and make creative use of the political activity generated by diversity and these demands for civic justice and equality: in short, citizenship will accommodate itself to the reality of multiple identity.

DEMANDS, PROPOSALS AND POLICIES IN BRITAIN

Since the late 1980s much publicity and debate has surrounded the topic of citizenship in efforts to give the status improved practical application. This activity falls into five categories:

Box 2.4

It has often been asserted that what binds citizens together in their citizenship is cultural homogeneity. However, as states become increasingly multicultural in composition, this assumption can no longer hold true. Professor Parekh gives his prescription for dealing with these new conditions:

What we need in contemporary Britain then is a new spirit of partnership, a spirit of what the Romans called civic friendship, between the majority and minority communities. The majority must accept the minority communities as rightful members of British society, create space for their growth, cherish their heritage just as much as they do, and establish the economic, educational, social and political conditions under which alone they can remain vibrant, proud, and self-confident and self-critical. For their part the minorities must pledge their loyalty to Britain, accept and cherish its great historical heritage as their own, and make room for themselves without subverting its basic character. (B. Parekh in Andrews, 1991, pp. 203–4)

---

1. The Conservative Government's attempts to foster active citizenship (see Chapter 6).
2. Plans to introduce clear programmes of citizenship education in schools (see Chapter 8).
3. The Speaker's Commission on Citizenship (see Chapters 8 and 10).
4. Demands for constitutional reform, notably by Charter 88.
5. The production of citizen's charters by the three main political parties.

As the first two types of activity are dealt with in other chapters, readers are referred to those relevant pages. A few extra words may be useful here regarding the Speaker's Commission. This was an attempt to advance the idea of citizenship by a prestigious, non-partisan body. It was promoted by the Speaker of the House of Commons, took evidence from a very wide range of experts and produced a succinct report of its work and recommendations (Commission on Citizenship, 1990).

The Commission's report, however, gives scant attention to a problem which has exercised many people, concerned with what they see as Britain's current malaise, namely, the urgent need for constitutional reform. In 1988 a movement was founded, calling itself

---

Box 2.5

The following is the ten-point agenda of Charter 88:

We call, therefore, for a new constitutional settlement which would:

Enshrine, by means of a Bill of Rights, such civil liberties as the right to peaceful assembly, to freedom of association, to freedom from discrimination, to freedom from detention without trial, to trial by jury, to privacy and to freedom of expression.

Subject executive powers and prerogatives, by whomsoever exercised, to the rule of law.

Establish freedom of information and open government.

Create a fair electoral system of proportional representation.

Reform the upper house to establish a democratic, non-hereditary second chamber.

Place the executive under the power of a democratically renewed parliament and all agencies of the state under the rule of law.

Ensure the independence of a reformed judiciary.

Provide legal remedies for all abuses of power by the state and the officials of central and local government.

Guarantee an equitable distribution of power between local, regional and national government.

Draw up a written constitution, anchored in the idea of universal citizenship, that incorporates these reforms.

Charter 88, by reference to the English Revolution of 1688 and the Czech human rights body Charter 77. Its programme is for a drastic overhaul of the constitutional system of the United Kingdom as listed in Box 2.5. The relevance of these plans to citizenship is the belief that an effective flourishing of citizenly behaviour and enjoyment of citizen rights is currently impossible given the constraints of Britain's archaic constitutional system. Thus the final item in the movement's agenda refers to a written constitution 'anchored in the idea of universal citizenship'. Charter 88 has attracted considerable support, though left-wing critics are sceptical of its relevance to enhancing the egalitarian principle of citizenship and, in particular, the social rights which many believe should adhere to the status.

In the meantime, all three main political parties have argued that, in their different ways, their doctrinal traditions fit them to promote citizenship. They have presented their interpretations in their own charters.

These were produced in July 1991 and were entitled respectively, *The Citizen's Charter: raising the standard* (Conservative); *Citizen's Charter: Labour's better deal for consumers and citizens*; and *Citizens' Britain: Liberal Democrat policies for a People's Charter*. Much of the discussion prior to these publications had been conducted at an academic, theoretical level. These party pamphlets were designed as plans for action; though the differences in their emphases clearly revealed some deep disagreements concerning the core meaning of the word 'citizen'.

Although the Government document was issued as an official White Paper and was warmly commended by John Major in his capacity as Prime Minister, *The Citizen's Charter* bore the unmistakable doctrinal stamp of the Conservative Party. It was composed of four main themes:

QUALITY – A sustained new programme for improving the quality of public services.

CHOICE – Choice, whenever possible between competing providers, is the best spur to quality improvement.

STANDARDS – The citizen must be told what service standards are and be able to act where service is unacceptable.

VALUE – The citizen is also a taxpayer; public services must give value for money within a tax bill the nation can afford (p. 4).

The whole point of the Government exercise was to ensure that the public services provided the individual with the best possible

---

Box 2.6

The British Conservative Party's perception of citizenship in 1991 is revealed in the Introduction to *The Citizen's Charter*:

Through the Citizen's Charter the Government is now determined to drive reforms further into the core of the public services, extending the benefits of choice, competition, and commitment to service more widely.

The Citizen's Charter is the most comprehensive programme ever to raise quality, increase choice, secure better value, and extend accountability. . . .

Quality of service to the public, and the new pride that it will give to the public servants who provide it, will be a central theme. (p. 4)

service within their resources and competence. The areas covered were: the National Health Service, schools, housing, transport (roads, London buses and underground, and British Rail), the Post Office, police, criminal justice and the courts, local authorities, employment and social services. Indeed, this basic charter was supplemented by particular pamphlets such as the Patient's Charter (NHS) and the Parents' Charter (schools).

The Citizen's Charter emphasizes the individual's right to good service, information and channels of complaint. The good service element is embraced in the very purposes of the charter to ensure quality, standards and value. The right to information is underlined by the charter's reference to 'no secrecy' and 'accurate information' (p. 5). The right of complaint is categorically stated, for example, by reference to the requirement for 'a well-publicised and readily available complaints procedure' (p. 5). Together with the pronouncement that 'Services should be available regardless of race or sex' (p. 5), this agenda has a traditionally liberal tone. Citizens have rights; all should be able to enjoy them equally; and they should be able to hold officials accountable for their actions.

The area of civil rights is dealt with by proposals for improving court procedures: 'Measures are being taken to increase awareness and receptiveness to the needs of victims, witnesses and jurors' (p. 26). The principle of welfare-state social rights is reaffirmed: 'The Government continues to uphold the central principle that essential services – such as education and health – must be available to all, irrespective of means' (p. 4).

Furthermore, this stress on rights seemed to balance the duty-laden concept of the 'active citizen', which had dominated Conservative thinking on the topic two or three years before (see pp. 123–6). Even so, for all its use of the word, the White Paper is not really about citizenship in the proper sense at all. Citizenship is about a sense of community, about citizens acting in harmony. Yet even the very title of the document refers to the citizen in the singular, implying individual rather than collective action. Very few of the rights are enforceable in court. There is not a word about political rights. The passages relating to civil rights are confined to improvements to the machinery of justice, not the constitutional entrenchment of such rights. And the stated commitment to the preservation of the health and educational services is a feeble recognition of citizens' social rights compared with, for instance, the

European Community's Social Charter (to which Britain alone of the Twelve has refused to accede).

The Citizen's Charter is a set of proposals to advance the interests of the individual in accordance not so much with the principles of liberal citizenship as with those of liberal economics. There is much emphasis on market values. Under the heading 'delivering quality' we have an illustrative list of the benefits of privatization (p. 28). The fourth theme, as we have seen, is concerned with 'value for money'. The message is that public services must be operated as free-market systems. There are, indeed, a number of places in the text where this real purpose of the initiative is made plain by the use of the words 'customer' and 'client' instead of 'citizen'. It is quite possible that the individual will enjoy some real benefits as a direct result of the charter. However, it will be in their capacity as consumer, not citizen, that the improvements will be noticed. Alternatively, we may add 'consumer citizenship' to Marshall's triad and the demanded fourth dimension of industrial or economic citizenship. The problem then is that the term 'citizenship' is in danger of losing any precise politico–legal meaning at all.

Labour's *Citizen's Charter*, as its subtitle indicates, is rather more broadly conceived, identifying the individual as both consumer and citizen. The document lists nine rights:

(a) to choose;
(b) to quality;
(c) to safety;
(d) to be treated equally;
(e) to swift and fair redress;
(f) to citizen's action;
(g) to a voice;
(h) to know;
(i) to advocacy.

In many ways Labour's proposals repeat those of the Conservatives. On the other hand, there is some attempt to recognize the distinction between consumer and citizen, and to enhance the rights of the individual in the latter capacity. Some examples are given of plans to improve the rights of citizens *vis-à-vis* local and central government: true civil and political rights. To cite just two examples: the Labour Party committed itself to a Freedom of Information Act;

and to encourage 'All local authorities . . . [to] develop ways of consulting people and giving residents the chance to manage local services through neighbourhood councils, area committees or management committees. . .' (p. 29).

Even so, the distinction between consumer and citizen is not very clearly drawn and the emphasis is placed on the individual in the former role; perhaps because of the challenge of the Government's promises. The Liberal Democrats certainly claimed that there was little difference between the two documents:

> Labour and Tory ideas are pale imitations of what is required. They have confused Consumerism with Citizenship. They aim to make happier subjects, not true citizens. (p. 1)

The Liberal Democrat charter, unlike the other two, addresses citizens in the plural.

Citizens' Britain identifies political, social and economic facets of citizenship. In its first aspect, the party emphasizes the crucial importance of representative and open government (e.g. a Bill of Rights, devolution of power). In the second, the rights of individuals and groups to protection from prejudice and discrimination and entitlements to housing, education, health care and a basic income. In the third, the importance of protecting the needs of individuals as employees and consumers (e.g. profit-sharing by employees, regulation of providers of public services). So even the Liberal Democrats, for all their attempt at a purist definition of citizenship, also utter the language of consumerism. (Though, true, they see the individual acting as an enforcer of standards, as a citizen keeping the state up to scratch.)

This conflation of the categories 'citizen' and 'consumer' is unfortunate. Citizenship is a legal and political term. The sociologists, notably Marx and Marshall, showed that economic and social issues affect the nature of this legal and political status, it is true. Marshall insisted on social citizenship as an essential third element, and others have argued for a fourth, economic, dimension, though not every economic transaction is an expression of citizenship. It can be plausibly argued that the obligations which the state owes to its citizens in parallel to their responsibilities of loyalty and duties should embrace a guarantee of decent living wages. What cannot be argued *on the same grounds of citizenship* is the right of the individual to compensation for a delayed journey on British Rail. That is a *customer's* complaint expecting partial refund by an analogy with a discount on damaged goods. This is not to deny the need for improved public services; rather to insist that this need be argued on commercial grounds in order to protect the concept of citizenship from confusion and devalued meaning.

It is noticeable that much of the recent debate on citizenship has been conducted in socio-economic terms. We must not, nevertheless, forget the importance of defining the individual's legal position *vis-à-vis* the state. Much of the recent interest in citizenship has been expressed independently of any focus on a particular state. However, because in Britain the legal position of the individual is that of a subject of the monarch rather than citizen of the state, we need now to deal with that specific situation.

FURTHER READING

Andrews, G. (ed.) (1991) *Citizenship* (London: Lawrence & Wishart).

Barbalet, J. M. (1988) *Citizenship: Rights, Struggle and Class Equality* (Milton Keynes: Open University Press).

Mouffe, C. (ed.) (1992) *Dimensions of Radical Democracy* (London: Verso).

Oliver, D. (1991) *Government in the United Kingdom* (Milton Keynes: Open University Press).

3

STATES AND THEIR CITIZENS

SUMMARY

In this chapter we turn from historical and philosophical aspects of citizenship to start our consideration of some of the general legal principles governing the relationship between states and their citizens. First, citizenship in international law: states are prohibited from expelling their citizens, so citizenship in this sense has as a 'core' the right to live in one's state of citizenship. Although it has complex rules controlling immigration, English law makes very little distinction between citizens in the international law sense and other individuals lawfully resident in the country.

Second, the relationship between the individual and the state: as far as English law is concerned this is still influenced by the concept of the subject, which was referred to in Chapter 1. This ancient and now outdated relationship of sovereign and subject has not been replaced by any very developed concept of 'citizenship' as a legal (as opposed to social or political) status. A process of legal emancipation of subjects has taken place through the development of the rule of law. This substitution of emancipation for subjecthood may be seen as a step in the direction of the establishment of a concept of citizenship in the legal systems of the United Kingdom. However, emancipation is often viewed as being synonymous with individual autonomy, which carries with it the notion that individual rights are of supreme importance and that membership of a community with the responsibilities and obligations that it implies are somehow incompatible with autonomy and should not be imposed upon individuals. Thus emancipation from the control of others and individual autonomy are not the same thing as being a citizen in the classical republican sense.

INTERNATIONAL LAW AND CITIZENSHIP

Until this point in the book we have been considering the historical, philosophical and political aspects of citizenship. In this chapter we begin to sketch in the legal aspects of the status. In subsequent chapters we shall look in some detail at the legal protection of civil, political, social and economic rights of citizens – associated with themes one, two and three of our analysis; at the duties of citizens, which is an aspect of the classical ideal of our first theme; and at European dimensions, which are to do with nationality and multiple citizenship, themes four and five.

In discussing the legal aspects of relationships between states and their citizens we have to separate the relationship as it is conceived in international law, and the relationship in domestic law – the law which citizens can invoke against the state in the courts.

First, an issue of terminology: in international law the terms 'citizen' and 'national' are often used interchangeably. English law generally prefers the word 'citizen' to 'national', but it also employs the term 'subject', which we shall consider in due course in this chapter. For the sake of clarity we shall use 'national' and 'nationality' when referring to the position of the individual in international law and United Kingdom immigration law, and 'citizen' or 'citizenship' when referring to the substantive rights of individuals in English law.

The two most important rules about the relationship of the individual to the state in international law are that states are prohibited from expelling their nationals, and that they should be willing to receive their nationals if they are expelled by another state. Thus nationality in international law has as its core, a 'right' of nationals to reside in their country of nationality or, in English law terms, the 'right of abode'. These rules originated in customary international law, but they have been given additional force in various international declarations and covenants. For example, the European Convention on Human Rights (ECHR), which binds governments who have signed it (including the United Kingdom), provides by

Article 3 (1) of Protocol 4 that: 'No one shall be expelled . . . from the territory of the State of which he is a national.' Article 3 (2) of the ECHR provides that: 'No one shall be deprived of the right to enter the territory of the State of which he is a national.' Paragraph 4 of Article 12 of the International Covenant on Civil and Political Rights (ICCPR) of 1966 provides that: 'No one shall be arbitrarily deprived of the right to enter his own country.'

These rules about the rights of individuals to live in their country of nationality did not originate from any idea that states owe these duties *to their own nationals*. Customary international law recognized that states had the *right* to protect their nationals but not a *duty* to do so. The state's duty to allow its nationals to live in the country of nationality was originally owed to other states. This followed from the fact that individuals could not enforce international law obligations against states: only other states could do that. Any legally enforceable right of individuals not to be expelled from their own country of nationality could only be found in the domestic or municipal law of the country, and in the United Kingdom no such right existed that could be enforced on the application of an individual citizen or national in UK courts. Looked at in this way, we may say that these rules about the rights of nationals and the duties of states towards their nationals were primarily for the benefit of other states, who would not welcome large numbers of another state's nationals being driven across the borders and dumped on a neighbouring state.

It is relatively simple to formulate the general principle that states should not expel their nationals: what is not always so easy is to determine who a state's nationals are. Each state may determine who are its own nationals, subject to the constraints of international conventions, international custom, and the principles of law generally recognized with regard to nationality (Hague Convention on the Conflict of Nationality Laws 1930, Article 1).

Most states have rules about which persons are born with nationality, and how other people can acquire nationality, for example through 'naturalization'. As indicated in Chapter 1 there are two broad approaches to determining nationality. It either attaches to *jus soli*, the territorial principle, which makes a person born in a state's territory a national of that state regardless of parentage; or nationality comes from *jus sanguinis* according to which nationality is passed on by parents to their children by birth, and in no other way – an essentially ethnic definition.

Clearly the rule that states determine who are their nationals leaves room for loopholes, for people to slip through the gaps between different states' definitions of their nationals. It is not surprising that there are stateless people in the world, often victims of the dislocations of war. The International Convention relating to the Status of Stateless Persons, which came into effect in 1960, seeks to relieve their position, for example, by enabling people who would otherwise be stateless to acquire the nationality of their country of birth or of one of their parents at the date of birth.

ACQUISITION OF BRITISH NATIONALITY

In UK law a person may have any of four citizenship statuses: British citizenship of various kinds (see below); Irish citizenship; a new status of citizen of the European Community states – according to the Maastricht Treaty, 'Citizens of the Union' – which embraces British nationals, Irish nationals and nationals of other Member States, but not other aliens; and finally, alien status. A person may have more than one of these statuses – for example, a British citizen is also a citizen of the European Union. English law also permits dual nationality, so a person may, for example, be a national of the United Kingdom and of the United States of America.

The rules about the acquisition of British nationality at birth are extremely complicated, largely because until the end of the period of the Empire after the Second World War, all 'subjects' born in countries under British sovereignty were regarded as citizens of the United Kingdom both in international law and in English law. All of them had the legal right to live in the United Kingdom, and indeed in any of the 'dominions' of the Crown. In this respect Britain was following the example of Rome which extended citizenship to the non-Roman peoples whom it conquered (see Chapter 1). As the countries of the Empire and Commonwealth became independent and obtained the right to grant nationality to their own citizens, rules, often extremely complex, had to be devised to deal with problems of dual or incompatible nationality. This sort of problem is common in states going through the process of the end of Empire – the states of the former Union of Soviet Socialist Republics are current examples (see Chapter 1).

At the same time as Commonwealth states were gaining their

independence, immigration into the United Kingdom led the Government to introduce immigration controls which affected what had been the rights of British subjects or Commonwealth citizens in the Commonwealth to live in the United Kingdom. In some cases the law effectively denied people a home, as with the East African Asians (Box 3.1). This case illustrates how something that many of us take for granted, the fact that somewhere in the world we have a right of abode, can become of vital significance in the lives of ordinary law-abiding people, and yet can be denied them by a panicky Government.

This is not the place for a detailed examination of the ways in which the right of abode may be acquired, for this, though important, is by no means the heart of what citizenship means, as we have seen in previous chapters. It suffices to point out that the British Nationality Act 1948 established the following categories of 'British-ness': British citizen, British Dependent Territories Citizen, British Overseas Citizen, British Subject and British Protected Person. Only the first category enjoys the right of abode in the United Kingdom. These complex rules are largely concerned with satisfying both the demands of international law about a state's treatment of its nationals, and the concerns of Government to limit immigration from former colonies and dominions and Commonwealth countries.

The matter is complicated by the fact that the 1971 Immigration Act introduced the category of 'patrials', and they have the right of abode: they include anyone, one of whose parents or grandparents was born, adopted, registered or naturalized in the United Kingdom. A woman married to a patrial also has the right of abode. People with five years' continuous lawful residence in the United Kingdom are also generally free of control after that period. So citizenship and the right of abode do not necessarily coincide in UK law, even though the latter is the core of the former in international law.

The impression a reader must gain from even this sketchy account of the law relating to nationality and the right of abode is that English law is very complicated about these matters. However, once a person is lawfully in the United Kingdom English law makes very little distinction between nationals (in the sense in which we have been discussing it so far, the international law sense) and other individuals – aliens and others. Aliens are at risk of deportation if the Home Secretary deems that it would be conducive to the public good – a very vague ground over which the courts have little control. Subject

Box 3.1 The East African Asians case

Until Kenya won independence from the United Kingdom in 1963 Kenyans were first British subjects and then, with the passing of the British Nationality Act 1948, citizens of the United Kingdom and Colonies. They were legally entitled to come and live in the United Kingdom if they wished to do so.

When Kenya became independent the Constitution provided that anyone born in Kenya and one of whose parents had been born there would automatically become a national of Kenya. There was a large Asian population in Kenya, some members of which did not qualify for Kenyan nationality under this provision. Those who did not qualify were given two years within which to register as Kenyan citizens if they had a close connection with the country (for example, by birth, naturalization, registration or ordinary residence). Meanwhile they remained citizens of the United Kingdom and Colonies or retained any other nationality they already had.

In 1967 the Kenyan Government passed laws that subjected those who had not acquired Kenyan nationality to controls such as work permits and restrictions on where they could trade. This resulted in emigration, some of it to Britain, their country of citizenship.

The press and some politicians, both Labour and Conservative (there was a Labour Government at the time), became concerned that up to 200,000 Asians from Kenya (and many more from Uganda and Tanzania) would settle in the United Kingdom. The panic pushed the Government into persuading Parliament to pass the Commonwealth Immigrants Act 1968. This placed controls on British subjects in the form of entry vouchers for which there was a quota unless the subject, or at least one of his or her parents or grandparents, was born, adopted, registered or naturalized in the United Kingdom. This was clearly indirect racial discrimination.

Although this measure did not technically remove the East African Asians' nationality, in effect it removed the 'right of abode', which as we have seen is the core of nationality. They had nowhere else to go because no other country needed to admit them, especially since they were technically British citizens.

The case was taken to the European Commission of Human Rights (discussed in Chapters 7 and 9) by a group of East African Asian citizens of the United Kingdom and Colonies, alleging that they had been subjected to inhuman and degrading treatment and that the 1968 Act had been racially motivated. The case was found to be admissible by the Commission, but its decision was never officially published. The British Government, under pressure, increased the quota of vouchers and admitted individual complainants. Yet the 1968 Act remains on the statute book. The East African Asian citizens of the United Kingdom remain deprived of their right of abode.

to that, their legal position is very similar to that of full UK citizens. (This is discussed further in Chapters 4 and 5.) In this respect nationality, the fourth strand in citizenship theory we identified in Chapter 1, is not central to the status of citizenship in the United Kingdom.

CITIZENSHIP AND SUBJECTHOOD IN THE UNITED KINGDOM

We have seen that modern terminology uses 'citizen' and 'national' to designate those who have the right of abode in their country of citizenship and other entitlements recognized in international law – to diplomatic protection, for example. Nevertheless, the term 'subject' was used in English law to embrace these concepts until relatively recently. The British Nationality Act 1948 first introduced the 'Commonwealth citizen' as an alternative name for 'British subject', which had until then been the legal term used to describe the relationship between the individual citizen and Government. As we shall see, the relation of subject to sovereign was far removed from any of the theories of citizenship that we identified in Chapter 1.

The crux of the relationship was that subjects owed allegiance to the sovereign, who owed protection to these subjects. It was essentially a personal and reciprocal relationship. The first question we need to ask is, who were subjects, and what other people owed allegiance to the sovereign?

The *jus soli* applied and subjects were often referred to as 'natives' to distinguish them from aliens and 'denizens'. ('A denizen is an alien born, but who has obtained *ex donatione regis* letters patent to make him an English subject' – Blackstone, 1803, Vol. I, ch. 10, p. 373.) An important point about the *jus soli* is that, unlike *jus sanguinis*, it was not discriminatory – all those born within the realm, regardless of race or ethnicity were equally subjects. So all of those born 'within the dominions of the crown of England' – to adopt the words of Blackstone in his *Commentaries on the Laws of England* (1803, Vol. I, ch. 10) – were regarded as subjects.

However, it was not only subjects who owed allegiance to the monarch at common law. In the case of *DPP* v. *Joyce* (1946) the Lord Chancellor Lord Jowitt said of the extent of the duty: 'Allegiance is owed to their sovereign Lord, the King, by his natural born subjects;

so it is by those who, being aliens, become his subjects by denization or naturalization; so it is by those who, being aliens, reside within the King's realm. . . .' The reason for imposing duties of allegiance was given as follows in *DPP* v. *Joyce*:

> Whether you look to the feudal law for the origin of this conception or find it in the elementary necessities of any political society, it is clear that fundamentally it recognises the need of the man for protection and of the sovereign lord for service.

The Lord Chancellor then went on to emphasize this reciprocal aspect of the duties between king and those owing allegiance:

> The principle which runs through feudal law and what I may perhaps call constitutional law requires on the one hand protection, on the other fidelity: a duty of the sovereign lord to protect, a duty of the liege or subject to be faithful.

We can see here that subjecthood was conceived as an essentially personal relationship between the individual and the sovereign. What were the obligations and rights in this relationship? In return for allegiance, British subjects had the right of abode and certain rights to protection when outside the realm through diplomatic channels. They received a degree of protection while within the realm, under 'the King's peace', but this was pretty minimal: there was no police force until the nineteenth century. The state made very little provision for social services – health services, education and the like. These were primarily the responsibility of civil society – families, churches and private charities (see Chapter 6). The very restricted duties of the sovereign to subjects is reflected today in the Coronation Oath. They are to govern her peoples according to their laws and customs; to cause law and justice in mercy to be executed in all judgments; and to preserve the Protestant religion, the Church of England and the Presbyterian Church in Scotland. (We consider the Christian aspects of the sovereign's duty in Chapter 9.)

As far as participation in politics was concerned, subjects were entitled to petition Parliament – a right which, as we shall see in Chapter 7, is also granted to citizens of the European Union who may petition the European Parliament under the Maastricht Treaty. This right seems to be taken as one of the marks of citizenship. However, ordinary subjects had no right to participate directly in government decisions or to vote for Members of Parliament. That privilege was reserved to very few subjects until the Reform Acts of the nineteenth century and later Representation of the People Acts introduced first partial, sex- and property-based voting rights and ultimately universal adult suffrage.

The duty of allegiance imposed various burdens on subjects and others owing allegiance. They were liable to be prosecuted for treason and sedition; to be 'impressed' into service in the navy, or 'enlisted' in the army; they could be called upon to do jury service; and they had to pay taxes.

Allegiance, then, implied a duty of blind obedience and loyalty, the lack of rights to criticize government. The granting of arbitrary power to the king, in the sense that he could make many laws by proclamation without obtaining the consent of Parliament, or could exercise his powers without giving reasons or consulting those affected in advance, implied in theory that subjects had no rights to participate in decisions either directly or through elected representatives. There was no concept of citizenship whether in a liberal, republican or social sense in this relationship.

As we shall see in Chapter 6, beliefs about governors and the governed have been influential in theories of citizenship. The sovereign–subject relationship, as it was embodied in the law, carried with it certain beliefs and assumptions about the king on one hand, and ordinary human beings on the other. As far as the king was concerned, Blackstone put it thus: 'Besides the attribute of sovereignty, the law also ascribes to the king, in his political capacity, absolute *perfection*. The king can do no wrong' (Blackstone, 1803, Vol. I, p. 245). This assumption of perfection derived in part from the doctrine of the Divine Right of Kings. It meant that much of what the monarch decided to do was beyond the reach of the courts, who had no right to question it. Nor did Parliament have the right to challenge the king for many centuries, until the 'Glorious Revolution' of 1688–89 finally secured the supremacy of Parliament over the Crown.

On the other hand, the idea of subjecthood involved the notion that the governed, ordinary individuals (as opposed to peers of the realm, who had seats in the House of Lords) were ignorant, unreliable and incapable of making valid judgements for themselves either about how they should conduct their own lives, or how the country should be governed.

SUBJECTS, SOVEREIGNS AND THE RULE OF LAW

We have painted an extreme picture of what the relationship between king and subject involved. As indicated in earlier chapters, T. H. Marshall (1950) argued that subjects won first civil rights and freedoms in the eighteenth century, followed by political rights and freedoms in the nineteenth century. The achievement of the immediate post-Second World War period was the addition of social rights. Marshall's interpretation of these three sets of rights was that they produced a form of legally recognized and underpinned citizenship. We can see that it has elements of a number of concepts of citizenship – liberal, republican and social – in it.

The legal device through which the status of subject and the power of the monarch have been transformed is the subjection of the state to the rule of law. Despite its name, this is a constitutional doctrine or principle rather than a law; but it is a principle that profoundly affects the substance or content of laws. The basis of the rule of law is that individuals are free in their relations with the sovereign, the Government or the state (and indeed in their private relationships) to do anything that is not unlawful: the burden lies on the state to establish its right to interfere with the freedoms of individuals, and the courts will normally require that there be an Act of Parliament authorizing interference. This point is well illustrated by the case of *Entick* v. *Carrington* (1765; see Box 3.2).

The rule of law then requires that Government has specific legal powers from the legislature if it is to interfere with the liberties of individuals. This requirement reflects a move towards a liberal conception of citizenship. It is important because, given the elected nature of the House of Commons, it secures accountability to the people for the laws that are passed. It also imposes a procedure on the process of legislation, which should secure that laws are more considered than they would be if they could be changed by proclamations, which was how the sovereign would have changed the laws to authorize interference with the freedoms of subjects.

An important ingredient of the rule of law is a separate and independent judiciary. A separation of judicial power from the Crown was claimed by the judges in the *Case of Prohibitions* (1607) when they refused the King's claim to be entitled to sit as a judge on the hearing of a case on the ground that the King was not a lawyer and cases ought to be decided by legally qualified judges in accordance with the

---

Box 3.2 *Entick* v. *Carrington* (1765)

The King's Secretary of State suspected that John Entick, who was the author of a number of papers that were critical of the Government, was in possession of documents which, if disseminated, might stir up political 'clamours and sedition'. He issued a warrant to a King's Messenger, Carrington, authorizing him to seize Entick and his books and papers and bring them to the Secretary of State. Entick sued Carrington in trespass alleging that the Secretary of State had no power to issue the warrant.

The Lord Chief Justice, Lord Camden, decided that Entick must succeed unless the defendant could establish legal authority for the search and seizure. 'If he (Carrington) admits the fact, he is bound to show by way of justification, that some positive law has empowered or excused him.' There was no express authority in any Act of Parliament for such a warrant and the courts ought not to imply such authority in the common, or judge-made, law. Carrington argued that warrants of this kind had often been issued before and the courts had never found them to be illegal so it ought to be presumed that they were lawful; and that 'it is necessary for the ends of government to lodge such a power with a state officer; and that it is better to prevent the publication before than to punish the offender afterwards.'

Lord Camden responded to this:

with respect to the argument of state necessity, or a distinction that has been aimed at between state offences and others, the common law does not understand that kind of reasoning, nor do our books take notice of any such distinction.

The case is important on a number of grounds. It shows that a public servant cannot hide behind the claim that he was only obeying orders. Government has to produce specific legal authority if it wishes to interfere with the liberties of individuals; it cannot rely on the fact that it has often done such things before; and a mere claim that 'it is in the public interest' or 'state necessity' will not serve to make something lawful that is otherwise unlawful.

---

law: the King himself was thus subject to the law and could not make rulings affecting the legal rights of his subjects.

A number of important Acts of Parliament in the seventeenth and eighteenth centuries further established the subjection of the Crown to the rule of law, thus giving protection to individuals against arbitrary exercises of power. The Bill of Rights 1689 required the consent of Parliament to the imposition of taxation and removed the King's suspending and dispensing powers. The Act of Settlement 1700 gave the judges security of tenure, thus securing their independence from the Executive. As Parliament achieved sovereignty over the monarch it became possible for legislation to be passed placing new legally enforceable duties on the Government beyond the ancient, unenforceable duties of protection in exchange for allegiance. Yet there is something of an irony in the fact that the legal supremacy that originally belonged to the King has now passed to Parliament, which in effect 'can do no wrong', although the dominance of the majority party in Parliament in effect transfers that power to the Government – the modern version of the monarch. In some respects the doctrine of perfection and executive supremacy has turned full circle.

EMANCIPATION, AUTONOMY AND CITIZENSHIP

One way of interpreting the process of subjecting the state to the rule of law is as a process of emancipation. It will be one of the themes of our discussion (linked with liberal citizenship theory) that if individuals are not to be subjects they need to be emancipated from the arbitrarily exercised control of others – government, parents, employers, even professionals with whom they have dealings. So the concept of emancipation as used here requires further explanation. In Roman law, emancipation referred to the freeing of sons from paternal authority (*patria potestas*). It was commonly used also to refer to the freeing of slaves. Its general meaning is freeing from the personal restraint, control or power of another. It is in this sense that the process of erosion of the power of the king over his subjects – a very personal power, as we noted above – may be interpreted as a process of emancipation.

Similar processes of emancipation or freeing from control or the power of others to those that have taken place between Government and governed may be detected in other, private relationships. These have often reflected changing ideas about human nature which parallel those that have affected the king–subject relationship. The legal trends have been in the direction of, first, acceptance of the intrinsic equality of individuals, regardless of their sex, age, or class;

second, acknowledgement that individuals may be capable of making rational and responsible decisions about their own interests and public interests; and third, appreciation of the fact that individuals may be endowed with qualities of 'civic virtue' (see Chapters 1 and 6). These legal trends are not always of course reflected in practice – there are still widely held assumptions that people are not and cannot be treated as equal, rational, responsible and virtuous. However, the law has, in some respects, led the way in establishing these foundations of citizenship.

So, for example, the relationships between men and women, husbands and wives, parents and children and masters and servants have undergone radical legal reforms in the last century and more. These have freed or emancipated wives, children and employees to a considerable extent from their position of subjection to control.

A few examples will make the point. At common law, wives were the subjects of their husbands; husbands did not commit rape if they had forced intercourse with their wives – this rule was only abolished in 1991 (*Reg.* v. *R.* (1991)); husbands alone were regarded as having rights in respect of their children – since the Children Act 1989 both parents have shared responsibility rather than rights; husbands owned all of their wives' property – since the Married Women's Property Act 1882 the regime has been one of separate property.

In employment relationships too employees were subjects of their masters. At common law, employees could be dismissed at will; now they are protected to a degree by redundancy provisions and 'unfair dismissal' rules. Employees had to obey their employers' orders; now the unfair dismissal rules give them some protection against having to obey unreasonable orders.

Lastly in our examples, the relationship between children and parents. At common law, children born in wedlock were regarded virtually as the property of their fathers; fathers, and as from 1973 mothers, of children born in wedlock had equal 'parental rights' over their children: they could control and punish them, and determine their religion, and they were entitled to their services. Now, as indicated above, parents are regarded as having 'responsibilities' rather than rights in respect of their children (Children Act 1989). Also, since the decision in the *Gillick* case (1986; see Box 3.3), children, as they achieve a sufficient degree of intelligence and maturity, may make certain decisions for themselves, and are generally entitled to have their views taken into account when

---

Box 3.3 *Gillick* v. *West Norfolk Area Health Authority and the Department of Health and Social Security* (1986)

In this case Mrs Gillick was concerned that a medical practitioner might prescribe contraception for one of her daughters under sixteen years of age without her consent as a parent. The Department of Health had issued a circular advising doctors that, although normally they should consult parents before issuing such a prescription, in exceptional cases it was for the doctor exercising his clinical judgement to decide whether to prescribe contraception even if the parents were not involved. Mrs Gillick argued that it would be an interference with her parental rights if a doctor should do such a thing.

The Law Lords decided that parental 'rights' derived from parental duties and existed for the benefit of children and not of parents. Parental rights existed only in so far as they were required for the child's benefit and protection. The extent and duration of the rights could not be ascertained by reference to a fixed age (unless the law stated a particular age, as it does with the age of marriage, for example, and the age at which young people may purchase alcohol or tobacco, or be tattooed). The question as to whether parents could dictate what happened to a child or whether the child could make its own decision depended on the degree of intelligence and understanding of the particular child. It followed that there was nothing unlawful in the guidance issued by the Department and Mrs Gillick was not entitled to a declaration that the circular infringed her parental rights.

---

decisions about them are being made by the courts or by local authorities when they are in care.

It is clear therefore, that English law has adopted a strongly liberal approach to the relationship of individuals to the state and in private relationships. (In subsequent chapters, we discuss the other theories that are embodied in the very eclectic legal system of Britain.) There cannot, of course, be complete, unrestricted autonomy in any legal system, and we now consider briefly some of the dilemmas a legal system is likely to face where there are conflicts between autonomy and the interests of the individual or others with whom a person is in relationship.

Each person's autonomy has to be limited in various ways, specifically in order to protect the autonomy of others. This is recognized, for example, in the European Convention on Human Rights, which provides that rights such as respect for private and family life, freedom of thought, conscience and religion, peaceful assembly and association may be subjected to conditions or restrictions in order to protect the rights of others. As we shall see, especially in our discussion of civil and political, social, economic and environmental rights and civic virtue, individual autonomy often has to be limited in the general public interest. However, restrictions of this kind do not 'subject' individuals to control by other individuals or by the state for its own purposes, in the way that subjection to the monarch and other powerful individuals considered above has done. The control of the law is generally impersonal. Nevertheless, there remain cases where individuals are subject to control of a very personal, individualized kind; this is true, for example, of prisoners, of young children in their relations with parents and teachers, and of patients in their relationships with medical practitioners or judges deciding cases (see Boxes 3.4, 3.5 and 3.6 for examples).

In such cases parents, prison authorities, medical practitioners and the courts override the wishes of individuals. The decisions are very personal in the sense that they depend very much on the particular circumstances of each case and the decision-maker adopts a highly protective, paternalistic approach. On the other hand, there has been a trend in recent cases for the courts to accord considerable autonomy to young people wishing to choose where they live and to 'divorce' their parents. Given the problems inherent in trying to draw a firm line as to when autonomy is appropriate, it is not surprising that elements of subjecthood remain in the law.

The last point in our consideration of emancipation is that it implies changing ideas about Monarch and Government, and about the essential nature of individuals or, in the relationships considered above, of wives, employees, children (see Chapter 6). Monarchs and their government and public officials are no longer to be regarded as possessing the quality of perfection referred to by Blackstone; and individuals are not to be assumed to be ignorant, irresponsible and incapable of making judgements about their own lives and about government. Women are not to be regarded as inferior to men, employees as necessarily subordinate to employers, children as incapable of making any decisions for themselves and as being essentially the property of their parents.

Box 3.4 The anorexia case: *In re W (A minor)*
(Medical treatment: court's jurisdiction) (1992)

A sixteen-year-old girl was suffering from anorexia nervosa. The local authority, in whose care she was, wanted to transfer her from the adolescent residential unit where she was living to a unit specializing in the treatment of eating disorders. The authority wanted to commence new treatment despite her refusal to consent to the new treatment. She objected.

The court decided that in principle minors who have a sufficient degree of maturity and understanding have a right to refuse treatment, but that such refusal cannot override the giving of consent by a parent or guardian or the court. However, in this case although the girl, when well, had a sufficient degree of maturity and understanding to make the decision for herself, she was at that time severely ill, so that her ability to make a judgement about treatment was removed. The court felt justified in ordering that treatment should be administered as it would be in her best interests even though she did not agree. However, generally the courts should not override the decisions of minors who were well enough and of sufficient maturity to make the decisions for themselves. The order for her transfer to new treatment was upheld.

FROM EMANCIPATION TO CITIZENSHIP?

The freeing of individuals from subjection through the process of emancipation has substituted for the concept of subjecthood that of autonomy as the basis of the relationship of the individual with the state. However, the recognition that people should not be subjected to the control of others has led to an almost opposite view, that the autonomy of individuals is the supreme value and that the purpose of constitutions is to secure that autonomy against any kind of infringement. This attitude is strongly manifested in Bills of Rights and international instruments that protect human rights.

One problem that flows from this placing of autonomy on a kind of pedestal is that it can operate to prevent evolution of the civic or communitarian aspects of citizenship in the classical sense. Citizenship theory, as we saw in Chapter 1, involves individuals having not

---

Box 3.5 Blood transfusions and religious objections: *In re T (Adult: refusal of treatment)* **(1992)**

T was twenty years old. Although not a Jehovah's Witness herself, she was under the influence of her mother who was. Jehovah's Witnesses object to blood transfusions. T was injured in a road accident. At the time she was pregnant. She had to undergo a Caesarean section for the delivery of her baby, and before going into the operating theatre she signed a form refusing a blood transfusion. At the time she did not expect to become seriously ill.

Her baby was stillborn, and her condition deteriorated so that she had to be placed on a ventilator and was in need of a blood transfusion.

T's father and boyfriend applied to the court for a declaration that it would not be an unlawful assault on her to give T a transfusion. The court decided that generally an adult patient is entitled to refuse consent to treatment. However, if the patient's capacity to decide had been diminished by illness (see *Re W*, Box 3.4) or misinformation or pressure from another person, as was the case here, the refusal did not bind doctors and they were entitled to treat the patient in accordance with their clinical judgement of his or her best interests. When she signed the refusal she had not appreciated that she might become so seriously ill.

Box 3.6 Refusal of surgery: *In re S (Adult: refusal of treatment)* **(1992)**

A woman had been in labour for three days and the life of herself and her unborn baby were in danger unless a Caesarean section was performed. She and her husband objected to surgery on religious grounds. The court decided that, in a situation in which the lives of mother and the unborn child would both be at risk if the operation were not performed it was open to the court to make a declaration that the operation could be performed notwithstanding the mother's lack of consent.

---

only civil but also political rights, and owing duties to the community and having responsibilities to others, including people outside their own families. It implies that individuals can and do participate effectively and responsibly in the decisions that affect their lives and their communities. A society that places the highest value on autonomy and the rights of individuals will be resistant to accepting legal or moral obligations of citizenship, and thus to the development of a mature effective citizenry. (We refer to this theme again in Chapters 6 and 10.)

In the next two chapters we shall look more closely at civil and political rights and duties (Chapter 4), and social, economic and environmental rights (Chapter 5) in English law. In Chapter 7 we widen the horizons of our legal survey to take in the European dimension which is of increasing importance in the lives of individuals. In Chapter 9 we consider how the legal foundations of citizenship might be strengthened, bearing in mind always that the law provides only part of the foundation of citizenship.

FURTHER READING

Dicey, A. V. (1885) *The Law and the Constitution* (London: Macmillan).

Dummett, A. and Nicol, A. (1990) *Subjects, Citizens, Aliens and Others* (London: Weidenfeld and Nicolson) ch. 1.

Gardner, J. P. (1990) 'What lawyers mean by citizenship' in Speaker's Commission *Encouraging Citizenship. Report of the Commission on Citizenship* (London: HMSO).

Lloyd, G. (1984) *The Man of Reason: "Male" and "Female" in Western Philosophy* (Minneapolis: University of Minnesota Press).

Maitland, F. W. (1908) *The Constitutional History of England* (Cambridge: Cambridge University Press).

Showalter, E. (1985) *The Female Malady. Women, Madness and English Culture, 1830–1980* (London: Virago Press).

Starke, J. G. (1989) *Introduction to International Law*, 10th edn, (London: Butterworths) ch. 12.

4

CIVIL AND POLITICAL RIGHTS AND DUTIES

SUMMARY

In this chapter we start our consideration of the rights and duties of citizenship. Rights may be divided into first, second and third generation rights, and we shall focus on the first generation, civil and political rights.

Citizenship in English law is eclectic, borrowing ideas from classical and liberal traditions, and from social citizenship theory. Although civil and political rights are important in liberal citizenship theory and in civic republicanism, in English law such rights are not protected in a very strong way since, unlike most countries, we do not have a written constitution or a Bill of Rights. So, for example, the protections of freedom of speech are weak. There is room both in law and in practice for discrimination against women and minorities. The value of the right to vote is undermined by the system for the distribution of seats and the counting of votes.

The law imposes *specific* duties of 'good citizenship' on citizens, for example, to pay taxes, in clearly defined circumstances. The question arises whether it should also impose *general* duties of good citizenship – to help the police, to pay taxes, for example. It will be suggested that such duties would undermine the rule of law, on which, as indicated in Chapter 3, the emancipation of individuals from ꜱᵁᵇ... ꜱtion rests.

state also owes duties to its citizens, and the law has a role in ꜳ that it does not fail in those duties.

THE RIGHTS OF CITIZENS: FIRST GENERATION RIGHTS

In this chapter we are concerned with civil and political rights. These are commonly regarded as 'first generation' rights, in the sense that they were the first to receive legal recognition in the English legal system in the eighteenth and nineteenth centuries. In Chapter 5 we shall consider 'second and third generation' rights. Social and economic ('second generation') rights are those that are recognized in the welfare state – rights to education, housing and health care, and to an income. In the last decade or so 'environmental' rights have come to be regarded in many quarters as fundamental, 'third generation' human rights.

It is convenient to follow the classification used by T. H. Marshall (see Chapters 1 and 2) and to divide first generation rights into civil or legal, and political. Taking civil or legal rights first (freedom of the person, freedom of association, freedom of speech and so on), these are, as we have seen in Chapter 1, of central importance in the liberal tradition of citizenship. The kernel of these is the rule of law, the right to protection in the exercise of rights by the courts. All individuals present in the United Kingdom are, generally speaking, entitled to the protection of the law without discrimination on grounds of nationality or citizenship: there are some exceptions – an 'alien' may be deported, for example. However, in normal everyday life, as one would expect, all individuals are entitled to the protection of the ordinary law in relation to contracts, torts and the criminal law, and in dealing with disputes about property, etc. (see *Entick* v. *Carrington* (1765), Box 3.2).

Political rights are central in both the classical or republican, and the liberal traditions of citizenship. These are generally taken to include the right to vote or stand for election, and rights to participate in political activity, for example, through freedom of expression and membership of political parties and pressure groups of various kinds.

In the United Kingdom, people are relatively free to engage in this sort of activity. This is an example of how 'nationality' (theme four in the debates about citizenship theory that we identified in Chapter 1) is not to any great extent determinative of rights and the relationship between the individual and the state in the United Kingdom. For example, as well as British citizens, citizens of the Republic of Ireland and Commonwealth citizens have the vote in UK parliamentary and

local government elections, and in European Parliament elections if
they are resident in the United Kingdom (voting rights will be
extended under the Treaty of European Union – see Chapter 7); as
far as the rights to stand for election and to be members of elected
bodies are concerned the rules vary depending on the body in
question. The general rule is that anyone who is twenty-one years old
or older is qualified to be a member of the House of Commons, a
local authority or the European Parliament, as long as they are 'not
alien'. There is no requirement for a local connection as far as
candidates for the House of Commons or the European Parliament
are concerned, but local government candidates must have a local
connection. Disqualifications – of peers from the House of
Commons, for instance – do not detract from this general principle.

In sum, the political rights of citizenship extend beyond the class
of citizens or nationals of nation-states, and an embryonic form of
supranational, multiple, citizenship is developing (the fifth theme in
citizenship theory identified in Chapter 1).

PEOPLE EXCLUDED FROM FULL CITIZENSHIP RIGHTS

In Ancient Greece and Rome, women and slaves were not regarded
as citizens with any civil or political – or social – rights at all. These
are examples of defects in systems that had, in other respects, highly
developed traditions of citizenship. In England too, certain classes
have been granted only partial rights: the imposition of a property
qualification for the vote was an example. The denial of the vote to
women was another.

The history of the legal position of women provides a particularly
strong example of exclusion from citizenship. In Chapter 3 we
considered the process by which they have been broadly emancipated, as far as the law is concerned, from subjection to their
husbands. In public life too, they were under a particularly strong
form of subjection. It was not until the late years of the nineteenth
century that women were regarded as entitled to participate in public
life – life outside the domestic sphere – at all (see, for example, Box
4.1). In the case of *Chorlton* v. *Lings* (1868–9) a woman claimed the
right to vote under the Reform Act 1832 as read with the
Interpretation Act 1850. The 1832 Act gave the vote only to certain

---

Box 4.1 Women and public life in the nineteenth century

As late as 1889, in the case of *Beresford-Hope* v. *Lady Sandhurst* (1889), the Master of the Rolls, Lord Esher, said: 'I take it that by neither the common law nor the constitution from the beginning of the common law until now can a woman be entitled to exercise any public function.'

'males'. The 1850 Act provided that 'words importing the masculine gender shall be deemed to include females unless the contrary is expressly provided.' The court held that in the case of the franchise 'male' did not include 'female'. Women had never been entitled to vote at common law, and the court held that it would require a clear statute to reverse this position. So it was not until 1918 that women won the parliamentary vote (restricted to certain categories of women aged over thirty until 1928, when women won the vote on the same terms as men).

Women were not even entitled to join the professions until the Sex Disqualification (Removal) Act 1919. In 1862 London University refused to allow women to be admitted to degrees under its new Charter, and thus Elizabeth Garrett (later Elizabeth Garrett Anderson) who eventually became the first woman doctor, could not obtain a London MD. In 1864 when she wished to be permitted to take the examinations of the Royal College of Physicians, the College took legal advice on the matter. The advice was to the effect that the College was precluded by the terms of its Charter from admitting women. One of the avowed aims of the Tudor founders of the College had been to exclude women from their profession. The Royal College of Surgeons treated her in a similar way. She had to obtain her qualification in France: it was then recognized in England.

Although most disqualifications for women have been removed, they continue not to be treated equally with men, either in law or in reality. While the Treaty of Rome, the Equal Pay Act 1970 and the Sex Discrimination Act 1975 are supposed to provide equal pay for work of equal value, in practice women are paid at lower rates than men, partly because they tend to enter low-paid work and partly because of continuing discrimination. The reduced rights of part-time workers to security of employment hit women more than men. This is a form of legally sanctioned indirect discrimination.

Institutionalized and condoned discrimination against minorities (blacks, homosexuals, Catholics in Northern Ireland) provide further examples of the denial of full and equal citizenship, and recognition as members of the community to certain classes of people.

These examples indicate how important it is for the law to recognize all persons as having equal citizenship rights in both the classical and liberal senses, in order to secure their emancipation from subjection to the state and other powerful individuals (employers, husbands, parents, and so on), and to ensure social cohesion so that all who wish to do so have the opportunity to participate in public life.

We must also realize that formal legal equality, though of central importance in citizenship, cannot by itself guarantee substantive equality between members of the community. Some people, women in our example, continue to be regarded as unfitted for participation in the community, in effect as second- or third-class citizens, despite their formal legal equality. There are limits to what the law can do about this. Here the civic culture, fostered by civic virtue and education (discussed in Chapters 6 and 8), also needs to be called in aid.

There remain today certain classes of individuals who are expressly denied full rights: children (see Chapter 3), prisoners, who are denied the vote as well as their freedom, public employees, many of whom are denied freedom of speech in that they may not criticize their employers or communicate official information to others. Many civil servants and local government officers are also denied the right to engage in political activity. Certain ministers of religion are denied the right to sit in the House of Commons. Although some of these disqualifications may be justified, for example, to protect children, or to secure the neutrality of the civil service, any measure that denies individuals citizenship rights needs to be justified.

RIGHTS IN THE UNITED KINGDOM

There is no Bill of Rights or written constitution in the United Kingdom. This means that there are no legally enforceable rights that citizens have that cannot be interfered with quite simply by Parliament passing legislation in the ordinary way, or indeed by acts of the Government, police or other state bodies, as long as they are not 'tortious'. This position needs some explanation.

We saw in Chapter 3 (Box 3.2) that Government in the United Kingdom may only interfere with the liberties of individuals if there is clear legal authority, generally in an Act of Parliament, for such interferences. Thus, it is commonly said that in the United Kingdom everything is lawful unless some specific law says that it is unlawful. Individuals are free to do whatever they like, including the activities we commonly associate with citizenship such as joining political parties or campaigning groups, demonstrating for or against some public policy, criticizing Government and so on, unless there is a rule of the common law or an Act of Parliament or a rule of European Community law which forbids the act. This contrasts with the position in the former Soviet Union, for instance, where effectively citizens had to justify everything they did and were acting unlawfully unless they could point to legal authority for their acts.

There are, of course, very many rules that prevent people from acting as freely as they wish: they must not take other people's property, injure them negligently or on purpose, break contracts. Free speech is limited by the laws of libel and slander which protect people's reputations; incitement to violence or to racial hatred are crimes. Demonstrations are regulated by rules designed to maintain public order and prevent traffic disruption, and so on. The upshot of the collection of rules which limit individuals' freedom is that freedom is 'residual' in the United Kingdom: it is the freedom to do those things that are left once all the things one is not allowed to do are taken into account.

Some statutes do give individuals civil and political 'rights' over and above the residual liberties of the common law – for example, the Representation of the People Acts give people the right to vote (subject to registration requirements) and to stand for office. So it would be unlawful for these rights to be denied, and a voter or would-be candidate could obtain a remedy in the courts if these rights were denied them – for example, by the Registration Officer or the Returning Officer in an election. So 'rights' set out in statutes are closer to being 'rights' in the usual sense than the residual freedoms mentioned above.

However, both rights and residual liberties, though they are extensive, are vulnerable to erosion in the United Kingdom. Acts of Parliament can remove people's statutory rights and limit people's freedom as citizens. This is because in the English legal system, Parliament is 'sovereign' (see Chapter 3). Acts of Parliament that interfere with rights and freedoms are no different in their legal status or in the procedure that Parliament has to follow in enacting them from other Acts which, for example, impose speed limits. All that is required is that the Bill be 'read' three times, and pass through a committee stage and a report stage in each of the two Houses of Parliament, receiving majority support at each stage. If the House of Lords refuses consent then it can be bypassed and a Bill can receive the Royal Assent – a formality nowadays – and become part of the law of the land on the basis of a majority in the Commons only.

Given that our electoral system normally gives one party a majority in the House of Commons the effect of this position is that a Government can generally rely on being able to have whatever measures it wishes enacted by Parliament, even if they erode civil and political rights. In reality, the sovereignty of the monarch has been transferred to Parliament, and hijacked in Parliament by government.

This position in relation to the legal protection of 'rights' can be contrasted with that in many countries with written constitutions (only the United Kingdom, New Zealand and Israel do not have written constitutions). In such documents there are certain provisions which cannot be altered by simple majorities in the legislature. Many written constitutions have Bills of Rights which are protected in this way. Under such systems citizens have 'rights' in the sense that they are legally free to do certain things that are set out in the constitution or Bill of Rights, and that legal freedom cannot be taken away unless a special procedure is followed. In the Republic of Ireland, for example, a referendum has to be held if the Constitution is to be amended. In the United States there are complicated provisions requiring the consent of a number of the states to amendments to the Constitution, including the Bill of Rights, and special majorities in Congress. Provisions of this kind, 'entrenching provisions', mean that the civil and political rights normally protected in a Bill of Rights or a Constitution cannot be easily interfered with by the Government of the day using its parliamentary majority to push through changes that reduce the freedoms or rights of citizens. It is because the United Kingdom has no such special legal protections for citizenship rights that we speak generally not of 'rights' but of 'freedoms' in this country.

Whether they have the status of 'rights' or 'freedoms', there are certain aspects of the relationship between the citizen and the state that are of special civil and political importance. For example, the access that an individual has to the courts for the resolution of disputes with state officials, or with private bodies such as employers with whom the individual has dealings, is vital to the maintenance of the rule of law. This, as we saw in Chapter 3, has been an important tool in the emancipation of the individual from state control, and indeed from the control of other powerful individuals and bodies. However, access to the courts is effectively limited in various ways: legal aid is available only to those with very low incomes and few capital resources; legal costs are high; in judicial review cases against public bodies, there are extensive procedural hurdles such as the need to apply to the court within three months of a decision and to obtain leave to apply for judicial review. Of course, it does not follow from the fact that a person is legally free that in practice people are or feel themselves to be free to exercise their liberties.

To be more specific about the importance of legal and civil and political rights to citizenship, freedom of speech may be viewed as part of civic republicanism (the first of the themes in citizenship theory identified in Chapter 1) in enabling individuals to participate in the political process. The freedom to criticize the Government, and freedom of association, including the right to form and join political parties and various pressure and campaigning groups, are clearly important to that process. Freedom from discrimination both at the hands of the state and by private employers and others may be regarded as an important entitlement of citizenship in that it enables all individuals regardless of sex, race, ethnic or national origin, religion and so on to participate equally in the political process and in membership of the community. It may also be regarded as part of the civil rights of individuals in that it reinforces their emancipation from the exercise of state and private control. As indicated earlier, the formal legal protection of such rights is important, but it is not self-executing. Discrimination is not abolished by outlawing it. The passing of laws is only one step in a complex process.

FREE SPEECH IN THE UNITED KINGDOM

The point was made above that liberties in the United Kingdom are residual, but that the extent of that residue is considerable. However, there are important restrictions on the exercise of civil and political liberties which undermine the ability of individuals to be citizens. We can consider here only some of the most important restrictions on these liberties. First, what is commonly referred to as freedom of speech or freedom of expression. Before we embark on a consideration of the legal position, we need to have a picture of why freedom of speech is important to citizenship. It needs to be viewed broadly, and includes the right to receive and impart information. The exercise of free speech can have a formative effect on public opinion, and thus it can, theoretically at least, be abused. It can stultify the thinking of the public, or encourage uniformity of views, especially through the mass media if they fall into hands which only represent a narrow range of views. It can allow for the dissemination of anti-democratic, anti-citizenship views – racist and sexist beliefs, for example. This line of thinking might be taken to justify the limitation of free speech, requirements that the media publish a range of views or eschew certain opinions.

Such arguments against free speech, however, imply a low opinion of the ability of ordinary individuals to form their own views and be critical of what they read in the press or see or hear on the broadcast media. Another view, and one to which we subscribe, is that, although some restrictions on free speech may be justified (see below), individuals are not so easily duped that they need to be protected against 'unacceptable' information. If educational processes (Chapter 8) and the civic culture (Chapter 6) are designed to encourage individual responsibility and the acquisition of political skills, then there is little to fear from free speech.

The European Convention on Human Rights (Box 4.2) provides a helpful criterion against which to measure freedom of speech in the United Kingdom.

Many of the limitations of freedom of expression in English law fall well within the exceptions that will be necessary in any legal system, such as those set out in para 2 of Article 10 of the ECHR (Box 4.2). For example, there are statutory restrictions making it a crime to disclose official information to do with security and intelligence, defence, international relations, crime and special investigation powers, and information entrusted in confidence to the Government by other states or international organizations (Official Secrets Act 1989). There are also restrictions on the publication of obscene material and on incitement to racial hatred, which are crimes, and on defamation, which is a tort.

Box 4.2 Article 10 of the European Convention on Human Rights

This Article sets out freedom of speech as follows:

1. *Everyone has the right to freedom of expression. This right shall include freedom to hold opinions and to receive and impart information and ideas without interference by public authority and regardless of frontiers. This Article shall not prevent States from requiring the licensing of broadcasting, television or cinema enterprises.*
2. *The exercise of these freedoms, since it carries with it duties and responsibilities, may be subject to such formalities, conditions, restrictions or penalties as are prescribed by law and are necessary in a democratic society in the interests of national security, territorial integrity or public safety, for the prevention of disorder or crime, for the protection of health or morals, for the protection of the reputation or rights of others, for preventing the disclosure of information received in confidence, or for maintaining the authority and impartiality of the judiciary.*

However, these provisions do not give the full picture of the extent of the legal limitations on freedom of expression in the United Kingdom. For example, by their terms of employment civil servants are under duties of confidentiality which mean that they cannot disclose any information at all about Government unless the disclosure has been authorized by the responsible minister. Disclosure would be a disciplinary offence for which they could be punished, and which would damage their careers. Disclosure of confidential information is also forbidden by the common law, quite apart from situations where a contract of employment imposes a duty of confidentiality. If information is received in circumstances where a duty of confidentiality is implied, then disclosure of that information can be prevented by a court order; or, after disclosure, anyone who profited by the disclosure may be required to hand over the profits to the 'confider' (for an example, see Box 4.3).

Thus the freedom of expression for civil servants, possible sources of important information about Government, is severely restricted and the freedom of citizens to receive information referred to in Article 10 of the ECHR (Box 4.2) is correspondingly limited. The upshot of these and other limitations on the freedom to give and

---

Box 4.3 *Spycatcher*

The 'Spycatcher' affair illustrates some of the legal restrictions on freedom to communicate information about government.

Peter Wright had been a member of MI5. After his retirement he wrote his memoirs in *Spycatcher* in which he disclosed information about MI5's operations and was highly critical of them. The Government, through the Attorney-General, sought to prevent the publication on the ground that Wright had owed a lifelong duty of confidentiality to the Crown because of his employment, so the material ought not to be published, and further it would be damaging to the morale and credibility of the service if publication took place. The English courts granted interim (temporary) injunctions stopping publication in England.

The book was published in many countries around the world. The British Government tried to obtain court orders preventing its publication abroad, for example, in Hong Kong and Australia. These proceedings were unsuccessful and the whole fuss caused the sales of the book world-wide to spiral.

Eventually the English House of Lords decided in the case of *Attorney-General* v. *Guardian Newspapers (No. 2)* (1990) that Wright had indeed had a lifelong duty of confidentiality, but they lifted the interim injunctions and refused to grant permanent injunctions because the information had lost its quality of confidentiality by being published round the world and being freely available in the United Kingdom. It would have been pointless to grant injunctions in such circumstances. However, the courts also held that an order for an account of profits should be taken from the publishers, Heinemann, since they had made the profits from publishing the book in breach of confidentiality.

---

receive information is that citizens are commonly not in possession of the information they would need to participate effectively in the political process, and potential 'whistle-blowers' are deterred. Thus, in many respects, the law hampers the practice of civic republicanism.

THE RIGHT TO VOTE

The second area where political rights are restricted in their effectiveness is the electoral system. An aspect of the right to vote which is clearly important to citizenship in both classical and liberal theories, is the effect that the votes of individuals have on the outcome of an election. One of the fundamental principles of a democratic electoral system and of a concept of equal citizenship is supposed to be that the value of a vote is the same regardless of where or by whom it is cast: as we saw in Chapter 1 (Box 1.3) this was one of the demands of the Chartists. This principle is enshrined in law in the provisions for the redistribution of seats (Parliamentary Constituencies Act 1986, Schedule 2) which seek to ensure that each constituency is close to a norm as to the number of voters within the area. These provisions are not perfect for a number of reasons, one being the requirement that parliamentary constituency boundaries should not normally cross local government boundaries. Another reason is that the Boundary Commissioners are to take account of 'local ties' in drawing boundaries. There is also currently an in-built 'Celtic preference' in that Scotland, Wales and Northern Ireland have proportionately more MPs than England does. Also London is over-represented by about 13 MPs.

There is, it is clear, a conflict in our electoral arrangements between the idea that MPs represent individuals, a liberal idea, which should mean that each individual's vote is worth the same, and the idea that the MP represents communities, which suggests that community ties – important elements in classical theory – are relevant in drawing boundaries.

The liberal principle of 'one vote one value' is further undermined by the operation of the first past the post system for parliamentary elections. In each constituency only one MP can be elected, and that is the person who achieves more votes than any of the other candidates. As the supporters of the two main parties tend to be concentrated in 'safe' constituencies, it is very difficult for supporters of parties whose support may be substantial but is more thinly spread (the Liberal Democrats and the Greens, for example) to win seats. In this respect their votes are not of equal value to those of supporters of the two main parties.

CIVIC DUTIES

We have focused so far on the civil and political rights and liberties of citizens in the United Kingdom; another important aspect of citizenship is the duties that the status imposes – civic virtue in various forms. In considering this topic it is necessary to distinguish between legally imposed duties and 'moral' ones. The latter were considered briefly in Chapter 1 when we looked at the classical citizenship tradition – theme one in our analysis. It will be considered further in Chapter 6. In this section, however, we are concerned with legally imposed duties of citizenship.

The range of duties that the law imposes on individuals include, briefly, the duty to obey the law, to pay tax, to do jury service, and in time of war or when legislation provides for conscription, military service. These duties can raise difficult legal problems, and issues arise from time to time about the clashes between different notions of citizenship and the relationships between 'good citizenship' in the classical sense and the liberal emphasis on individual autonomy. We can illustrate these issues by considering some of the leading cases in two areas of the law relating to civic duties – the questions (a) whether citizens have duties to assist the police in keeping the peace and detecting and dealing with crime; and (b) what is the extent of the duty to pay taxes?

In principle, it might be said that the good citizen ought to have a duty to assist the police in their work in keeping the peace and detecting and preventing crime. Whether this is or should be a legal as opposed to a moral or social duty is, however, a difficult issue (see for example, Box 4.4).

Not only do individuals have the right in law not to answer police questions, they also have the right to use reasonable force to defend themselves against intrusions by the police or other officers of the state. So, for example, in *Kenlin* v. *Gardiner* (1967) plain-clothes police officers became suspicious of the behaviour of two boys who were going from door to door to the homes of members of their school rugby team to remind them of a match. One officer approached the boys and asked them what they were doing. He told them he was a policeman and showed them his warrant card, but they did not register this information. One boy tried to run away but was restrained by the officer, and struck him to escape. They were charged with assaulting an officer in the execution of his duty. It was held that the police had no power to detain people to question them unless they went through the proper procedure for arrest, and so the officer was not acting in the course of his duty, and the boy was not guilty.

Box 4.4 *Rice* v. *Connolly* (1966)

Police officers were patrolling late at night in an area where there had recently been a number of burglaries. They observed Rice loitering in the streets and asked him where he was going, where he had come from, and for his name and address. They were not satisfied with the information he gave them and asked him to go with them to have the information checked. He refused to move unless arrested, and they then arrested him for wilfully obstructing them in the course of their duty. It was held that he was not guilty. The police were acting in the course of their duty, because this includes the duty to take all steps which appear to them necessary for keeping the peace, for preventing crime or for protecting property from criminal injury. However, Rice was not acting 'wilfully' since that involves acting without lawful excuse. In effect the court gave precedence to Rice's autonomy as opposed to placing him under a duty of 'good citizenship'.

In giving judgment in this case Lord Chief Justice Parker said:

It seems to me quite clear that though every citizen has a moral duty or, if you like, a social duty to assist the police, there is no legal duty to that effect, and indeed the whole basis of common law is the right of the individual to refuse to answer questions put to him by persons in authority, and to refuse to accompany those in authority to any particular place; short, of course, of arrest. . . . In my judgment there is all the difference in the world between deliberately telling a false story – something which on no view a citizen has a right to do – and preserving silence or refusing to answer – something which he has every right to do. . . .

These cases raise a number of issues. First (as we saw in *Rice* v. *Connolly*, Box 4.4), individuals have a right of silence, a right not to answer questions. This is part and parcel of the presumption of innocence, and recognizes that the burden is on the state to prove guilt, not on the individual to establish innocence. This reflects both a view of the individual as not to be presumed to be an offender – a bad citizen – and a view of the police and prosecuting authorities as being fallible.

On one view it might be said that it is contrary to ideas of good citizenship that people should be entitled to refuse to help the police; but there are a number of rationales for the legal position. The police would be placed in a position of even greater power and authority over individuals than they are now if they were entitled to demand that people answer questions and arrest those who refused to do so. The state is not to be presumed to possess the quality of 'perfection', to use Blackstone's expression (see Chapter 3) previously attributed to the monarch, and safeguards for the individual are required against abuse of power by the state.

Our second example of the problems that can flow from legally imposed duties of 'good citizenship' is in the field of liability to pay taxes. This duty again raises conflicts between good citizenship and autonomy. Most individuals prefer not to pay taxes, or to minimize their liability; yet surely a good citizen will accept the need to make a contribution to the good of the community?

The duty to pay taxes is, in principle, imposed by specific taxing statutes which are often very technical and detailed. Since the Bill of Rights 1689, liability to pay tax may only be imposed by parliamentary authority, not by executive 'fiat' (see Box 4.5).

Problems arise when statutory measures imposing tax liability are not clear, and this raises issues about whether there is or should be a

---

Box 4.5 Article 4 of the Bill of Rights 1689

This article provides that 'levying money for or to the use of the Crowne by pretence of prerogative without grant of Parlyament for longer time or in other manner than the same is or shall be granted is illegal'.

This provision put an end to the previous claims of successive kings to be entitled to raise taxation without the consent of Parliament, for example, through the imposition of duties on imports, forced loans, demands for 'ship money' and so on.

Article 4 encapsulates a number of important basic principles of constitutional law. Since Parliament would not be willing to grant the Crown the right to tax unless and until it had shown itself willing to deal with the grievances of Parliament and of subjects, it implies 'that there shall be redress of grievance before the granting of supply'. Clearly it means there shall be no taxation without representation, and the courts have drawn from it a presumption in favour of the subject when it comes to interpreting and applying a taxing statute, to the effect that a statute shall not be construed as imposing a liability to tax without clear words.

general duty on citizens not to seek to reduce their tax liability by artificial means – short, of course, of fraud and the like, which is clearly unlawful.

What about the attitude of the courts to complicated arrangements made by individuals to minimize their tax liability? The two conflicting ideas in such cases are on the one hand the principle of individual autonomy, that people may arrange their lives as they wish with the minimum of interference by the state (for example, see Box 4.6); and on the other hand, the idea that 'good citizens' should pay taxes and make the contributions to the common good that Parliament intended.

A number of cases may be taken to illustrate how the courts have altered their approach in recent years so that the balance is moving in the direction of a duty to pay taxes as a matter of good citizenship. In the Duke of Westminster's case (*IRC* v. *Duke of Westminster* (1936)), the Duke employed a gardener and other servants to whom he paid wages out of his taxed income. He decided to save himself tax by entering into covenants with these employees to pay them annuities or sums of money equivalent to their wages instead of actual wages. The effect of making payments under covenant was that the money was regarded as not having been part of the Duke's income so he did not have to pay tax on it. The staff, of course, did have to pay tax on what they received.

The majority in the House of Lords in this case, was hostile to the claim by the Revenue that the court may ignore the legal position and regard what it called 'the substance of the matter'. In this case, it was alleged, the reality was that the gardener and other staff were serving the Duke for something equal to their former salary or wages,

---

Box 4.6 The Duke of Westminster's case

Lord Tomlin, in the majority in the House of Lords, in this case stated:

Every man is entitled if he can to order his affairs so as that the tax attaching under the appropriate Acts is less that it otherwise would be. If he succeeds in ordering them so as to secure this result, then, however unappreciative the Commissioners of Inland Revenue or his fellow taxpayers may be of his ingenuity, he cannot be compelled to pay an increased tax.

so that the payments should be treated as salary or wages and not as covenanted annuities. The majority of the Law Lords accepted the form of the arrangements, and so held that the Duke did not have to pay tax on the payments he made to his staff as if they formed part of his income. One Law Lord, Lord Atkin, however, was of the view that the court should look at 'the substance of the transaction'. He felt that on the evidence this was an arrangement for the payment of remuneration for work to be done by employees, and the Duke ought to be taxed on that basis.

In this case the majority were clearly not of the opinion that there was anything like a legal or even a moral duty of good citizenship in preparedness to pay taxes; so there would be no justification in the courts going behind the legal forms adopted by a taxpayer to look at the substance or reality of an arrangement to see whether it attracted a liability to pay tax.

In the case of *Furniss* v. *Dawson* (1984), the refusal of the court in the Duke of Westminster case to look at 'the substance of the matter' was modified. The taxpayers, a father and two sons, wished to sell their shareholdings in two small family companies. In order to minimize their tax liability they entered into an elaborate scheme designed to defer liability to pay capital gains tax. This was not a 'tax avoidance scheme' but 'a simple and honest scheme which merely seeks to defer payment of tax until the taxpayer has received into his hand the gain which he has made' (per Lord Brightman in the House of Lords). However, some of the steps in this series of transactions had no commercial or business purposes other than deferring a liability to tax. The question was whether the courts could go behind the forms and look at the substance of the arrangements in order to impose a liability to tax.

The House of Lords decided that the steps having no commercial purpose other than deferring a liability to tax could be disregarded for tax purposes, the end result of the series of transactions being looked at and taxed according to the terms of the particular taxing statute. In his judgment of the case, Lord Brightman identified a 'new approach' in tax cases: if there were a preordained series of transactions or one single composite transaction in which steps were inserted which had no commercial (business) purpose apart from the avoidance of a liability to tax, the inserted steps are to be disregarded for fiscal purposes. The court must then look at the end result in deciding how the transaction was to be taxed.

This decision may be regarded as imposing something of a duty of good citizenship – or perhaps more accurately, entitling the judges to presume good citizenship – on the part of individuals, in the sense that it makes it difficult to avoid or defer paying tax by entering into complex transactions with the sole purpose of doing so.

Yet *Furniss* v. *Dawson* has caused a number of legal difficulties, which illustrate the problems that a legal duty of good citizenship can cause for the rule of law and the emancipation of 'subjects', which we discussed in Chapter 3. Since transactions or a series of transactions of this kind may have effects in law, for example, on property rights, it is inconsistent for the law to treat them in one way for tax purposes and another way for other legal purposes. In effect, it subjects individuals to what may be unpredictable and arbitrary decisions by the Inland Revenue about their tax liability, thus undermining their freedom of action and reimposing a degree of 'subjection', to use the terminology introduced in Chapter 3.

So, in a number of cases since the *Furniss* v *Dawson* decision in 1984 the courts have narrowed down the principle. Under the law as it now stands a distinction is to be drawn between 'mitigation' of tax liability, which is acceptable, and 'unacceptable tax avoidance schemes'. On this basis, the Duke of Westminster was mitigating his tax, not indulging in unacceptable tax avoidance, because he did actually make, and was legally obliged to make, the covenanted payments to his servants. Unacceptable tax avoidance, by contrast:

> typically involves the creation of complex artificial structures by which, as though by the wave of a magic wand, the taxpayer conjures out of the air a loss, or a gain, or expenditure, or whatever it may be, which otherwise would never have existed. These structures are designed to achieve an adventitious tax benefit for the taxpayer, and in truth are no more than raids on the public funds at the expense of the general body of taxpayers, and as such are unacceptable. (per Lord Goff in *Ensign Tankers* v. *Stokes* (1992))

We have here a concept of the good citizen as one who does not 'raid' public funds and other taxpayers for their own selfish advantage.

From the cases about the duty to pay tax and the scope for taxpayers to take steps to minimize their tax liability, we see the courts seeking a balance between different ideas of citizenship and autonomy. On the one hand there are notions that autonomous individuals are entitled to mitigate the amount of tax that they pay in their own interests, and that the rule of law requires certainty about the extent of tax liability and the effectiveness of legal transactions; and on the other hand there is the view that it is unacceptable for individuals to raid public funds at the expense of other citizens. So, in cases of highly artificial transactions, tax liability will be determined according to the purpose of the transactions, and a duty of 'good citizenship' will be imposed.

THE RULE OF LAW AND THE DUTIES OF THE STATE TO ITS CITIZENS

Our attention has been focused in the discussion in this chapter on the rights and liberties of citizens and their duties to the state. A third dimension to the relationship between citizen and state is the extent of duties owed by the state to its citizens. Some aspects of this dimension are considered in Chapter 5 (the social and economic rights of citizens). However, there are wider issues about the general nature of the obligations of state to individuals, especially given the original legal assumption of a subject–sovereign relationship under which, as we saw in Chapter 3, the sovereign owed no more than protection to subjects.

Part of the duty of the state to the individual is for the state itself to obey the law – a crucial aspect of the rule of law considered in the previous chapter. A case which illustrates the importance of government itself complying with the law and giving individuals remedies where they have not done so, whether deliberately or not, is *Woolwich Equitable Building Society* v. *Inland Revenue Commissioners* (1992), another tax case.

The facts were that the Inland Revenue had demanded that building societies pay tax on their depositors' money in accordance with new regulations. The Woolwich Building Society took the view that the regulations were invalid, but they paid the money under protest and then sought to recover it from the Revenue. It was held that the regulations were indeed invalid as being outside the rule-making power given in the enabling Act, and the moneys paid were repaid by the Revenue. However, the Woolwich wished also to recover interest on the money for the period during which the Revenue had had the use of it. The Revenue agreed that interest should be paid as from the date of the court's judgment to the effect that the demand had been unlawful, but not as from the date the money had been paid by the Woolwich to the Revenue. The Woolwich sued the Revenue for interest back to the date of payment (many millions of pounds) and succeeded in the House of Lords. The majority of the Law Lords decided that interest was payable, recognizing a right of recovery based on payment of money pursuant to a demand that had been wrongly exacted by a public authority. Lord Goff of Chieveley relied, in part, on Article 4 of the Bill of Rights (see Box 4.5) holding that:

> Retention by the state of taxes unlawfully exacted is particularly obnoxious, because it is one of the most fundamental principles of our law ... that taxes should not be levied without the authority of Parliament, and full effect can only be given to that principle if the return of taxes exacted under an unlawful demand can be enforced as a matter of right. ... In any event, it seems strange to penalise the good citizen, whose natural instinct is to trust the revenue and pay taxes when they are demanded of him.

We see here recognition of the importance of protecting the good citizen and his property against the state, similar in some ways to the protection of individuals and their personal freedom from the police discussed above.

CONCLUSIONS

The cases discussed in this chapter illustrate a number of points about the relationship between individual rights and 'good citizenship'. First the basic starting point in English law leans in favour of the individual's rights, including rights not to help the police, and to minimize tax liability, as opposed to imposing or assuming general duties of good citizenship. It contains elements of liberal citizenship theory. However, in some areas of law, and taxation law is one, the courts have modified this position to a degree, as in *Furniss* v. *Dawson*, introducing some elements of classical 'civic virtue' into the law. Here, as in other areas such as the duty to assist the police discussed above, attempts to impose a legally recognized duty of good citizenship except by clear, express terms in a statute undermine legal certainty and thus the rule of law. This principle involves not only that individuals should know with reasonable certainty what their legal rights and duties are, but also that the state itself should govern according to law, as the *Woolwich* decision shows.

Not only is the rule of law important to good government, but, as indicated in Chapter 3, it is also one of the foundations of the emancipation of subjects. Good citizenship in the sense of the acceptance and performance by individuals of duties to the state and the community cannot be imposed by broadly stated general legal principles, only by clear legal duties. 'Civic virtue' is essentially a moral, not a legal, obligation. If individuals were under very generalized duties of 'good citizenship' – duties to pay as much tax as the Revenue or the Customs and Excise deemed due, duties to help the police with their inquiries and assist in law enforcement as demanded by the police – rather than the relatively closely defined duties imposed under the present legal tradition, then in effect subjecthood in the sense of owing duties of obedience to an arbitrary power would be reintroduced into the legal system, in the guise of 'good citizenship'.

This completes our survey of the legally supported civil and political rights and duties of citizens and the legal imposition of duties on the state. We continue our discussion of legal rights in the next chapter, which is concerned with the protection of second and third generation rights.

FURTHER READING

Ewing, K. D. and Gearty, C. (1990) *Freedom under Thatcher. Civil Liberties in Modern Britain* (Oxford: Clarendon Press).

Hansard Society (1990) *Women at the Top* (London: Hansard Society).

Maitland, F. W. (1908) *The Constitutional History of England* (Cambridge: Cambridge University Press).

Manton, J. (1965) *Elizabeth Garrett Anderson* (London: Methuen).

Okin, F. M. (1979) *Women in Western Political Thought* (Princeton: Princeton University Press).

Oliver, D. (1991) *Government in the United Kingdom. The Search for Accountability, Effectiveness and Citizenship* (Milton Keynes: Open University Press).

Rawlings, H. F. (1988) *Law and the Electoral Process* (London: Sweet and Maxwell).

Robertson, G. (1989) *Freedom, the Individual and the Law* (Harmondsworth: Penguin Books).

Wollstonecraft, M. (1975) *A Vindication of the Rights of Women* (Harmondsworth: Penguin Books).

5

SOCIAL, ECONOMIC AND
ENVIRONMENTAL RIGHTS

SUMMARY

Social and economic rights belong to the 'second generation' of rights. They enable individuals to participate in the life of the community and in politics, and so are an aspect of 'social citizenship'. Giving legal effect to these rights raises difficult issues of resource allocation which make their legal protection more complex than that of civil and political rights. Rights to health services provide a useful example and case study of social rights.

The legal forms of protection for social rights are restricted, but there are non-legal methods of protecting them. Some of these are to do with the 'empowerment' of individuals, in education for example, which provides a helpful case study. However, the question arises whether 'empowerment' is consistent with established notions of citizenship, or whether it is rather to do with the autonomy of individuals.

Environmental rights belong to the 'third generation' of rights: they have come onto the political agenda as a result of the increasing pollution of the environment in the late twentieth century. They differ from first and second generation rights in a number of respects. First, their protection requires international cooperation, since pollution will often cross the boundaries of nation-states; second, there are difficulties in granting individuals remedies for damage suffered from environmental pollution; third, their recognition imposes responsibilities for their neighbours on private as well as public bodies, and imposes new limitations on individual autonomy.

THE NATURE OF SECOND AND THIRD
GENERATION RIGHTS

In this chapter we turn from civil and political, 'first generation', rights, to those of the second and third generations: social, economic and environmental rights. Social and economic rights make up the social element of Marshall's notion of the citizenship of entitlement, discussed in Chapters 1 and 2. They cover

> the whole range from the right to a modicum of economic welfare and security to the right to share to the full in the social heritage and to live the life of a civilised being according to the standards prevailing in society. (Marshall, 1950, p. 11)

The idea that citizenship involves environmental rights is of much more recent origin, and has been influenced by concern about the effect on people's lives of pollution. We consider these towards the end of the chapter.

We need to have a picture of the scope of social and economic rights. Social rights include entitlements to services such as education, health services, housing, social services. Many of these rights were introduced in the United Kingdom during and after the Second World War, although the foundations of the welfare state were laid in the early twentieth century.

The phrase 'economic rights' is ambiguous; it may be used in three main senses. First, it can refer to people's rights in the market-place – to own property, to earn and spend money, to exercise choice in the purchase of goods and services. It is debatable whether these are rightly regarded as elements of citizenship rather than of autonomy. We saw in Chapter 1 how in the Greek classical tradition, economic rights were associated with citizenship. Such rights gave – and still give – citizens a stake in society: this stake encourages people to take an interest in public affairs, or at least to desire the opportunity and freedom to do so. In Greece and Rome they were used as a test or qualification for citizenship, with the result that it was an exclusive status (exclusivity in citizenship theory is also found in systems where nationality is the basis for rights, and in 'multiple' or 'new' citizenship theory, discussed further in Chapters 7 and 10).

Since the early twentieth century in the United Kingdom, citizenship in the liberal sense has been regarded for most purposes as a universal status, and civil and political rights are enjoyed regardless of economic status. An example of an exception to this is the fact that the property qualification for jury service, one of the duties of citizenship (see Chapter 3) was not abolished until 1974. Nowadays, however, economic rights in this first sense are essentially regarded as rights of consumers, not of citizens in the civic republican or liberal senses.

The second sense of 'economic rights' attaches to the rights of workers to participate in the management of the workplace: the Liberal party has a longstanding commitment to workplace democracy through worker participation in decision-making. The European Community's Social Charter (which was adopted in December 1989 by all the Member States of the Community except the United Kingdom) provides that 'Information, consultation and participation for workers must be developed along appropriate lines, taking account of the practices in force in various Member States'. However, the forms that worker participation may take are varied, from board membership for employees to provision for representation in collective agreements. This sort of economic right may be regarded as a form of 'private' democracy based in civil society, designed to enhance the autonomy of workers, and without the national public and political dimensions generally associated with citizenship.

The third sense in which the phrase 'economic rights' may be used is in relation to entitlements to welfare benefits paid by the state – pensions, social security, child benefit and the like. It is in this sense that the phrase will be used in the rest of this chapter. In some respects this form of economic right is closely related, in its citizenship aspects, with those of the first category, property and contract rights: one commentator, for example, has called pensions and other privileges and benefits conferred by the state 'The New Property' (Reich, 1964) to make the point that they serve the same purpose as property in ancient Greek democracy, giving people security, and enabling and entitling them to participate in the government of their society.

Next, let us place social and economic rights in the context of the 'nationality' theme of citizenship. As with civil and political rights, we find that eligibility for the social elements of citizenship is not dependent on whether a person is a British national. All children resident in the United Kingdom, whatever their nationality, have access to state schools – indeed their parents are under a duty to secure that they receive efficient full-time education as long as they are of school age. Students in further and higher education are entitled to mandatory grants to meet their tuition fees and, subject to parental means, maintenance grants, on the basis not of nationality but of 'ordinary residence' in the United Kingdom for three years before they start their course (Education Act 1962, Section 1(1) as amended by Education Act 1980, Section 19 and Schedule 5). European Community students are entitled to have their fees paid like home students because Community law prohibits discrimination on grounds of nationality.

In other areas too, eligibility for welfare benefits does not depend on British nationality. Many non-UK residents are entitled to National Health Service (NHS) treatment. All persons in the country are entitled to receive treatment, but charges may be made to certain non-residents such as overseas visitors. Treatment free of charge is available to citizens of Member States of the European Community, but other countries too (Austria, for example) have reciprocal arrangements with the UK Government under which their nationals are eligible for NHS treatment while in the United Kingdom and British nationals will be eligible for treatment in the other country if they fall ill there. Eligibility for welfare benefits paid in cash in the United Kingdom – child benefit, old age pensions, unemployment benefits, income support – is also not normally dependent on British nationality.

The idea that individual citizens have social and economic 'rights' does not tell us how those rights are to be met. The delivery of these rights can take a number of forms: one is the actual provision by the state of welfare benefits and public services; this was the form of delivery favoured by the legislation that introduced the welfare state after the Second World War. Other methods of providing for these rights include local authorities and other public bodies 'enabling' the provision of service, by contracting with private enterprises for services – street cleaning, school meals and so on. Alternatively, the provision of these rights may be 'facilitated', for example, by enabling voluntary or charitable bodies to make the provision, as is the case with housing associations and voluntary aided schools; or by enabling citizens to purchase public services in a market of some kind by giving them vouchers, cash or other 'tickets' to the service. Each of these techniques implies different views of the relationship between the individual and the state or the community.

RATIONALES FOR SOCIAL AND ECONOMIC RIGHTS

A number of rationales or justifications may be advanced for ensuring that social and economic 'needs' are met in society; in other words, that those 'needs' become 'entitlements'. Not all of these rationales are to do with the idea of citizenship as a universal and equal status. Marshall saw social and economic rights as necessary to enable all individuals to participate in the life of the community, thus making their civil and political rights a reality: persons who are destitute, disabled or homeless will, in practice, be limited in their ability to engage in political activity or become involved in community activities unless they receive assistance. Social and economic rights should remove this barrier to citizenship.

The inability to participate in political or community life is damaging because it affects social cohesion and national identity, which, as we saw in Chapters 1 and 2, are important elements of citizenship. Individuals or groups in the population who feel themselves excluded by poverty, homelessness or lack of education from membership of the community are likely to feel alienated, and this can be a cause of crime, a subculture of drug-taking and so on. This concept views social and economic rights as forming a vital core of civic republican-style universal and equal citizenship.

Quite apart from considerations of expediency to do with preventing alienation, common humanity and compassion may be said to require that relief be given to those in need. However, this rationale for rights does not necessarily imply equal and universal citizenship.

Before the growth of what we now regard as the welfare state from the mid-nineteenth century, the meeting of social and economic needs was not recognized as something of any great concern to the state. Needs were met in an unsystematic way by, for example, the Poor Law Commissioners, by families and by voluntary and charitable activity. The provision which enabled charitable trusts to operate (the preamble to the Charitable Uses Act 1601, now repealed) translated considerations of common humanity as the rationale for this sort of activity into a concept of 'general public benefit'. As a result, charitable status was available to trusts engaged in activities such as the relief of poverty, the advancement of education or religion and for other purposes beneficial to the community (Lord Macnaghten in *Income Tax Special Purposes Commissioners* v. *Pemsel* (1891)). Looked at in this way, the relief of various kinds of hardship and the meeting of needs for education, health care and the like could be seen as a proper concern of 'good citizens', for example, those endowing charitable trusts on a voluntary basis or those working for such institutions, rather than the concern of the state.

A desire, motivated by compassion, to meet certain basic needs of individuals differs from Marshall's justification for securing social and economic provision as a rationale for these rights, in a number of respects. First, as far as the standard of provision is concerned, the rationale of compassion might be taken as a justification for minimal social and economic provision designed simply to save people from destitution. By contrast, the need as advocated by Marshall to secure that all individuals have the opportunity and the wherewithal to participate in the community would indicate a process of equalization and a level of social and economic provision above the minimum.

Second, reliance on charitable and voluntary provision cannot produce rights or entitlement to such provision: such benefits are bound to be distributed in a haphazard way. Third, the compassion rationale for social and economic provision focuses on the position of the giver as 'citizen': the receivers are not themselves perceived as citizens with entitlements to benefits and rights of participation in decisions that affect them, but rather as passive beneficiaries of largesse. Indeed, this is seen as one of the problems with voluntary provision of social benefits as an alternative to public provision, since voluntary agencies such as housing associations and churches are often paternalistic in their organization and attitudes, and tend to treat the recipients of their favours as subjects, allowing little scope for the beneficiaries of their provision to be involved in the running of their activities.

So, although the rationale of compassion for the meeting of social and economic needs has many appeals, it says little about the citizenship of recipients as opposed to givers, and is not connected to any idea of citizenship as a universal and equal status – indeed, it can be quite incompatible with such a concept. A depersonalized relationship based on entitlement is essential if recipients of services and benefits are to be citizens rather than subjects.

What the welfare state has done is to depersonalize this function of giving, to convert it from a voluntary act by a few 'good citizens' into a duty on the part of all citizens who can afford to do so to contribute to the Exchequer in payments of tax (discussed in Chapter 4) and so secure that the needs of the body of the citizenry are met as of right.

LEGAL PROVISIONS FOR SOCIAL AND ECONOMIC RIGHTS

In Chapter 4 we considered how civil or legal and political rights can be safeguarded in the legal system. Social and economic rights cannot be dealt with in the same way. It does not follow that they are any less important than civil and political rights – that is a matter of lively debate into which we shall not enter here. However, it is important to appreciate why the legal protection of second generation rights has to be different from that of the first generation.

First, social and economic rights cannot be 'residual' in the way that important civil and political freedoms such as freedom of speech and association, for example, can be (see Chapter 4): social and economic rights must be found in positive law, such as statutes and regulations which establish rights and the mechanisms for their payment, together with authorization for Government to raise taxation and earmark it for the provision of these benefits.

Second, social and economic rights impose costs on the state or the community in a more direct and often a more expensive way than civil and political rights do. The resource implications of meeting the social and economic needs which the welfare state seeks to transform into rights are generally much higher than the costs of maintaining civil and political rights: decisions about the allocation of resources to meet social and economic needs raise even more difficult political and economic issues in a liberal system than decisions about resourcing civil and political rights.

This perception is reflected in the fact that policy decisions about the content of social and economic rights are generally regarded as the province of politicians, Parliament and ministers, rather than the courts; whereas decisions about civil and political rights have historically been regarded, at least until relatively recently, as matters that can, even should, be left to judges. The point may be illustrated by the fact that the civil and political freedoms that survive have been created by the judges through the common law (see the discussion of this in Chapter 3). There is virtually no legislation giving individuals civil and political rights. (A major exception is the Representation of the People Acts, which make provision for the exercise of the right to vote.) The common law has not established any social or economic rights because these require action rather than inaction by the state and require the raising of taxation and allocation of resources which the courts have not seen it as their function to provide.

This point about the resource implications of social and economic as opposed to civil and political rights needs some elaboration. Of course civil and political rights or liberties – freedom of speech, freedom of the person and so on – do impose some cost on the state in the sense that they require a police force and the court system for their protection: but this cost is indirect and impersonal, and not linked to the needs of particular individuals. By contrast, the cost of welfare benefits, for instance, is directly imposed on the state and is often directly linked to the needs of particular individuals. Moreover, even if there were few or no civil or political rights and liberties, the state would probably still have to provide a police force and court system, if only to protect itself and assert its authority. Also, it is not possible to calculate the cost of a particular individual's civil and political rights to the state, whereas the cost of social and economic rights may more easily be allocated to individuals – the cost to the state of an operation for appendicitis or of a school place can be calculated more readily than the cost of protecting the freedom of speech of A or the freedom of association of group B.

The resource implications of civil and political rights or liberties for the state are usually less problematic than the resource implications of providing social and economic rights: the cost to the Exchequer and local authorities of providing education, health services, welfare benefits, and so on can be enormous, virtually open-ended, and much greater than the cost of maintaining civil and political rights and freedoms. Difficult political choices need to be made about the allocation of limited resources to these services as opposed to making them available to industry for investment, or to individuals for their own consumption, for example.

The difficulties considered above in giving protection to social and economic rights explain why enforceable Bills of Rights do not usually extend to such rights. Yet there are a number of international instruments which bind states that are parties to them to secure the availability of some of these rights. For example, the United Nations

Declaration of Human Rights and the European Social Charter (produced by the Council of Europe, a body quite separate from the European Community and not to be confused with it) both cover social and economic rights; and the Treaty of Union (the Maastricht Treaty) contains a 'Social Chapter' from which the United Kingdom has 'opted out'. (See Chapter 9 for further discussion of the European Social Charter.)

THE 'RIGHT' TO HEALTH SERVICES: A CASE STUDY

Health services provide good examples of the ambiguities in any discussion of social and economic rights, and of the choices that have to be made as to how social rights are to be enforceable and how extensive they should be. Thus, this topic provides a useful case study of the workings of a system of social or economic rights.

The Beveridge Report of 1942, the blueprint for the welfare state for over forty years, aimed to abolish, among other evils, disease. The Institute of Public Policy Research's Commission on Social Justice, reviewing the welfare state in *The Justice Gap* (1993), identifies 'the opportunity to enjoy good health' as one of the 'five great opportunities' that should be the basis of social cohesion and economic security. How should such aspirations be achieved?

One method – but it is only one of a possible range – is through the right of an individual to receive health services, which is discussed below. However, such rights have to be seen in the context of the broader question as to whether individuals ought to have not just a right to treatment if they are ill, but a 'right to good health'. (Similarly the right to schooling is but a concrete aspect of a right to education, and a right to unemployment benefit a concretization of a general right to what Marshall described as 'a modicum of economic welfare'.)

The case could be made that individuals have a 'right to good health' and that, in aid of that right, governments have a duty to promote the good health of the population. Such broad duties raise complex resource problems. For example, the prohibition of tobacco advertising or advertisements for alcohol would reduce their consumption and promote good health. However, the Government would lose substantial sums in revenue and many sporting and other events would lose sponsorship. A decision to ban such advertising is not a simple one.

Another example of the problems raised by imposing duties on the Government to promote good health is the degree to which it is legitimate for Government to interfere with the rights or freedoms of individuals to make their own decisions on these matters. For example, the requirement that drivers and passengers in cars wear seat belts promotes good health by reducing the injuries suffered in accidents both by drivers and their passengers. Yet it interferes with their autonomy. The same is true of the requirement for crash helmets to be worn by those on motor cycles.

The question arises of the justification for such measures: is it that they save the National Health Service costs that would otherwise be borne in treating more serious road accident injuries? If this is the justification, it is linked to ideas of good citizenship – citizens must accept some limitation of their freedoms for the sake of the common good. However, the common good has to be weighed against the duty of the state to respect the autonomy and philosophical convictions of individuals. In recognition of this argument Sikhs are released for reasons of religious conviction from the obligation to wear crash helmets.

Or is the justification for rules about wearing safety belts and crash helmets that Government knows best what is good for drivers and passengers, and is entitled to impose that on them – a paternalistic justification? An aspect of these two justifications for limiting a person's autonomy might be that the restriction on individual freedom is minimal and has no implications for the freedom of individuals to participate as citizens in politics and community activity. So, it could be argued, to limit individual freedom in order to protect the public purse or do what Government thinks best for individuals is not inappropriate as long as it does not interfere with 'citizenship' in the classical or liberal–political senses; and it may be waived for those who have religious convictions, thus leaving room for individual autonomy and respect. Most importantly, this sort of interference is impersonal and of general application: in this respect it is not equivalent to treating people as 'subjects' which, we suggested in Chapter 3, involves essentially personal control by the sovereign or superior.

Let us now turn from the difficulties involved in imposing general duties on Government to promote good health (or good education, a modicum of welfare and so on) and the consequent 'rights' of individuals to have their good health, etc., promoted, to the rights of particular individuals who are in need. This too raises difficult questions, to do with the allocation of resources. Health services are a good example. Some medical treatments clearly depend on the availability of resources – transplants, blood transfusions are obvious examples. There is little that Government can do about this particular service in a system which respects individual autonomy, save conduct publicity campaigns to encourage people to be donors. Equipment for other treatments is limited unless a Government is prepared to allocate very large sums of money to health services, which no Government is likely to do – the limited availability of kidney dialysis machines illustrates the point. Technology is another limitation. So, too, is general staff time and equipment – waiting lists for medical treatment are almost inevitable unless major injections of resources are to be made.

The legal position reflects these problems. Individuals do not have a legally enforceable right to treatment either against the NHS or against a particular doctor (for an illustration of this point, see Box 5.1).

Although there is no legally enforceable right to treatment, there

---

Box 5.1 *In re Walker's Application* (1987)

A baby with a hole in the heart was waiting for an operation. The operation had been postponed on five previous occasions. On the sixth the mother applied to the court for judicial review. The judge decided the decision to postpone the operation was not unlawful. There was a lack of specially trained nurses and accompanying facilities which did not allow the expansion of intensive care. The baby was at no risk at present. Other more urgent cases had to be dealt with.

Technically the judge was right. The case leaves open the question about whether legislation *ought* to give patients rights to particular treatment. It also leaves open what the position would be if a patient were in urgent need of treatment but was not given it.

Note that the 'Patient's Charter' is misleading on this point in that it recites that every citizen has the right to receive health care.

are some legal remedies available to a patient who is not satisfied with the NHS. Decisions whether to give treatment are essentially for medical practitioners, and are discretionary. Sometimes the decision as to whether or how to treat a patient will be taken by a doctor on the basis of a professional clinical judgement regarding the appropriate treatment. If a patient suffers injury or damage as a result of such a decision, he or she may sue the doctor for negligence. The decision will then be judged according to whether the doctor adopted a practice which a responsible body of skilled medical practitioners accepted as proper (*Bolam* v. *Friern Barnet Hospital Management Committee* (1957)). There is thus no right to be cured, or to receive the 'right' treatment – if there is such a thing.

Nor is there a right to receive particular treatment, even if it is available, unless the doctor responsible for the patient considers that it is in the best interests of the patient: so in the case of *Re J (A minor) (Medical treatment)* (1992), the court held that it should not order a paediatrician caring for a severely handicapped baby to give mechanical ventilation if he considered that it was not appropriate to do so.

Even more difficult questions arise where treatment is refused for non-clinical reasons. A doctor may wish not to give a patient treatment for infertility, *in vitro* fertilization (IVF), for example, because the patient is regarded as an unsuitable parent. This happened in the case of *R.* v. *Ethical Committee of St. Mary's Hospital (Manchester), Ex parte H* (1988). H had been refused IVF because the hospital consultant believed that she would not be capable of providing proper care and upbringing for a child (she had criminal convictions for offences to do with prostitution and had not been successful as a foster parent). The court decided that it was for the consultant to decide whether treatment should be given; the consultant had rightly given H the opportunity to put more information about herself to him before he made the final decision. The court also said that his refusal could not be said to be one that no reasonable consultant could have come to, and it would not therefore intervene. The case illustrates again the fact that there is no right for an individual patient to receive the treatment they desire, even if it is available, and suitable from a medical point of view.

If treatment is given without a patient's consent, then he or she may be able to recover damages. However, as we saw in Chapter 3 (Boxes 3.4, 3.5 and 3.6) even this basic requirement that treatment should not be given without the patient's consent raises some difficult issues about individual autonomy and paternalism in the system.

We see from this discussion that there are difficulties in giving patients directly legally enforceable rights to health services. Very similar problems arise in relation to other social 'rights' – to education, housing, social service support and so forth. It is unlikely that there will ever be an absolute legally enforceable right to receive a particular form of treatment, education, housing or social services because of the resource problem. Questions about the allocation of resources for health and other services are essentially political and should, we suggest, be resolved through the political process. They should not be resolved by giving all individuals legally enforceable substantive rights to treatment, let alone to be cured of a particular disease, housed in a particular place, educated at a named school or university. We shall see in Chapter 9 how the legal position of patients and others claiming social rights could be improved in various ways short of trying to give them specific, substantive legally enforceable rights.

EMPOWERMENT AND CITIZENSHIP

We referred earlier to the range of ways in which public services may be made available as of right to individuals – provision by a local authority, through contracting out of services, through vouchers, etc. Measures have been introduced in the last decade or so to strengthen the position of the individual in relations with the state, in education, housing and health, and in other publicly provided services. For example, the *Citizen's Charter* (see Chapter 2) gives people the right to information about public services, and rights to complain or appeal if they are dissatisfied with them. Parents are represented on school governing bodies. Such provisions may be regarded as giving people a 'voice' in the services they receive.

Other provisions give people greater 'choice'. Parents may express preferences about the school that their child should attend; they are not limited to sending them to schools in their own education authority area; and they may appeal if dissatisfied with the allocation. However, they have no absolute right to send their child to their preferred school.

Such measures as these form part of a strategy of 'empowerment' of individuals which raises important issues about citizenship. In some respects, it enhances the autonomy of the individual. Another intention behind measures of this kind has been to expose public services such as schools to market pressures, so as to ensure that weak schools lose support unless they improve their performance, and that strong schools are rewarded. So in a way the empowerment of citizens or consumers is used to pressurize public services to meet the wishes of consumers. Empowerment is an alternative to control of these services by professionals – teachers, managers, officials – or 'democratic' control through local authorities or ministers account-able to Parliament (which is to do with the classical and liberal theories of citizenship). However, 'empowerment' begs all sorts of questions.

First, choice, to be effective, must be informed. However, the information on which, for example, parents are supposed to make decisions about schools is only partial. It does not cover the background and home situations of children, which can affect their performance and which is not the responsibility of the school. Nor is information required to be made available about the standard reached by pupils at the time of entry to the school. Without this information it is not possible to ascertain the 'added value' the school has given to the pupils' performance: children who enter a school with a strong record of achievement are, of course, much more likely to do well than those who have weaker records – one thing about a 'good' school is its ability to *improve* the performance of children at whatever point they start.

Second, these provisions assume that certain aspects of a school are more important than others and these assumptions may be questionable. Are exam results as important as opportunities for personal development, participation in non-academic activities, the acquisition of social and political skills, all of which, as we see in Chapter 8, can take place in schools?

Another point sometimes taken about the increase of parental choice in schools, is whether parents are good judges of the quality of schools and of what is best for their own children. The answer depends, of course, on the purpose or purposes of education (see Gutmann (1987) and Chapter 8). It is suggested that it would be unnecessarily patronizing to deny parents all choice and information on this basis, and arrogant to assert that professionals – teachers and various experts – necessarily know best what is good for a particular child. Ideally, we believe, this sort of decision should be taken jointly. If it were left entirely to teachers and 'experts', both parents and children would in effect be being treated as 'subjects' rather than autonomous individuals.

CHOICE IN EDUCATION: THE CLEVELAND SCHOOL CASE

One side-effect of increasing parental choice could be the segregation of schools.

The *Cleveland* case (Box 5.2) raised important issues about the boundaries between individual autonomy and citizenship, about the extent to which duties of 'good citizenship' should be imposed by law (see Chapter 4), and about the reasons for the state to be responsible for the provision of education.

A range of reasons for state education, indeed for education at all, could be put forward: for example, Article 29 of the UN *Convention on the Rights of the Child* states that the education of the child should be directed to 'the preparation of the child for responsible life in a

---

Box 5.2 Parental choice and segregation in schools

In *R. v. Cleveland County Council, ex parte Commission for Racial Equality* (1991) a local education authority complied with a request from a parent for a child to be transferred to a different school. There was some suggestion that the parental choice might have been motivated by considerations of the racial composition of the intake of the present school, which was predominantly Asian. The court decided that the local authority's duty under the Education Act 1980 to give effect to parental choice was mandatory, whatever the parent's subjective motive for making the request; that compliance with the parent's request for the transfer of the child did not amount to segregation by the authority; and that there was no question of the local authority itself being motivated by race, but only by its legal duty to comply with parental choice.

If large numbers of parents sought to place their children in schools where their own ethnic group predominated, or sought to avoid certain ethnic groups, this could result in segregated schooling, which would undermine social cohesion.

free society, in the spirit of understanding, peace, tolerance, equality of sexes, and friendship among all peoples, ethnic, national and religious groups and persons of indigenous origin'. In Chapter 1 consideration was given to the view that state-provided education is essential to the creation of a true citizenry: an 'ignorant citizen', it was suggested, is a contradiction in terms, because such a person would be unable to participate in politics and government effectively. In this sense education is an instrument for democratization.

A connected objective of education was also considered in Chapter 1 and will be further developed in Chapter 8: to produce people who can make the most of the rights that they have, perform their civic duties and behave with due loyalty and responsibility. This approach involves inculcating into pupils senses of obligation to the community, the skills necessary to take part in communal activities, ultimately political skills. These, in turn, engender senses of 'belonging' and social cohesion. On this approach to education, the legal framework has to allow for a combination of inputs from public policy and its conception of the duties of citizenship: from pupils themselves, and parents, exercising and, in so doing, learning to exercise responsible choices; and from teachers who can convey the information and the setting for learning about citizenship and democracy. The legal framework could include provisions, essentially political in nature, about whether and how social cohesion should be promoted. (What does the *Cleveland* case, Box 5.2, tell us about that?)

Democratization and the fostering of social cohesion are not the only set of rationales that could be advanced for compulsory schooling. Others are to do with promoting the interests of the individual pupil – an essentially liberal justification. Education enables children to realize their own potential, to develop their talents and thus to live fulfilling lives. This rationale is to do with individual autonomy and respect, and involves giving pupils opportunities to do all sorts of things, some of which may be of no value – social, economic or political – to them or to society: learning to enjoy listening to music, to appreciate art and so on. However, it is not self-evident that this rationale justifies compulsory education, interfering as it does with the autonomy of the child and its parents.

To return to the *Cleveland* case, if the promotion of self-fulfilment were the only justification for education, the decision to be made would be: 'Which school can best enable this particular child to realize its potential?' and presumably that decision should be taken for each child by parents, perhaps by teachers or experts, and possibly with some input by the child. (The *Cleveland* case, Box 5.2, leans towards this conception of the purpose of education.)

Another justification for educating children is that the community needs useful and productive members: this essentially economic rationale involves the idea that pupils should learn usable skills and not things which are unlikely to have economic value – learning to appreciate music again provides an example. This justification treats the interests of society as paramount over the interests of the individual pupil. It regards pupils as essentially economic actors rather than independent autonomous agents or citizens participating in public decisions other than those taken in the market: this concept of the person fits well with the *Citizen's Charter* idea that individuals are 'consumers', an economic activity (and with the concept of European Community citizens as economic actors, which we consider in Chapter 7). If this were the only rationale for education we would expect the state to have the power to impose its own decisions as to which school a pupil should attend and what the curriculum should contain.

Are these purposes of education necessarily mutually incompatible? Some, especially those who object to the way in which pupils and their parents are treated as consumers, fear that this will make it difficult for the first objective, democratization and the promotion of social cohesion, to be achieved. For example, if many parents were to exercise their choice to send their children to schools where the pupils came predominantly from their own racial or ethnic group, this could, in the long run, damage social cohesion and convey the 'wrong message' to parents and children, that it was acceptable to wish to avoid being educated with members of other groups. The separate education of Catholic and Protestant children in Northern Ireland must have reinforced the divisions in the community there. If, on the other hand, few parents choose to place their children in such schools, the parents' right to choose is unlikely to be a problem and could be a concession to individual autonomy. It could also enable members of groups within society, especially minority groups, to maintain their culture through the education system. This issue again poses problems in resolving the possible conflict between social cohesion and individual autonomy, pluralism and national identity, absorption and assimilation, considered in other chapters.

It is not entirely clear what concept of the purpose of education the *Cleveland* case (Box 5.2) embraced. This sort of parental choice seems not to put the promotion of social cohesion as high as other objectives. However, it is not possible to generalize about such choices when there may be special circumstances in a given situation which would not be present in others. The issue for those who are critical of the result in the *Cleveland* case is whether the need to promote social cohesion is a persuasive argument for removing parental choice of schools. The case poses starkly the difficulty in drawing a line between the autonomous individual of liberal theory and the citizen of classical theory, deciding which concept of the place of the individual in society is to be preferred and how it is to be promoted – legally, by example or by exhortation.

SOCIAL AND ECONOMIC RIGHTS AND THE *CITIZEN'S CHARTER*

It has been suggested in previous chapters that citizenship is essentially a relationship between the individual and the state or the community. The last question we pose in this chapter is, does it follow that everything about that relationship is an aspect of citizenship? The question is posed because a point commonly made about the *Citizen's Charter* is that it treats the individual as a consumer, with power of the kind that might be found in the market – the power of choice (see Chapter 2). If this is so, does the *Citizen's Charter* undermine true citizenship by treating individuals as consumers in their relations with the state?

One response to that question would be that we are all of us consumers in many of the relations that we have in our daily lives – with retailers, service industries and the like; having consumer-like rights in our relations with the state is unlikely to add to the level of consumer-orientation of individuals in a way that undermines citizenship.

One effect of the *Citizen's Charter* initiative is supposed to be to improve the efficiency of public services, to the benefit not only of individuals having dealings with them, but to the general public benefit. In this respect, it may be said that the initiative is supportive of social citizenship rather than anathema to it, as some of its critics suggest.

In one respect the Charter may undermine the political aspects of citizenship: we are encouraged, by the Charter, to complain as consumers do rather than take collective political action, which is what citizens might do if dissatisfied with public services. So the Charter approach may be said to encourage individualism (reflecting liberal citizenship theory) and discourage political activity (associated with classical theory). Against this, it may be said that it is and has been for many years Utopian to suggest that taking political action can do or ever has done much to improve public services, and it certainly is not a very effective way in which individual grievances can be dealt with. Joining a rail users' group, writing to an MP, letters to the press, will very rarely help an aggrieved individual and almost never result in any broad improvement in a service. A change of Government may have that result but this prospect, it is suggested, is no reason not to do what the *Citizen's Charter* suggests, use established complaints mechanisms, apply for compensation and so on. Looked at in this way, the *Citizen's Charter* may be seen as adding a dimension to citizenship, or, perhaps more accurately, to the relations between the citizen and the state, rather than subtracting from citizenship.

ENVIRONMENTAL RIGHTS

As we have seen civil and political rights are generally enforceable by individuals in the courts. Social and economic rights are only enforceable if they are sufficiently clearly phrased, and, because of limited resources, they will often not give rise to specific rights such as to be educated at a particular school, or to receive particular medical treatment from a particular medical practitioner. Subject to these limitations such rights can be claimed in the courts. (In Chapter 9 we consider how these rights might be strengthened.)

Environmental, 'third generation', rights pose different problems, and have new implications for the notion of citizenship. These 'rights' may take a number of forms. Sometimes they give rise to rights to compensation to individuals from private bodies or the state. The law of nuisance, for example, gives owners of land the right to be free from unreasonable interference with their use and enjoyment of their land (for example, freedom from noise, vibrations, fumes, etc.) and the right not to have it damaged by some forms of pollution. Compensation, even injunctions putting a stop to the interference, may be awarded to the victim.

Such 'rights' not to have one's environment polluted are relatively rare in the law. An exception is a case in February 1993 of a woman who suffered from permanent bronchitis and breathing problems because she had been working in an environment in which she was exposed to passive smoking. She claimed compensation for the damage to her health from her employer and the claim was settled in her favour. (As it was settled it will not reach the Law Reports.) The implications of the case are far-reaching. The woman was, in effect, entitled to an unpolluted environment; the responsibility of the employer for harm caused by a firm's employees was increased, and it extended to controlling the activities of the smokers in the company. The case gave rise to speculation that children might sue their parents for damage caused by smoking: if this were to be the case this sort of right would clearly limit the autonomy of smokers in the interests of others, and impose duties to those with whom they come into close contact – an extension of the duty to respect the interests and rights of others, thus increasing the responsibility of citizens for one another. Of course, a right to smoke has nothing to do with the classical, political concept of citizenship. Smoking thus provides a useful illustration of ways in which limits on autonomy will not always interfere with 'citizenship' if it is taken to mean participation in collective decisions.

Generally problems posed by the pollution of the environment do not lend themselves to claims for compensation by individuals. These problems need to be dealt with by high level governmental and intergovernmental action and cooperation. Much pollution is caused by companies whose actions need to be regulated by Government: allowing individuals to sue for nuisance and interference with their enjoyment of their land is not an adequate way of controlling pollution.

Pollution knows no political boundaries – the discharge of waste into the Danube and other great rivers on the continent of Europe, for example, affects all of those who live downstream. The discharge of carbon dioxide and greenhouse gases into the atmosphere can affect life many miles and continents away and even alter the climate of the world. Realization of the scale of problems caused by large-scale pollution has produced international agreements to try to reduce the level of greenhouse gases, to protect the rain-forests and biodiversity, and so on.

What has all of this to do with citizenship, though? The answer is that it has led to claims that humanity, not as a large collection of individuals but as occupants of 'Planet Earth' has a collective right, at least a moral right, and to a degree legal rights, to a healthy, unpolluted environment. This claim finds its expression, for example, in Tony Benn MP's Commonwealth of Britain Constitution (see Chapter 9) where the Charter of Rights provides that every citizen shall have the right to 'a healthy, sustainable, accessible and attractive environment and to clean water and air'. (This is treated as one of the citizen's social rights in that Charter.) However these 'rights' are essentially claims that are communal rather than individual and the community that claims them is not necessarily based within nation-states. Also, nation-states are not always the appropriate bodies to meet these rights.

The implications of this set of 'rights' are many. They indicate that neither the individual nor the nation-state or its organs can be the only or even the main protector of the environment. There have to be international and cooperative agreements on the ways of dealing with the problem and collective rather than individual action against pollution. This suggests that, in some respects, individuals need to see themselves as 'citizens' of the Planet and of international organizations, and that it is inappropriate to regard citizens as simply politically active individuals in a nation-state, as opposed to members of the whole human race, crucially affected by the pollution which is often the result of human action. We have here an argument for 'multiple citizenship', our fifth theme in citizenship theory.

Concern for the environment also implies limitations to the autonomy of individuals to the extent that this entitles them to contribute to pollution. The restrictions on the exercise of individual rights 'for the protection of rights of others' in the European Convention on Human Rights, for example (see Chapters 3 and 9) must be supplemented by restrictions in the broader public interest. The European Convention allows interference with the rights it proclaims if they are necessary in a democratic society in the interests of national security, public safety, public health or morals. What it does not do is spell out the justification for restricting the exercise of such rights to autonomy in the interests of mankind and the world environment. This is probably because at the time that it entered into force (1953) the problem of global pollution and the need to protect the environment were not recognized.

CONCLUSIONS

This brings us to the end of our consideration of the place of rights, civil and political, social, economic and environmental, in citizenship theory. We have seen how they raise issues to do with each of the six themes outlined in Chapter 1. The law plays an important part in forming and promoting citizenship, but the law alone cannot produce a true status of citizenship. In the next chapter we resume our consideration of the non-legal aspects of the subject, which can complete the picture and fill the gaps that the law cannot fill.

FURTHER READING

Coote, A. (ed.) (1992) *The Welfare of Citizens* (London: IPPR/Rivers Oram Press).

Montgomery, J. (1992) 'Rights to Health and Health Care' in A. Coote (ed.) *The Welfare of Citizens* (London: IPPR/Rivers Oram Press).

Plant, R. (1991) *Modern Political Thought* (Oxford: Blackwell).

Plant, R. (1992) 'Citizenship, rights and welfare' in A. Coote (ed.) *The Welfare of Citizens* (London: IPPR/Rivers Oram Press).

6

'CIVIC VIRTUE' AND 'ACTIVE CITIZENSHIP'

SUMMARY

Citizenship, in the fullest sense of the word, means not just a status but an attitude. Citizens should be persons who want to behave in such a way as to bring benefit to their community – in short, be good citizens. A difficulty arises, however, because there is so much disagreement about what is meant by 'good' in this context.

The traditional view is often called 'republican civic virtue' or sometimes 'communitarianism'. From the Greeks to the eighteenth century particularly, there was a belief that a citizen should undertake certain duties and responsibilities and be loyal to the state rather than pursue his own selfish interests. The writings of Aristotle, Machiavelli and Rousseau, for example, expound this point of view.

It has often been thought that the alternative, liberal view of citizenship is so concerned about the rights of the individual that it has little room for this kind of virtue. That is not necessarily the case. Liberal qualities like tolerance and respect for others and a desire to defend freedom and impartial justice can mark out the good citizen in this tradition.

Very recently, the British Conservative Party has expounded the idea of the active citizen, with an emphasis on the virtue of voluntary service in the local community. Supporters of the communitarian and liberal styles of thought have criticized what they believe to be the weaknesses in each others' cases. It is possible also to criticize the concept of active citizenship. Nevertheless, it may be feasible to discern some common features across the various schools of thought. From this exercise emerges a picture of the good citizen as someone willing to defend freedom and perform useful public service in the local community.

THE GOOD CITIZEN

A citizen is not just someone who is endowed by law (or custom) with certain rights and expected or required to perform certain duties. A citizen, in the fullest sense, is someone who feels a moral commitment to the state and to perform the duties associated with the status. In short, a citizen, properly speaking, should be a good citizen, even though, as explained in Chapter 3, serious problems surround any idea of imposing civic duties by law.

A difficulty arises immediately, however, when we ask the precise meaning of 'good'. What attitudes should an individual have and what actions should they perform to warrant the use of that small adjective? It is a question which, as we saw in Chapter 1, lay at the very heart of the classical tradition of citizenship. A citizen had to be possessed of 'virtue', though the overtones of that word varied, as we shall see in the next section of this chapter.

All the commentators in this tradition over the centuries are agreed on several principles, however. One is that citizens have a *civic* duty to be loyal to the state and uphold its laws. Another is that in return, the state itself should be governed by proper constitutional rules, the rule of law (see Chapter 3) – it should be a *republic*, in the original sense of the word, not a despotism. Thirdly, the individual should be prepared to sink his self-interest in some respects in favour of the interest of the *community* at large. Consequently, this style of theorizing about and practice of citizenship has been called either 'civic republican' or 'communitarian'.

The decay of this tradition in the nineteenth and twentieth centuries has recently been deplored by writers who are saddened by the decline, as they see it, of civic virtue. The liberal emphasis on autonomy, individualism and citizens' rights, they argue, has undermined the old values of community and duties. This renewed interest in civic republicanism and its ideal of civic virtue and the good citizen has had four results:

(a) an attack on the liberal and social traditions of citizenship as selfish;

(b) a liberal response in defence of its own concept of the good citizen;
(c) a demand by communitarians for a renewed emphasis on a sense of commitment and duty;
(d) in Britain, the Conservative Party has propounded the idea of the 'active citizen'.

These are the themes of this chapter.

REPUBLICAN CIVIC VIRTUE

When individuals behave as good citizens are they behaving naturally? If civic virtue is not a natural habit, how may it be instilled? These questions concerning human nature must be our starting point in understanding the civic republican vision of the good citizen. All writers in this tradition accepted the need to mould the good citizen in some way, though different theorists had slightly different preconceptions about the task (as Dr Oldfield has shown in his study of authors in the modern era). For the sake of simplicity, throughout this section, we shall draw our illustrations from Aristotle, Machiavelli and Rousseau.

For Aristotle, virtue (a very rough translation of *areté*) meant excellence in a particular activity. Thus, there were particular qualities for a good citizen which would be different from those required of a good sailor, for instance. Nevertheless, he held to the general Greek view that there were four virtues which the good man and citizen should have. These were: temperance, justice, courage and wisdom. In displaying these virtues the citizen must also be adaptable: different constitutions require different behaviour patterns, therefore different styles of virtue; and because citizenship requires 'ruling and being ruled in turn', the citizen must display different qualities depending on his role at any particular time. Aristotle explained:

> Ruler and ruled have indeed different excellences; but the fact remains that the good citizen must possess the knowledge and the capacity requisite for ruling as well as being ruled, and the excellence of a citizen may be defined as consisting in 'a knowledge of rule over free men from both points of view'. (Aristotle, 1948, 1277b)

Box 6.1

The civic republican writers did not believe that civic virtue came easily. They believed that the good citizen had to be 'made' – for the benefit of himself as well as for the community of which he was part. The following three extracts illustrate this point of view.

There are three means by which individuals become good and virtuous. These three means are the natural endowment we have at birth; the habits we form; and the rational principle [i.e. the power to think] within us ... men are often led by that [rational] principle not to follow habit and natural impulse, once they have been persuaded that some other course is better. (Aristotle, 1948, 1332b)

In constituting and legislating for a commonwealth it must needs be taken for granted that all men are wicked and that they will always give vent to the malignity that is in their minds when opportunity offers. ... Men never do good unless necessity drives them to it. (Machiavelli, 1970, I, iii)

Whoever ventures on the enterprise of setting up a people must be ready, shall we say, to change human nature ... in a word each man must be stripped of his own powers, and given powers which are external to him, and which he cannot use without the help of others ... if each citizen can do nothing whatever except through cooperation with others, ... then we can say that law-making has reached the highest point of perfection. (Rousseau, 1968, pp. 84–5)

Aristotle firmly believed that human beings, by their very nature, are fitted to live in political communities. On the other hand, virtue, as we have seen, embraces knowledge. Therefore, this natural potential must be shaped by communal and educational influences to produce the truly good citizen.

Machiavelli had a much more cynical and pessimistic view of human nature than Aristotle. In contradistinction to the Greek philosopher, the Florentine politician believed that there was nothing in human nature which would give a spontaneous urge to altruistic communal behaviour. Men had to be cajoled, bribed and bullied into being good citizens; at best, they might be impressed by the *virtù* of a conspicuously good leader. However, he placed most reliance on the discipline of religion and military service.

Rousseau's understanding of human nature was much more complex. He believed that primitive man, man 'in a state of nature', was innocent of the corruption and vices which so characterized the human condition in his own age. True morality can only be achieved by the performance of duties in a political community, an experience unknown in the state of nature. Morality is therefore synonymous with civic virtue. Since the golden days of Sparta and Rome, mankind's potential for this behaviour had been undermined by evil social and political institutions. A restoration, in modern terms, of the ancient style of civic virtue was Rousseau's urgent message.

If the citizen's mind and heart had to be guided to the path of virtue, how was this to be achieved? Of prime importance is the creation of a sense of community, a recognition of interdependence. Aristotle expressed it thus:

> concord is . . . friendship between the citizens of a state, its province being the interests and concerns of life.
> Now this conception of concord is realized among good men, for such are in harmony both with themselves and with one another . . . for the wishes of good men . . . are directed to what is both good and expedient. (Aristotle, 1955, IX. vi)

In Machiavelli, this idea becomes one of equality and mutual respect as opposed to the divisiveness of a master–servant relationship. Rousseau echoes the Christian ideal of loving one's brother as oneself, extending into what became the ideal of fraternity in the French Revolution. Both Machiavelli and Rousseau fully appreciate that a sense of community cannot flourish if the laws and institutions of the state are divisive in character.

Aristotle and Rousseau recognize the value of education to enhance the civic spirit – for adults in the case of Aristotle, for children in the case of Rousseau. Rousseau saw the purpose of education as to accustom the citizens 'in good times to the rules, to equality, to fraternity, to competitions, to live in the sight of their fellow-citizens and to desire public approbation' (quoted in Oldfield, 1990, p. 71).

Another recommended cohesive force is religion. Machiavelli was disappointed with Christianity; he sought rather a religion which would school citizens to sacrifice themselves, if necessary, in combat for the good of the state. (Military discipline, Machiavelli recommended, would also be conducive to this kind of virtuous self-sacrifice.) The idea of a civil religion was central to Rousseau's thinking, to replace the distracting dichotomy between Church and state, and to act as a civic cement. He explains his conviction in such a creed:

> There is thus a profession of faith which is purely civil and of which it is the sovereign's function to determine the articles, not strictly as religious dogmas, but as sentiments of sociability, without which it is impossible to be either a good citizen or a loyal subject. (Rousseau, 1968, p. 186)

Once the citizen had been shaped into a virtuous mould by these means, how would that virtue express itself? How did the advocates of the civic republican ideal expect their good citizens to behave?

A good citizen is one who acts responsibly and with honour, whatever his station in the community. Aristotle, for example, expects officials to act honourably, if only out of self-interest; for they would be called to account when they revert to being private citizens. Machiavelli believed that, by acting honourably, good citizens would be a beneficial example to others.

A good citizen will also be courageous. Aristotle, analysing different kinds of courage, allocates first place to 'civilian courage . . . the courage of the citizen soldier . . . because it is inspired by moral excellence . . . and the desire of a noble thing, honour' (Aristotle, 1955, pp. 97–8). Machiavelli, in turn, believed that the creation of a citizen-army would stimulate the valour of its members and canalize it for the good of the state:

> some people who were unarmed and dispirited, but united . . . become warlike and courageous; others who were previously given to faction . . . turn against the enemies of their country those arms and that courage which they used to exert against each other. (quoted in Oldfield, 1990, p. 42)

A citizen-soldier will fight for his country's freedom and protection unlike the mercenary, who could be used by a despot for his own ends. Rousseau expressed the matter epigrammatically: 'All citizens should be soldiers as a duty, not as a career' (quoted in Cobban, 1964, p. 119).

For the good citizen is, in the republican tradition, a patriot, proud to help enhance his country's greatness and glory. Machiavelli's purpose was to encourage this spirit in an Italy debased by self-seeking. In his advice to the unhappy state of Poland, Rousseau wrote, 'Every true republican takes in with his mother's milk the love of his fatherland. . . . This love forms all his existence' (quoted in Oldfield, 1990, p. 71).

It has often been asserted that the civic virtue entailed by communitarianism is absent from the alternative, liberal tradition (see p. 128). Yet liberal citizenship is not, in fact, devoid of a moral dimension worthy of the label 'virtue'.

LIBERAL VIRTUE

The assumption by theorists of the communitarian school of thought that their style of citizenship has a monopoly on civic virtue led the American scholar Stephen Macedo to present a rejoinder in his book *Liberal Virtues*. His starting point is that freedom, the very foundation stone of liberalism, requires very positive moral contributions from the ordinary citizen: 'tolerance and respect for the rights of others, self-control, reflectiveness, self-criticism, moderation, and a reasonable degree of engagement in the activities of citizenship' (Macedo, 1990, p. 2). In order to balance the communitarian case it will be useful to examine some of the main features of liberal virtue as discerned by Macedo.

The freedom which to the liberal is the highest good is not licence: its enjoyment requires that the free individual respects institutional procedures and the reciprocal freedoms of others. Furthermore, freedom must be protected. In the words of the great American judge, Justice Brandeis, the Founding Fathers believed 'that the greatest menace to freedom is an inert people; that public discussion is a political duty' (quoted in Macedo, 1990, p. 100). If freedom involves the morality of respect and duty, the liberal citizen can hardly be accused of being devoid of virtue.

Indeed, the very theoretical bases of liberal representative government assume the ideal of virtuous civic behaviour. Both ordinary citizens and those in public office may be lazy and/or corrupt. That is because human beings are not perfect. The classical contract theories and the constitutions of modern liberal states alike assume and cultivate a certain altruism in the conduct of public officials, and an alertness among the citizenry in ensuring that certain standards are maintained. Precisely how much latitude may be allowed to the people's representatives and how much intrusive vigilance is permissible to the news media acting on behalf of the ordinary citizen, has been a live issue in Britain recently as the tabloid press has unmasked the immoral behaviour of some MPs.

But is there a sense of moral *community* in the liberal state? Or is the virtuous behaviour which is required by liberal theory required only of individuals acting in isolated cases, without an overarching ethic? Macedo argues that for all the individualism and pluralism of the liberal tradition, a unity of general principle is provided by the related concepts of reasonableness and impersonal justice.

The politics of liberalism is rooted in the assumption that the actions and decisions of politicians and judges are derived from fair reasoning and not, for instance, from prejudice or self-interest. Good citizens, therefore, are those who take a sufficient interest in public affairs so that they can understand the decisions made; and then demand that those in public office give reasons for their action by way of public justification. By the same token, the arguments proffered in justification must satisfy the test of general acceptability, not merely acceptability for particular individuals or groups.

Liberal justice also contributes to a public morality. It presupposes that citizens are involved in creating, interpreting and criticizing the law. All citizens, therefore, have a common duty to test the law and its implementation against the yardstick of a common justice. This is engagement in a common civic morality. This principle must be pursued to its logical end. Liberal virtue, therefore, not only allows, but positively encourages, campaigns of civil disobedience pursued from motives of common benefit, though not for a sectional interest. To take an extreme example: during the Cold War an individual who demonstrated in defiance of police authority in the belief that great general benefit would derive from Britain's abandonment of nuclear weapons, would be counted a good citizen; an individual whose motive was to render Britain malleable to Soviet foreign policy would by this criterion be a bad citizen. The good liberal citizen is expected to make impersonal judgements about laws and policies, and voice an opinion and/or take action if that judgement suggests the beneficial need for change.

However, in operating the principles of reasonableness and impersonal justice the liberal citizen is not behaving in a regimented manner. The liberal citizen combines responsibility with autonomy. The liberal citizen is expected to be able to have the freedom to choose; not to be forced to be free, in the Rousseauean civic republican sense.

To be a truly good citizen in this liberal sense inevitably presupposes certain personal characteristics. Some of these traits have already appeared in the quotation on page 120. Let us now outline a few of the most important in relation to the nature of liberal public morality.

We may say that the ideal liberal good citizen has five broad characteristics. The first relates to the individual's self-knowledge. Liberal citizens are expected to be able to shape their own lives by using the reasoning faculty for self-criticism. They will neither be dictated to nor act irresponsibly. Any fanatical or extremist impulses will therefore be kept in rein by an adequate measure of self-control. Excess, even of principle, even of virtue, is to be avoided: the good liberal citizen, echoing Horace, loves the golden mean. Moderation should be the keynote of political life.

One implication of this life of moderation is an attitude of tolerance and impartiality. People are different. These differences should be treated with tolerance, not antipathy; with impartiality, not prejudice. Liberal citizens therefore have a breadth of sympathy and respect for their fellow citizens and can empathize with their points of view. This flexible frame of mind also ensures a willingness to enter into dialogue to understand and resolve disagreements; and, just as importantly, to adapt, to experiment and to change one's own convictions and habits.

Liberal virtue is realistic, not prescriptive. It recognizes that modern states are pluralistic, not inhabited by citizens whose ideas of the good life are cut from the self-same moral template. Individuals *are* different and imperfect. However, the liberal message is that conniving at this uncomfortable lack of conformity is preferable to the constraints of a strictly conformist ethic. In the words of Stephen Macedo, 'Quiet obedience, deference, unquestioned devotion, and humility, could not be counted among the liberal virtues' (Macedo, 1990, p. 278). But, then, those virtues can be dangerously corrosive of freedom.

The distinction between the republican or communitarian and liberal styles of civic virtue is not just a theoretical matter.

Box 6.2

A good citizen in liberal political theory is one who lives by the liberal ethic. The following extract explains this style of civic morality.

In a liberal community people disagree about goals, lifestyles, and religious beliefs. Such a community may, nevertheless, flourish in a liberal way and, if it does, it will have a discernible shape because liberal justice is not neutral among human goods or ways of life: it exerts the positive requirement that every citizen's 'good' includes certain features: a willingness to 'live and let live', to subordinate personal plans and commitments to impartial rules of law, and to persuade rather than coerce. . . .

Liberal pluralism, tolerance, change, and freedom do not stand for a moral void of arbitrary values and the will to power. (Macedo, 1990, pp. 265 and 283)

Exhortations by government ministers in Britain in the late 1980s made the issue a live matter of practical policy.

ACTIVE CITIZENSHIP

From 1988 to 1990 the British Conservative Government undertook a campaign to revive civic virtue in the country, using the term 'active citizenship'. What prompted this initiative? And what did the Government hope that the active citizen would undertake?

We cannot be sure of the motives, though given the priority concerns of the Government at the time, we may indulge in informed speculation. Five considerations may be identified:

1. Perhaps most importantly was the need to find a replacement for the 'nanny state'. This argument had both pragmatic and ideological sides. The steadily rising life expectancy is placing a mounting burden on medical, paramedical and social services. If more voluntary help could be recruited, the costs borne by the state could be eased. In any case, the New Right Conservatives were scornful of the 'dependency' mentality which they believed had been encouraged by the 'socialist' welfare state. This mood needed to be counteracted by an emphasis on self-help and responsibility, including that of the family to all its members.

Box 6.3

The leading exponent of the Conservative concept of active citizenship was the Home Secretary, Douglas Hurd. The following extract from a newspaper article provides an authoritative definition.

Active citizenship is the free acceptance by individuals of voluntary obligations to the community of which they are members. It cannot be conjured up by legislation or by political speeches – although both can help. It arises from traditions of civic obligation and voluntary service which are central to the thinking of this Government and rooted in our history.

The need to foster responsible citizenship is obvious. Freedom can only flourish within a community where shared values, common loyalties and mutual obligations provide a framework of order and self-discipline. Otherwise, liberty can quickly degenerate into narrow self-interest and licence. (Hurd, 1989)

---

2. This self-help could be most effective through local community collaboration. Central government had whittled down the autonomy of local government authorities. Active citizenship envisaged greater use of small-scale functional groups like Neighbourhood Watch and school governors.
3. Neighbourhood Watch schemes were particularly relevant because, despite sizeable increases in spending on the police, crime rates were inexorably rising. Citizens should be mobilized to protect each other and each other's property.
4. Citizens in their capacity as parents and teachers should ensure that the schools made a better job of training the younger generation to be good citizens. Apathy and delinquency were too rife.
5. Indeed, underlying these particular concerns was a generalized worry about the social malaise of selfishness and lawlessness which seemed to be permeating the country. To reverse this trend there was a need to resuscitate respect for morality, service, discipline and authority.

The Home Secretary, Douglas Hurd, launched the idea of active citizenship in 1988 in a speech at Tamworth to mark the 200th anniversary of the birth of Robert Peel. The significant sentences in this address were:

We have to find, as the Victorians found, techniques and instruments which reach the parts of our society which will always be beyond the scope of statutory schemes. I believe that the inspiring and enlisting of the active citizen in all walks of life is the key. (quoted in Carvel, 1988)

Following Hurd's Tamworth address, both he and his junior minister, John Patten, made statements in articles and speeches which provide us with pieces of evidence for building a composite picture of the active citizen. This picture has three facets: the character of the active citizen; how the active citizen fits in to the established social and political context; and the actions expected of such a person.

The active citizen is someone who has a sense of 'civic obligation' (Hurd, 1988), 'personal responsibility', 'self-discipline and respect for others' (Hurd, 1989). The vision was to create 'a third force' of 'talent and energy' mobilized into voluntary activity 'outside both the public and private sectors' (Patten, 1988).

Such a development was seen as consonant with the Conservative philosophy of the 'diffusion of power' (Hurd, 1988). Furthermore, by this means, local allegiances would be strengthened as a complement to national patriotism. Schemes like Neighbourhood Watch 'recreate a sense of neighbourhood and revive in back streets the instincts of a traditional village'. 'National and civic loyalties are strengthend by a thriving personal and local sense of community' (Hurd, 1989). Active citizenship is also a consistent reflection in political terms of the Conservative economic policy:

> The idea of active citizenship is a necessary complement to that of the enterprise culture. Public service may once have been the duty of an élite, but today it is the responsibility of all who have time or money to spare. Modern capitalism has democratised the ownership of property, and we are now witnessing the democratisation of responsible citizenship. (Hurd, 1989)

The active citizen is clearly someone to be admired. How can the individual acquire this coveted soubriquet? To put the matter negatively, this state of civic grace cannot be purchased. In a speech at a Lions Club conference, Patten declared that it 'is not just a matter of writing cheques'. He had earlier provided a succinct definition: 'The active citizen is someone making more than a solely economic contribution to his or her community; nothing more nor less' (Patten, 1988). In a positive sense active citizenship means self-help and involvement to improve education, housing and crime prevention: Hurd (1988) commended 'governing bodies, tenants' co-operatives, housing associations, neighbourhood watch schemes'. The idea was to build on activity already under way in these three spheres:

> Greater opportunities for active citizenship are being offered and being taken up. Parents are having more say over the way in which their children's school is run. Council tenants have new powers to share in the management of their estates. Our action against crime and against drugs relies increasingly on a partnership between statutory agencies, the relevant professions and public-spirited citizens. (Hurd, 1989)

Beyond citizen-initiated schemes, the ministers commended the 'Volunteers' project sponsored by a Trust founded by the Prince of Wales for young community volunteers. They also praised 'Active Businesses' who help their local communities (Patten's Lions speech) and second 'skilled staff to a voluntary organisation' (Hurd, 1989).

The momentum of publicity for the ideal was not sustained. As we shall see below, there were problems in the concept, not least the inconsistency that civic altruism was being dressed in partisan party political clothes. The active citizen was superseded by the 'consumer citizen' of the *Citizen's Charter* (see pp. 47–9).

COMPARISONS AND PROBLEMS

Having presented these different notions of the good citizen, we may now ask a number of questions by way of correlating and assessing them. As the republican argument tends to draw upon theories and practices of past centuries, we need to look at its relevance today. This will lead in to a consideration of the communitarian criticism of liberalism. In response, the liberal case against the republican tradition will be surveyed. There follows a critical assessment of the concept of the active citizen. Finally, we attempt to identify some common features across these diverse ideals.

1. The relevance of civic republicanism

The good citizen of republican tradition was held to be imbued with a sense of community and a feeling of patriotism, eager to participate in political activity and defend the country. Attempts to translate the classical tradition into contemporary terms have been stimulated by concern, especially in the United States, that these virtues have decayed. Yet an exact replication of an ideal Roman or Rousseauean state, for example, is quite impractical. The modern state is large and complex, precluding direct political participation; it lacks a civil religion to cement a sense of community; by no means all citizens undertake military service, and most would probably resent it if so required.

It follows that, if the ideal of civic virtue is to be recaptured (if ever it really existed in practice!), modern equivalents are necessary. These could be in several forms. Decentralization of power ('subsidiarity' in the terminology of the European Community) would multiply the potential for participation and enhance the motivation for civic action. Education for citizenship in the schools could be a substitute for civil religion. Mobilization of the citizenry for community service could perform a similar function to military discipline.

However, something more intangible is also necessary – what the

---

Box 6.4

One of the core problems in any process of translating the classical ideal of civic virtue into the modern state is to know how the necessary goodness is to be instilled into essentially self-centred individuals. The conclusions of one authority are as follows:

The lesson from the civic-republican tradition is that it is the will to engage in the practice [of citizenship] that is crucial. Now within civic republicanism this will was to be generated and sustained by religion. . . . [But in the modern world when such civic faiths] are devised with intent and consciously propagated, [they] are not effective in encouraging a rational commitment to a practice of citizenship. . . .

This suggests that one must build on whatever religion is available, and that a different social institution must be brought into focus: education. (Oldfield, 1990, p. 154)

French writer Tocqueville called 'habits of the heart'. Good citizenship in the communitarian spirit needs the underpinning of customs and understanding, and the expectation that the citizen will act for the good of the community as a whole. The republic may exert pressures of laws and opinion to this end, but the will to act in their support must be present in each individual citizen for this pressure to be truly effective.

2. Criticism of the liberal tradition

The effort to adapt the civic-republican tradition to modern conditions appears worthwhile to modern communitarians because of the weaknesses, as they see them, in the prevailing liberal system. One American commentator has declared:

> The liberal legacy has troubled generations of American intellectuals. Individualism seemed to leave America without a sense of moral community and pluralism without a sense of national purpose. (J. P. Diggins, quoted in Macedo, 1990, p. 131)

Communitarian criticism identifies a number of features of liberal citizenship theory which would tend to inhibit the efflorescence of citizenly virtue.

In the first place, liberalism is an abstract, universal theory which is bound to be weak in fostering a commitment to the citizen's particular community and its traditions. The qualities of fraternity and social solidarity are consequently likely to be feeble in a society based on the liberal ethic. For liberal citizens are guided by the subjective desire to protect their individual rights, not by the commitment to an objective public moral code.

Liberalism, communitarians further complain, is too apolitical. It tolerates the wish of too many to be 'private citizens'; the duty to behave as a good citizen is thus pushed to one small corner of the individual's conscience. This emphasis on the pursuit of a self-interested good life leads to a shallow happiness of an essentially materialist nature. It leads also to the 'free-rider' mentality – of taking from society and giving nothing in return. This is a condition, they argue, which is the very antithesis of civic virtue and destructive of that communal harmony which is the prerequisite for its cultivation.

3. Criticism of communitarianism

On the other hand, the defenders of the liberal style of citizenship find faults in the communitarian alternative. Part of the criticism is based on historical arguments; part, on arguments of principle.

Even if the civic republican ideal of virtue had been suitable for the city-state of Greek experience or Rousseau's imagination, it is by no means pertinent to the modern nation-state. Modern states are not socially and culturally homogeneous, and are not sufficiently compact for constant direct political participation. Yet the classical ideal of civic virtue was founded on the twin premises of a tightly-knit community and politically active citizens.

Even if the socio-political conditions were apposite, the liberal would still find the application of the precepts of republican virtue objectionable. If strictly applied, it is too intrusive into private life. It demands an austere commitment to public duty and a strict rein on the pursuit of individual rights and interests. By confining one's social and political horizons to the established conception of the communal good, there is danger of dulling one's critical faculty. The citizen is paternally guided by the state's demand for what it conceives to be the proper discharge of obligations and duties. Moreover, in so far as the atmosphere of civic virtue generates in the individual a personally motivated desire to be civically 'good', there lurks the peril of enthusiasm. Enthusiasm, in the eighteenth-century sense of over-excited faith, can so readily spill over to fanaticism; and fanaticism is the very antithesis of those qualities of tolerance and moderation which are the twin foundations of the liberal conception of civic morality.

4. Criticism of active citizenship

Is, then, the British Conservative Party's notion of active citizenship a more balanced view of civic morality? It is difficult to give a thorough answer to this question because the concept has not been expounded in any detail. The desire to encourage a greater emphasis on responsibility and duties, to balance what the Conservatives have diagnosed as an unfortunate bias towards rights, is assuredly a basic message in favour of good citizenship. When, however, one examines the activity required of active citizens, it is clear that their virtue is expected to be highly concentrated. No vigilance is necessary in defence of democracy or justice. The virtue of the active citizen is the altruism of voluntary social service. The impression is given that in order to become a *good* citizen, the individual must surrender positive, critical political interests. The active citizen is a depoliticized voluntary worker in his or her local community. This version of good citizenship is clearly different from either the communitarian or the liberal style. (It is, however, in harmony with the traditional Conservative vision of an apolitical society in which most individuals are freed of political concerns in order to pursue their own good lives.)

5. Synthesis

We may now therefore attempt some comparisons across these three schools of thought. As we have explained in Chapter 2, interest in the whole topic of citizenship has intensified in recent years. Part of the objective of the academic analysis and political rhetoric has been an attempt to re-emphasize the moral element in the concept and status of citizenship. If true citizenship entails the discharge of responsibilities, duties and obligations, it is necessary to explain what these are, justify the demands on the citizen to perform them and suggest how the citizen can be motivated to such virtuous behaviour.

For all the evident differences, indeed antagonisms, between the three schools of thought we have reviewed in this chapter, it is possible to compile a composite picture of a good citizen which might be acceptable to all – a kind of lowest common multiple of civic virtue. The three traditions would not need to adapt too much to accommodate themselves to the following definition: a good citizen is one who enjoys freedom and is vigilant to defend it against the abuse of power; and participates as effectively as possible in public affairs, especially in the local community.

Emphasis on the defence of freedom needs no explanation in terms of the liberal tradition. The right to both negative and positive freedoms is fundamental to the liberal philosophy. It would be a poor citizen who did not feel it his or her duty to protect them from attack or erosion. Now, although the civic republican tradition appears to place a greater emphasis on duty to the community than enjoyment of individual rights, Quentin Skinner has cogently argued that the reason writers such as Machiavelli emphasized this duty was precisely to defend liberty (see Box 6.5). Unless the citizen is ready to protect

---

Box 6.5

Professor Quentin Skinner has argued that the equation of liberalism with rights and civic republicanism with duties is a false dichotomy. Civic-republican writers urged the performance of duties by citizens in order to defend their freedoms. It is a message relevant to today.

Politics is a profession; unless politicians are persons of exceptional altruism, they will always face the temptation of making decisions in line with their own interests and those of powerful pressure-groups instead of in the interests of the community at large. Given this predicament, the republican argument conveys a warning which, while we may wish to dismiss it as unduly pessimistic, we can hardly afford at the present juncture to ignore: that unless we act to prevent this kind of political corruption by giving our civic duties priority over our individual rights, we must expect to find our individual rights themselves undermined. (Q. Skinner, in Mouffe, 1992, p. 223)

---

the freedom of the state against external attack and internal civil liberties from the assault of power-hungry autocrats, the citizen would decline into a condition of servitude. Defence of freedom can also be plausibly read into the Conservative concept of active citizenship. Citizens are to be freed from the over-intrusive functions of the state and be free to construct a good society by their own efforts at the level of the local community.

This brings us to the matter of the display of civic virtue at the local level. It is often held against the communitarians that their attempt to resuscitate the ancient civic republican morality is bound to fail because of the size and complexity of the modern state. However, if the state, by a process of decentralization of power, is reconstituted as 'a mosaic of smaller collectivities' (Marquand, 1988, p. 239), then the classical conditions of the duties of citizenship being performed in a compact community can be revived. There is nothing in the liberal tradition which would find this objectionable. Indeed, the above quotation is taken from a British academic who may reasonably be placed in the liberal category. Of course, the whole Conservative concept of active citizenship is based on the notion of local community voluntary work.

Differences of emphasis do exist of a very real nature. However, the need for a coherent and broadly acceptable idea of good citizenship is urgent and could surely be sought along the lines we have suggested.

Even so, it must be recognized that an individual cannot display citizenly virtue in a vacuum. The moral dynamic must be generated by a social or political entity and be directed to its welfare. Is the European Community yet sufficiently well formed in fact and in citizens' minds to be such an entity? What does it mean today to be a European citizen? These are the questions which we now need to address.

FURTHER READING

Macedo, S. (1990) *Liberal Virtues: Citizenship, Virtue and Community in Liberal Constitutionalism* (Oxford: Clarendon).

Oldfield, A. (1990) *Citizenship and Community: Civic Republicanism and the Modern World* (London: Routledge).

7

THE EUROPEAN DIMENSIONS OF CITIZENSHIP

SUMMARY

Since the end of the Second World War in 1945, a European aspect has been added to citizenship in the United Kingdom. This represents a move away from citizenship being regarded as centred on the nation-state. The development flows partly from UK membership of the Council of Europe and the concomitant jurisdiction of the European Commission and Court of Human Rights at Strasbourg to deal with complaints that the law of the United Kingdom does not conform to the European Convention on Human Rights; and partly from UK membership of the European Community.

Originally the Community was primarily concerned with the market and not with the political and civil rights of nationals of Member States. Since the Single European Act of 1978 and the Treaty of Union (the Maastricht Treaty), the Community has been developing the political side of its activities and seeking to create a European citizenship. The European Parliament, elected by citizens of the Member States, its members owing their duties to their citizens and not to national governments, has achieved greater influence over the Council of Ministers and the Commission.

The European Community has treated individuals as economic actors rather than political ones. However, under the Treaty of Union, citizens of Member States will be 'Citizens of the Union', entitled to vote in local government and European Parliament elections in the state in which they reside, even if it is not the state of which they are nationals. Individuals will be able to petition the European Parliament and complain to a newly established European Ombudsman about the conduct of European Community institutions. They may receive diplomatic protection abroad from the Governments of other Member States.

The conception of European citizenship is exclusive: it does not benefit the many people of nationalities outside the Community who reside within it. Some of the Member States and some citizens fear that the growth of the Community will undermine the nation-state. The Maastricht Treaty seeks to promote 'subsidiarity' which would protect the powers of Member States, but it is difficult to give this principle legal meaning.

Freedom within the Community and a non-exclusive conception of citizenship are also made difficult by the need to take concerted action against international crime – drug smuggling and terrorism – and to prevent large-scale illegal immigration into the Community. These problems have conjured up the fear of a move to 'Fortress Europe'.

CIVIL AND POLITICAL RIGHTS AND EUROPEAN CITIZENSHIP

Previous chapters in this book have considered a range of aspects of citizenship – historical and philosophical, legal and political, which, though operating in a framework of international law, have developed within the notion of the city- or nation-state. As we saw in Chapters 1 and 3 in particular, they have been influenced by exclusionary considerations – nationality, sex, civil status. They have also been primarily concerned with the participation of those individuals who are citizens in the political process, their duties, and the enjoyment of civil and political, social, economic and environmental rights.

In the years since the end of the Second World War, a new legally-based dimension of citizenship has been developing in Western Europe, which is not strictly based in international law, nor is it based on the concept of the state. In this chapter we shall be concerned with the notion of European citizenship.

The first stage in this development of a legal concept of European citizenship came with the signing of the European Convention on

Human Rights and Fundamental Freedoms in 1950. The United Kingdom ratified this document in 1951. It has the status of an international instrument and is therefore binding only on governments in international law. The European Court of Human Rights in Strasbourg has jurisdiction to hear allegations that one of the states that are party to the ECHR has been in breach. Initially such cases could only be brought by other states and not by individuals, unless a particular state had granted individuals the right to bring cases by petition, as was permitted by Article 25 of the Convention. It was not until 1966 that the Government of the United Kingdom recognized this right of individual petition. This has to be renewed every five years. The effect was to give rights to individuals in the United Kingdom, enforceable in the Court at Strasbourg, and thus to enhance the status of what, without such a right of individual petition, was simply an instrument binding between governments. These rights do not depend on the nationality of the individual concerned.

The European Convention on Human Rights protects the ordinary civil and political rights of individuals, including the right to life, to liberty of the person, freedom of thought, conscience and religion, expression, association, privacy and family life, the right to a fair trial and to effective remedies for breach of these rights. It is not much concerned with second or third generation rights, though it does guarantee 'a right to education' (see Chapter 5).

In some countries, the ECHR has domestic effect, so that an individual who complains that the rights and freedoms protected by the Convention have been violated, may pursue that claim in the courts of the state in question. However, in the United Kingdom the Convention does not have such effect, and so those complaining of a breach must take the case to the Court at Strasbourg – a slow and expensive process. (In Chapter 9 we consider the case for incorporating the ECHR into the domestic law of the United Kingdom.) A number of important cases has been taken successfully to the European Court of Human Rights at Strasbourg against the British Government.

The British Government has had to get Parliament to alter our law in order to bring it into line with the requirements of the Convention in some cases. For example, telephone tapping used not to be either a crime or a civil wrong in the United Kingdom, but as a result of the European Court of Human Rights' decision in the *Malone* case the

---

Box 7.1 *Gaskin* v. *United Kingdom* (1989)

This case illustrates how the right of individual petition and the ECHR work. Gaskin had been brought up in the care of a local authority from the age of three until he reached eighteen. He had been placed with foster parents for much of that time, and he alleged that he had been ill-treated and abused by them. He wanted access to the local authority's records concerning him, to enable him to learn about his past and overcome his emotional and psychological problems. The Council was not prepared to show him records unless contributors of the information consented. He claimed that refusal of this access was in breach of his right to 'respect for his private and family life' under Article 8 of the ECHR, and his right to receive information under Article 10.

The European Court of Human Rights found that there had been a violation of Article 8, but no violation of Article 10. Although it was accepted that confidentiality of information was important, there ought to have been an independent authority to decide whether access had to be granted if a contributor failed to answer or withheld consent. The right to receive information only covered situations where the owner of the information wished to impart it to a person, in which case the state should not prevent it. It did not mean that a body such as the local authority which held information should be compelled to impart it to an individual. Gaskin was awarded his legal expenses and a sum of compensation for the emotional distress and anxiety he may have suffered from the absence of an independent procedure to review the question of access to his files.

British Government had to get Parliament to pass an Act putting telephone tapping on a formal legal basis so that it could only be permitted in strictly limited circumstances and required official authorization.

The European Convention on Human Rights, as we have seen, has a legal status stronger than a purely international obligation where states who are parties to it have recognized the right of individual petition. The class of person who may bring a case under this right is not limited to, for example, nationals of the state in question, and in this respect it involves a broad view of the extent of the civil and political rights of individuals – in effect of who is a citizen. However, it does not grant social, economic or environmental rights. We have considered, in Chapter 5, the difficulties in giving individuals enforceable, broadly defined social and economic or environmental rights, and so it is not a criticism of the ECHR that it is confined to civil and political rights. However, the concept of the relationship between the individual and the state that it entails, is clearly a limited one: it protects individual autonomy and it enables individuals to participate in the political process through the freedoms of speech and association; so it embraces liberal and classical concepts of citizenship. It extends the rights of individuals to bring cases against governments, and it establishes a landmark in the development of a concept of legal rights of citizenship beyond that contained in domestic systems of law, a step towards the internationalization of citizenship rights, along the lines of the fifth strand of citizenship theory identified in Chapter 1.

CITIZENSHIP AND THE EUROPEAN COMMUNITY

The European Community represents yet another step in the development of a form of European citizenship – or more precisely, a relationship between the individual and the state or community institutions. It entails legally enforceable rights that go beyond the first, second and third generation rights we have considered in Chapters 4 and 5. It also goes beyond the additional protections afforded by the ECHR and the machinery of the Council of Europe. Citizenship in the European Community will be the subject of the rest of this chapter.

The United Kingdom joined the Community with effect from 1 January 1973. When the Community was founded in 1957 it was principally concerned with market matters – hence its original title 'The Common Market'. The 'constitution' of the Community was, and is, the Treaty of Rome, now amended by the Treaty of Maastricht ('The Treaty on European Union'). Most of the provisions of the original Treaty had little to do with citizenship, and the civil and political rights and freedoms associated with it. The 'constitution' of the Community was thus quite different from that of nation-states, being restricted in its scope and not claiming 'sovereignty'. It was concerned with the participation of individuals in policy-making and holding institutions to account only to a very limited extent.

The Community is based on the 'four freedoms', quite different from those normally associated with citizenship: these are free movement of workers, goods, services and capital. Note that the freedom of movement has been guaranteed primarily to individuals as workers – though it extends to their family members – thus introducing a new dimension to the relationship between the individual and public institutions, an essentially apolitical, economic relationship.

In 1993, the Member States of the European Community ratified the Treaty on European Union – the 'Maastricht Treaty'. It will have radical effects on many aspects of the relationship between individuals and the Community institutions and governments of Member States. For example, it seeks to extend the free movement rights: by Article 8a 'Every citizen of the Union shall have the right to move and reside freely within the territory of the Member States'. (This right, however, is subject to the limitations and conditions laid down in the Treaty and by the measures adopted to give it effect.) A number of directives has been issued by the Council of the European Communities in 1990, which extend rights of residence to nationals of Member States and their families as long as they are covered by sickness insurance and have sufficient resources to avoid becoming a burden on the social assistance system of the host Member State during their period of residence. These and similar provisions cover retired people and their families, provided they have a pension of an amount sufficient to avoid becoming a burden on the social security system of the host. Students and their families also have rights of residence in the country in which they are studying, again as long as they do not become a burden on the host. The emphasis in these provisions is on people as past or future economic actors, rather than as individuals with rights and needs that the Government of their place of residence should meet. Given that the Community itself does not provide social and economic rights, such rights form no part of European Community citizenship as such – in this respect too, it differs from the 'citizenship of entitlement' of Marshall.

The guarantees of free movement of capital, goods and services, to the extent that they give rights of mobility to owners of those assets and those who would wish to consume them, also imply that important facets of the individual in the Community are those of property owner, consumer and contractor. None of these measures is explicitly concerned with the role of the individual as a political actor, which we normally associate with citizenship.

Yet the Community, as initially conceived, did not entirely marginalize the civil and political roles of individuals. The Treaty of Rome established the European Assembly. It had no legislative power when it was instituted, but – a mark of the evolution of the Community – it was officially renamed in 1986 under the Single European Act as the 'European Parliament' (it had been called a Parliament unofficially since 1962). From 1979, direct elections to the Parliament were required (hitherto indirect elections had been permitted) and the Treaty of Rome requires adoption in due course of a uniform system of election. The Parliament is supposed to represent 'the peoples' of the Member States rather than the governments or the Member States themselves (Article 137). Thus the Treaty of Rome and the Single European Act give some political role to individuals in the Member States through the Parliament.

The European Parliament's functions have been broadly supervisory and advisory, based on consultation and cooperation. The Parliament has the power to pass a motion of censure over the Commission and if it achieves a sufficient majority, it may dismiss the Commission; this has never happened. The Parliament has the power to ask questions of the Commission and the Council, orally or in writing. It may debate the Commission's Annual Report on the Activities of the Communities. It debates the Commission's Annual Programme, and in cooperation with the Commission an agreed legislative programme and timetable for the year are drawn up. It is entitled to be consulted over major policy proposals, and before major Acts are adopted. It may propose amendments to legislation, but not insist upon them. It may request the Commission to submit proposals. If the Council intends to depart from an opinion of the Parliament on a matter with financial implications, a 'conciliation procedure' has to be followed.

As far as the budget is concerned, the Parliament may reject or amend some proposals and propose amendments to others. It may adopt or reject a draft budget. The Parliament does, then, have considerable powers, but their limitations are important. It has no right of legislative initiative nor a right to amend legislation put forward by the Council of Ministers or the Commission.

The implications of these arrangements are that individuals' civil and political rights are primarily matters for the Member States, and the representation of the interests of individuals in the Community takes place primarily through their governments as members of the

Council of Ministers rather than as individuals. This, in turn, seems to negate the idea that individuals may have interests as citizens of Europe as opposed to as citizens of the Member States. There is little concession to the idea of 'multiple citizenship' in these arrangements.

Under the Treaty of Union the powers of the European Parliament will increase. In some respects cooperation and consultation will be supplemented by 'codecision' (Article 189b). The Parliament will, from 1995, have the power to approve or refuse to approve membership of the Commission, and it is entitled to be consulted as to the nomination of the President of the Commission. It will be able to 'require' the Commission to submit proposals for new legislation (Article 138b). It will be able to set up a Committee of Inquiry to investigate contraventions of Community law (Article 138c). It will, in effect, have the power, subject to a conciliation procedure between the Parliament and the Council, to delay and veto legislation put forward by the Council of Ministers.

Although, as indicated above, the Community, when it was formed, was concerned principally with commercial matters, some aspects of the Treaty of Rome did have implications for civil and political rights. For example, Article 119 of the Treaty forbids discrimination on the ground of sex, at least in employment, and this article has been useful in the United Kingdom in strengthening the protection of women against discrimination in pay, retirement age, fringe benefits and so on. Article 7 of the original Treaty, now renumbered Article 6, also proscribes discrimination against citizens of Member States on grounds of nationality 'within the scope of application of the Treaty'.

However, the Community law protections against discrimination are, in other respects, narrower than those under UK statutes; there is very little protection against discrimination on grounds of race or religion. Protection is limited to the employment or commercial field. It only protects nationals of Member States; so, for example, it would not protect Commonwealth citizens working in the Community outside the United Kingdom. It is in this respect exclusive, and may be contrasted with the more liberal approach in English law generally which, as we saw in Chapter 3, makes little distinction between nationals and others lawfully resident in the United Kingdom.

The Treaty on European Union seeks to give greater precedence to civil and political rights, in an indirect way: by Article F,

The Union shall respect fundamental rights, as guaranteed by the European Convention for the Protection of Human Rights and Fundamental Freedoms ... and as they result from the constitutional traditions common to the Member States, as general principles of Community law.

It is not clear what actual effects this will have on the civil and political rights of European citizens.

THE EUROPEAN COMMUNITY, CITIZENSHIP AND THE NATION-STATE

There is some evidence that citizens of Member States in the Community regard its institutions as remote and inaccessible, and fear that they will be vulnerable if the powers of their own governments over their lives – governments which are generally far more accountable to their citizens than the Community's institutions are to Community citizens – are reduced and replaced by Community institutions. Thus, the people of Denmark in the first referendum on ratification of the Maastricht Treaty voted on 2 June 1992 by a small majority to reject it; and the French electorate in its referendum on 20 September 1992 voted in favour only by 51 per cent to 49 per cent. These referendums stimulated consideration in Community institutions and by governments of the Member States of how the Community could be made more accountable either to the governments of Member States or to the representatives of the peoples of the Community in the European Parliament, or the extent to which powers claimed by the Community could be reserved to the governments of Member States through the principle of 'subsidiarity' (see below).

The Treaty of Union (the Maastricht Treaty) seeks to develop the concept of European citizenship beyond the rather limited concept set out above. Article A of the Treaty is expressed to mark 'a new stage in the process of creating an ever closer union among the peoples of Europe, in which decisions are taken as closely as possible to the citizen'. Note the reference to 'peoples' rather than 'states' and to 'the citizen'. Article B sets out a number of objectives, which include 'to strengthen the protection of the rights and interests of the nationals of its Member States through the introduction of a citizenship of the Union'. Article F requires the Union to respect fundamental rights, as guaranteed by the ECHR (see above) and as they result from the constitutional traditions common to the Member States, as general principles of Community law. Thus a number of aspects of these general provisions set out important ideas about European citizenship: but they do not themselves give citizens any enforceable rights.

The provisions about citizenship of the Union are elaborated in Articles 8 to 8e of the Treaty of Union. 'Every person holding the nationality of a Member State shall be a citizen of the Union' and in that capacity shall enjoy the rights conferred by the Treaty and be subject to the duties imposed thereby. Some of these rights are not yet effective but the Treaty commits Member States to implement them soon. The rights include the right of a citizen of the Union residing in a Member State of which he is not a national to vote and stand for election at municipal elections and for European Parliament elections in that state (Article 8b). Citizens of the Union are also entitled to diplomatic protection from the governments of other Member States in non-EC countries, and they have rights to petition the European Parliament and to apply to the Community Ombudsman, who is to be appointed under the Treaty.

These measures, together with other provisions of the Treaty and other European laws on, for example, social rights, when they are fully effective, will establish the framework within which European citizenship may develop. The version of citizenship that they imply is, in many respects, limited. First, partly for the reasons set out above, they do not contain the usual civil and political rights that are protected in one way or another in most of the Western democracies. The requirement referred to above, that the Union should respect fundamental rights, is too vague to be directly enforceable, though it may influence the exercise of discretion and the way in which the European Court of Justice decides cases. From time to time, the issue has been raised as to whether the Community itself ought to be a party to the ECHR, so that citizens affected by the actions of the Community institutions in a way that interferes with their civil and political rights would have a remedy, but this has not happened. Second, as indicated above, Community law focuses on individuals as workers, property-owners and consumers rather than as politically active people. Although the Treaty of Union increases the political rights of citizens by allowing them to petition the Parliament, and by increasing the powers of the Parliament in the various ways that have been summarized above, the political role envisaged expressly for citizens is limited.

Third, the rights and duties of citizenship of the Union are limited to the nationals of Member States, and are not available to all individuals regardless of nationality. There are large numbers of people living perfectly lawfully in the Member States who are not nationals of any of those Member States and are not entitled to these benefits, though they may, in practice, enjoy them under the law of the particular Member State in which they reside. As we saw in Chapter 3, there are many Commonwealth citizens living in the United Kingdom who have the right to vote in UK elections and who enjoy the civil and political, social, economic and environmental rights and duties of citizenship in the UK regardless of their lack of full British citizenship; yet they will not enjoy the benefits of European citizenship under the Treaty of Union, or under the Treaty of Rome. In Germany, there is a large Turkish population, in France a North African population, and in many of the Member States other groups who are nationals of non-EC countries who will be non-citizens in the European context. The exclusivity of citizenship in the European Community contrasts with the increasing inclusiveness in, for example, the United Kingdom, and it will result in unequal treatment and could encourage a climate of nationalism and racial discrimination.

There are additional provisions in Community arrangements for special interests and for regional representatives to have greater input into Community decisions. The Treaty of Union proposes a Committee of the Regions (Article 198a), to be consulted by the Council and the Commission; but it is not to be elected. The Treaty purports to give priority to the principle of subsidiarity, the idea that decisions of a governmental or public kind ought to be taken as near to the people affected as possible. However, this principle raises a number of difficult issues. First, it is very vague and almost impossible to enforce. As yet there are no firm rules about how decisions should be made as to the appropriate level for decision-making, nor which decisions should be taken at which level. Second, the British Government, coming as it does from a highly centralized system, sees subsidiarity as meaning that the governments of the Member States should take decisions for their own states and citizens, and does not acknowledge that there should be subsidiarity within states through, for example, strong local government, or English regional assemblies or assemblies for Scotland and Wales.

WHITHER COMMUNITY CITIZENSHIP?

In certain respects, citizens in Europe are regarded as having important functions in holding the Community and the Governments of Member States to account, and promoting the rule of law in the Community in a way that does not have a parallel in the United Kingdom. If a Government of a Member State does not comply with the requirements of European law which gives rise to individual rights, then an individual who has suffered as a result may apply to the courts in that Member State for a remedy against the Government in question, and the courts are obliged to give some kind of remedy. In accordance with the idea of subsidiarity, each Member State can have its own system of remedies as long as they are effective; so in some countries compensation will be available, in others only orders requiring the Government in question to comply with the law of the Community or to desist from breaking it will be available. The European Court of Justice has been quite explicit about the fact that citizens are allowed to bring these cases, not just to vindicate their own rights but also to put pressure on governments to obey the law.

Part of the programme of the Community relates to the development of social rights. The rationale for these has been the promotion of equal competition rather than any idea of the essential equality of individuals which citizenship suggests. Since the Single European Act provisions on Social Policy, the Community has been more active in promoting social policy. In 1989 it produced its Draft Community Charter of Fundamental Social Rights ('the Social Charter') enjoining Member States to secure improved living and working conditions, collective bargaining, vocational training, worker participation in management and so on. The British Government has refused to accept this. The Treaty of Union contains a 'Social Chapter' which adds to the legal force of these proposals, but the British Government persuaded the rest of the Community to agree to its 'opting out' of this chapter.

One problem with which the Community will have to grapple, and which affects civil liberties particularly, is that of international crime,

---

Box 7.2 The *Van Gend* case (1963)

A company, Van Gend, had been charged a customs duty when it imported material into the Netherlands from Germany. This was contrary to the Treaty of Rome's requirement of free movement of goods, one of the four freedoms of the Community. Van Gend applied to the Dutch court claiming reimbursement of the duty. The Dutch court referred the matter to the European Court of Justice for an opinion on whether a private litigant was entitled to assert rights under European law, as it was not clear in the early days of the Community whether it was possible to do so.

The European Court of Justice decided that the Community constitutes 'a new legal order' for the benefit not only of Member States but of their nationals. 'Community law ... not only imposes obligations upon individuals but is also intended to confer upon them rights which become part of their legal heritage.' Importantly the Court added that: 'The vigilance of individuals concerned to protect their rights amounts to an effective supervision in addition to the supervision entrusted by (the Treaty) to the diligence of the Commission and of the Member States.' Thus we have the idea of 'the citizen as enforcer' or guardian of the rule of law in the Community.

---

terrorism, drug dealing and illegal immigration. With internal boundaries between Member States being dismantled in 1993 with the arrival of the single market, the external boundaries become the main protection against these threats. In place of internal boundaries, there is likely to be pressure for the introduction of identity cards, with the police having powers to require their production, keeping central records of people's movements, etc. Such documents are already required in many of the Member States but not in the United Kingdom, which has a strong liberal tradition in such matters. It has been suggested that we may end up as 'Fortress Europe' as it becomes necessary to counter large-scale immigration from Eastern Europe; genuine refugees may find themselves labelled 'economic migrants', so that the liberal traditions of some of the European states will be undermined by fear of an unstoppable tide of immigration. Fear of drug trafficking may also increase external border controls and increase police powers of search and entry in the war against drugs.

CONCLUSIONS

In this chapter we have traced briefly the emergence of a limited, legally supported form of 'multiple' citizenship in Europe, the roots of which lie in the Council of Europe and the European Community. We have noted, however, how in many respects it concentrates on the economic rather than political roles of citizens, reflecting some of the more radical strains of liberal theory, and only recently acknowledging the role for classical theory. Nationality is central to it. The absence of strong protections for the civil rights of individuals in the United Kingdom or through the legal institutions of the Community may mean that individuals will find themselves ill-protected if pressures from international crime and migration push the European Community towards a 'Fortress Europe' set of protectionist policies.

In Chapter 9 we return to consider how the legal aspects of citizenship could be strengthened. First we turn to an important non-legal foundation, education.

FURTHER READING

Collins, L. (1990) *European Community Law in the United Kingdom* 4th edn (London: Butterworths).

Duffy, P. and Yves de Cara, J. (1992) *European Union. The Lawyers' Guide* (Guildford: Longman).

The European (1992) *Maastricht Made Simple* (Milton Keynes: *The European*).

Freestone, D. A. C. and Davidson, J. S. (1990) *The Institutional Framework of the European Communities* (London: Routledge).

Lasok, D. and Bridge, J. W. (1991) *Law and Institutions of the European Communities* 5th edn (London: Butterworths).

Nielson, R. and Szyszczak, E. (1991) *The Social Dimension of the European Community* (Copenhagen: Handelshojskolens Forlag).

Spencer, M. (1991) *1992 and All That* (London: Civil Liberties Trust).

8

CITIZENSHIP IN SCHOOLS

SUMMARY

The belief that schools have a vital role to play in preparing young people for citizenship has become widespread during the twentieth century. Democracy and nationalism have been powerful forces in this respect. Responses have varied: different terms have been used and in England, for example, a range of historical, political and social conditions have shaped the ways in which schools have discharged this responsibility.

Nevertheless, some aspects of citizenship education have not been universally accepted as an appropriate undertaking for schools. Despite evidence of widespread ignorance and prejudice among adolescents and the suitability of schools as institutions to combat this condition, doubts have been expressed: pupils are too young to handle political material and indoctrination is a possible peril.

Even in schools which accept the need for citizenship education, there has been little agreement about what this should entail. Should knowledge, attitudes and skills be taught covering basically political and legal subject matter? In a multicultural society like Britain, should the matter of the status of and relationships between the various ethnic groups be included? Should the temptation to include matter more germane to health education, for example, be resisted?

During the 1970s especially, a great deal of groundwork was undertaken in England in the field of political education. More recently, law education has been developed. By the late 1980s the Government was encouraging citizenship education, a term which had fallen into disuse since *c.* 1950. The topic was selected as one of the 'cross-curricular themes' for the National Curriculum. The key document to assist schools in this work, the National Curriculum Council's *Curriculum Guidance No. 8* gives a range of advice across the whole age spectrum 5–16. Nevertheless, criticisms of this booklet suggest that further development work is still needed.

BACKGROUND

If individuals are to be effective citizens, they must develop certain attitudes, learn certain knowledge and acquire certain skills. It is highly convenient that the foundations of this learning take place in schools. The realization that schools have this vital function to perform has become especially widespread throughout the world in the twentieth century. There are two main reasons for this.

In the first place, liberal democracy has become recognized, even if somewhat haltingly, as the most acceptable form of government. Democracy involves the participation of ordinary citizens in choosing their Government and a recognition by the Government of citizens' rights. It follows that citizens need to know how to participate in public affairs and what their rights are and how to defend them. Very commonly, governments have emphasized rather the need for citizens to act 'responsibly', that is, to support their 'betters' in their tasks of government, legislation and law enforcement. However 'democracy' has been interpreted – in the active or passive way – schools have been used throughout the world in the twentieth century to prepare young people for 'citizenship', even though in many cases a more apt word would be 'subjecthood'.

The second reason for the involvement of schools in this kind of teaching has been the prevalence of nationalism. Schools have been used to consolidate a sense of national identity and loyalty. This process has occurred in states such as the United States with a very large immigrant population. The schools have helped Irish, Italians, Chinese and Mexicans, for example, to learn how to be American citizens. The process has also been evident in former colonies like

---

Box 8.1

In the late 1920s, the distinguished American political scientist, Charles E. Merriam, commissioned nine studies of citizenship education: Soviet Russia, Great Britain, Austria–Hungary, Italy, Germany, Switzerland, France, the United States and primitive and ancient societies. Merriam himself summarized all this work. He wrote:

In conclusion one might be inclined to generalise to the effect that the newer the régime the more vigorous the use of the educational system for civic training, and cite the cases of Russia, Italy, and America. The older systems of France and Germany are exceptionally developed, however . . . And the English system, in the background, in spite of the general denial of an attempt at conscious utilization of the schools is a classic example at least of the indirect and unconscious employment of the educational system.

The fact is that in all cases the school system is the basic factor in the development of civic interest and loyalty, and the chief instrument for that purpose. (Merriam, 1931, p. 134)

Nigeria, where a new nation-state has had to be forged from an ethnically heterogeneous population.

One of the difficulties in studying and describing the work of schools in preparing young people for citizenship is that it has been given different titles and has been undertaken in different contexts. Are, for instance, 'civic education', 'social studies', 'political education', 'law-related education', 'moral education', 'personal education' the same as 'citizenship education'? And what have been the roles of the different disciplines such as history, sociology and politics?

We shall have more to say on these matters later in the chapter. What we need to point out here are two particular matters.

1. If the term 'citizenship education' is not used, it is wrong to assume that the school is failing to undertake that kind of work.
2. In the history of English education, the term 'citizenship' was used approximately from 1880 to 1950, disappeared for nearly half a century, and was revived *c.* 1990. Indeed, under whatever title, there was little interest in this kind of teaching *c.* 1950–70.

What factors, then, have historically shaped citizenship education in England? There have been five main influences: the lack of central direction, class structure, expansion of the franchise, consciousness and legacy of Empire, and war and peace. Let us look briefly at each of these in turn.

Until the introduction of the National Curriculum, which we shall deal with later in this chapter, central government issued no regulations or detailed guidelines concerning the curriculum. In so far as citizenship education was undertaken from the late nineteenth century onwards, it was developed by intermittent encouragement from the Ministry of Education, the writing of textbooks and the enthusiasm of individual teachers and, occasionally, local education authorities.

Lack of central government support in the area of citizenship education can be a blessing: there are so many examples, not least, of course, the Nazi and Communist regimes, of governments using their power to indoctrinate school pupils. On the other hand, there are also disadvantages in the refusal of central government to support civic education. The story of the Association for Education in Citizenship (AEC) is interesting in this respect. Created in 1935, the AEC was the most significant attempt ever to promote citizenship education in British schools. It was supported by many famous people, conscious that the democratic style of citizenship needed to be strengthened against the totalitarian threats of Fascism, Nazism and Stalinism so powerful at that time. Yet even the AEC could not obtain official support. The civil servants at the Board of Education were so nervous of sanctioning explicit political teaching and discussion in schools that they would not sanction central government involvement.

The second factor in the English scene has been the class system. This has been reflected in the division between the private, public schools and the state sector of education. From the mid-nineteenth century the public schools have provided a civic education of a kind through their emphasis on discipline and 'team spirit'. However, the objective has been overtly élitist – to forge the products of these schools not into 'ordinary' citizens but into citizen-leaders.

For two generations or so, from the late nineteenth century to *c.* 1950 the education of 'ordinary' young citizens involved training in deference and moral behaviour. As late as 1949, a Ministry of Education pamphlet stated:

There are forward-looking minds in every section of the teaching profession ready to reinterpret the old and simple virtues of humility, service, restraint and respect for personality. If schools can encourage qualities of this kind in their pupils, we may fulfil the conditions of a healthy democratic society. (Ministry of Education, 1949, p. 41)

(It is interesting to compare this statement with the discussion of subjecthood in Chapter 3.)

The third factor influencing education for citizenship in England has been the extension of the franchise. If the working class did not have the vote, there was little point in teaching working-class children about the British political system: teaching obedient behaviour, the duties of subjecthood, was sufficient. The various Reform Acts, which incorporated an increasing number of men, then women, into the voting classes, strengthened the argument for full citizenship education. Even then, however, there was for long the counter-argument that a number of years elapsed between the 'novice' citizen leaving school and obtaining voting rights: civic education in schools was therefore premature. The minimum school-leaving age was not raised to 16 until 1972–73 and the age of legal majority was not lowered to 18 until 1970.

The matter of the franchise was not, of course, peculiar to England. The extent of the British Empire was, however, unique. This brings us to the fourth factor. Much citizenship education up to *c.* 1960 involved inculcating pride in the Empire upon which the sun never set and a sense of duty to overseas subjects. Empire (later Commonwealth) Day was celebrated in all schools each year.

From the 1960s, because of immigration from former British dependencies, citizenship education has had to take into account the fact that Britain is now a multicultural society. The implications of this demographic change were the subject of the report of a committee which met under the chairmanship of Lord Swann in the early 1980s. Its title was *Education for All* (see p. 62).

Finally, the belief that young people should be educated as world citizens has been given considerable relevance during the twentieth century by the two world wars and the seeming threat of a third, nuclear, world war. Schools have been encouraged to adopt a global perspective by the Education Committee of the League of Nations Union (LNU) from 1919 to 1939 and its successor, the Council for Education in World Citizenship (CEWC) since 1939. The introduction of courses in Development Studies, Environmental Studies and

Peace Studies has also contributed to a sense of global responsibility.

In responding to each of these five factors and influences relating to citizenship education over the past century, the schools have often found themselves caught in arguments and controversy. It is to these problems that we now turn.

SHOULD CITIZENSHIP BE TAUGHT AT ALL?

To adapt the proposition at the beginning of this chapter: an individual who is grossly ignorant about political and legal affairs and/or is deeply prejudiced against social, cultural or religious groups to which he or she does not belong can hardly be considered to be an effective citizen. On the other hand, if people are denied the opportunity to learn citizenly behaviour, they will be accused of lacking the competence to enjoy the status.

There is considerable evidence of ignorance and prejudice among British youth. Summing up a series of investigations under the general heading 'Young people in society', Professor McGurk has written:

> Although the different projects are devoted to relatively diverse topics, there are a number of recurrent themes running through the findings. Perhaps the most salient ... is the political innocence, naivety and ignorance of British young people.... Stemming, perhaps, from such political ignorance is the overt racism which the research projects commonly reveal to be endemic among white youth in Britain. (McGurk, 1987, p. 6)

One might add, too, a feeling of alienation among certain sectors of Britain's youthful population. The reasons for ignorance, prejudice and alienation are complex and beyond the scope of this book. What we are concerned to report here is that evidence of this uncitizenly mentality has periodically led to calls for the schools to 'do something about it'.

There have, even so, been doubts about the appropriateness of schools engaging in teaching for citizenship. Ever since Aristotle, some commentators on the subject have argued that learning about public affairs is essentially an adult activity. The case has three main components:

1. Children and adolescents lack experience of the adult world and cannot therefore be expected to have an interest in or a comprehension of politics and law, which are the very stuff of citizenship.
2. Because these matters can be controversial, they can generate strongly-held opinions. It is dangerous to handle such emotionally-charged subject matter in schools; and, in any case, parents could justifiably complain. Citizenship education, like sex education, should be undertaken in the privacy of the family.
3. Teachers cannot be trusted to teach this material in an unbiased way.

There is, as might be expected, a contrary case.

In the first place, the argument relating to experience/interest/comprehension reveals a shallow understanding of teaching. If first-hand experience is essential for learning, history would not be taught at all and precious little geography and literature. Interest and

---

Box 8.2

The classical assertion that the study of political affairs is unsuitable for young people was made by Aristotle. He declared:

political science is not a proper study for the young. The young man is not versed in the practical business of life from which politics draws its premises and its data. He is, besides, swayed by his feelings, with the result that he will make no headway and derive no benefit from a study the end of which is not knowing but doing. (Aristotle, 1955, p. 28)

A contrary view was recently expressed by Dr Olive Stevens:

At seven many of them were able to take part intelligently in discussion about politics, to present limited but relevant information and introduce ideas. . . . By nine, children were showing increased ability to sustain a discussion and to contribute a wider range of political topics to it. . . . The ten-to-eleven-year-olds produced discussions that were able to deal with aspects of competing ideologies and to understand the economic dimension. . . as a causal effect and a dimension of policies. (Stevens, 1982, p. 168) comprehension depend on the style of teaching, including the careful selection of appropriate subject matter and practical activities, according to the age and aptitude of any given class. What is suitable for sixteen-year-olds is not suitable for ten-year-olds. What is suitable for a school in a wealthy middle-class area is not suitable in an area of high, long-term unemployment.

A great deal of research in a number of countries, most notably the United States, has shown that school pupils from the age of about seven upwards have potential for interest in and learning about civic affairs. Children are exposed to parents' conversation, even quarrels, about social and political issues; and they pick up scraps of information and perhaps ill-formulated ideas from television broadcasts. We also know that attitudes, including prejudices, gel at the late primary/early secondary age. Consequently, if schools are to be effective in helping to counteract prejudice and promote tolerance, then citizenship education is needed at comparatively young ages.

While it is true that many young people will be bored with lessons on the technicalities of British constitutional conventions, practical activity or lessons with practical application – role play and experiential learning – can command interest by virtue of their relevance. Although one should not over-emphasize the rights and entitlements associated with the principle and status of citizenship, they are a significant component. Many of the 'life skills' taught in some schools are very pertinent – organization, team-work, oral and written communication, for example. However, this is to encroach on the subject matter of the next section.

Now that a mere two years (16–18) separate the minimum school-leaving age and the age of majority, the argument that full citizenship is too far ahead to be pertinent to the school-pupil carries much less weight. Moreover, an increasing number of young people are now staying on in full-time education beyond 16 – 60 per cent by 1992 in Britain (and an even higher proportion in other industrialized countries). We must ask, therefore, how young people are to acquire understanding about and competence for citizenship if not through the schools.

On the other hand, can teachers be trusted? Will their own biases not show through? Will some not even positively attempt to indoctrinate their pupils?

Let us first of all be clear what these two words mean. 'Bias' means 'unbalanced'. If, for example, I teach almost entirely about citizens' rights, virtually ignoring the duties of a citizen, I would be guilty of bias. This bias may be the result of ignorance or incompetence. If, on the other hand, I have deliberately planned to withhold from my pupils the responsibilities, obligations and duties of citizenship in order to train them to be alert only to their rights, then I am guilty of indoctrination.

Most commonly bias is the result of selecting material. All lessons and textbooks are a selection from a huge range of possible subject matter. Where there are different facets to a topic, different policies or different points of view that are reasonable, they must all be fairly represented. This is easier to achieve when the subject matter is description than when judgement is introduced. For example, it is easier to avoid bias by describing race discrimination laws than by inviting discussion about their fairness in drafting and implementation. Excessive praise or condemnation, especially if the evidence does not warrant such judgements, would introduce bias into the lesson.

The problem is a sensitive one because there are plenty of historical examples of children being systematically indoctrinated; in ancient Sparta, in Nazi Germany and Stalinist Russia, for instance. During the 1980s in Britain, several right-wing politicians and academics made accusations that left-wing-motivated bias, even indoctrination, was rife in state schools.

One may say at once that 'indoctrination for citizenship', if anyone ever used the phrase, would be a contradiction in terms. Citizenship involves independent thinking, a process that is impossible if one has been 'programmed' to accept a particular point of view.

In any case, informed opinion suggests that there is little danger of indoctrination in British schools. There was virtually no evidence for the scares of the 1980s: teachers *do* have professional standards. Moreover, pupils gain information and ideas from other sources and most are too canny not to detect a teacher's purpose if he or she attempts to indoctrinate. Where successful indoctrination has taken place, in Hitler's Germany, for example, it has involved a combined effort of state, party, media and teacher to achieve the effect.

Genuine citizenship education should, in fact, enable pupils to realize that bias is endemic: a key responsibility of teachers is, therefore, to train their pupils to detect bias, whether it be projected by politicians, the news media or the teachers themselves. What is much more contentious is how a teacher should handle the expression of intolerance in the classroom. This is the pedagogical parallel of the political problem of how the democrat copes with anti-democratic organizations. Suppression of these ideas is a contradiction of the principles of citizenship education/democratic freedoms, yet to allow them free rein is to condone the undermining of one's values.

How is the conscientious teacher to discharge the responsibility of providing citizenship education, having been alert to all these doubts and pitfalls?

SCHOOLS AND SYLLABUSES

Much confusion has marked the development of citizenship education in many countries. Some schools appear to think of important topics for pupils' personal and social development and throw them into a syllabus labelled 'citizenship education'. Thus, one English survey found the following topics in different schools: health and safety; alcohol education; eating for health; smoking; body abuse; sexual relationships and decision-making; mental health studies (Commission on Citizenship, 1990, p. 84). We are not suggesting that these matters should be deleted from the curriculum, rather that they should be treated under other headings such as moral or health education. Citizenship is primarily about the relationship of the individual to the state and society; it is about politics and law. In so far as it concerns morality (and it very much does), then it is about the responsible behaviour of the individual in the community.

However, even if we adhere to a proper definition of citizenship, it still has a number of guises. It is therefore important to recognize these as essential components of any programme for preparing young people to be citizens. An American specialist in this area of education has made a useful analysis of 'six views of citizenship'. These are:

(a) nationalistic loyalty;
(b) exemplary behaviour (e.g. being responsible and just – a 'good' citizen);
(c) junior social scientist (training in social scientific methods of study);
(d) social criticism (development of an enquiring and sceptical mind);
(e) reconstructionism (aiming to make the world 'a better place');

(f) social activism (skills for participation)
(See Nelson and Michaelis, 1980, pp. 9–10.)

Clearly each of these different views requires different subject content and different modes of teaching. In so far as citizenship involves appropriate attitudes and behaviour, it is important to remember that it is not only classroom teaching that contributes to the learning process. What is sometimes called the 'ethos' of the school or 'the hidden curriculum' can also be a significant influence. The school is a micro-social or political community. The ethos or hidden curriculum means the way this community is run and the relationship of the pupils with the teachers. Let us illustrate the point by some negative statements. A school is a bad purveyor of citizenship if arbitrary punishment denies *justice*; if biased history or religious studies undermines *tolerance*; if orders are given to pupils deprived of the opportunity to *participate responsibly* in some decision-making; and if the faculty of *critical judgement* is cramped by too much giving of unquestioned factual matter by the teacher.

The qualities represented by the words emphasized in the previous paragraph are crucial for citizenship. Even so, no-one would suggest that teaching for these ends is easy or that factual knowledge and understanding are not equally important.

It is helpful to analyse learning into three categories: knowledge, attitudes and skills. Young citizens need to acquire information about the society in which they are growing up, particularly about the political and legal systems. They need to develop citizenly attitudes

---

Box 8.3

It is important to incorporate the full range of learning methods in any school programme of citizenship education. This has been highlighted in the official guidance pamphlet for the National Curriculum in England and Wales.

A policy on education for citizenship will cover the formal curriculum, the ethos of the school and relationships with the wider community. The most successful policies are likely to be developed in consultation with teachers, parents, governors and community representatives. Schools may also wish to consider the benefits of liaising with other schools where appropriate.
(National Curriculum Council, 1990, p. 14)

and modes of behaviour, such as responsibility and tolerance; and they need to acquire skills of collaboration and communication.

If citizenship is to be taught in the classroom, a decision has to be made about its timetabling. There are three options.

1. Through a single subject. This could be politics, though few schools have much space on the timetable to teach this subject separately. The most common vehicle for citizenship education has been history. Much can be learned through this subject, especially if the teacher clearly draws out the continuities and contrasts over time. However, the practical relevance of the here-and-now and of the necessary participative skills might well be missing from a history syllabus.
2. A component or theme in social studies or personal and social education (PSE). Citizenship would be built into a syllabus which also contains economics, environmental, legal, moral and health education, for example.
3. A cross-curricular theme. Facets of the topic are built into the syllabuses of the individual subjects wherever relevant (e.g. communication skills in English, civic responsibility in moral education, evolution of rights in history).

We shall have more to say about how citizenship education has recently developed in England in the next sections of this chapter. Before moving on to that, however, one more general consideration regarding the topic needs to be commented on here. This relates to what many commentators believe is the obsolescence of the nineteenth/early twentieth century style of nationalistic citizenship education. It is a twofold problem.

One component is the belief that the citizen's knowledge about and loyalty to the nation-state must be complemented by a notion of global 'citizenship' or 'planet consciousness'. If citizenship involves acting responsibly, then that sense of responsibility must extend beyond national frontiers to issues of development and environmental degradation world-wide. Schools, it follows, should incorporate a global dimension to their programmes of citizenship education.

The other component is a reflection of the effects of substantial migrations of people on the homogeneity of the nation-state. Traditional mass citizenship education presupposed that all the pupils shared certain basic traditions – either in fact or in ambition.

For example, all French children spoke French and honoured the republican style of government; all American children, from whatever ethnic background, wanted to be accepted as 'proper' American citizens. In multicultural and multifaith societies today, this is not necessarily true. Hispanics in the United States want to keep their Spanish language, Blacks in England want to preserve their Caribbean culture and Muslims in France adhere to their Middle Eastern focused religion. The function of the schools therefore changes from transmitting a traditional concept of national citizenship to forging a new and more flexible sense of identity. Citizenship education must include teaching all ethnic groups to understand and be tolerant of each other, and to recognize that, as citizens, all have the same rights and the same duties.

These issues have exercised the minds of educationists in many countries. We now need to look specifically at the recent discussions relating to the schools of England and Wales.

BEFORE THE NATIONAL CURRICULUM

During the period *c.* 1950–90, the term 'education for citizenship' was rarely heard. Sundry courses in 'Civics' and 'British Constitution' were taught in some schools. In an attempt to stimulate more widespread and interesting work in this area, a professional body called the Politics Association was founded in 1969. It has been sponsored by the Hansard Society for Parliamentary Government.

The 1970s was a period of great interest and activity. There were political as well as educational reasons for this.

1. The raising of the school-leaving age and the lowering of the age of majority made the preparation of school pupils for adult civic life more relevant.
2. A general mood of disillusionment with politicians bred a fear that the British people were becoming apathetic and alienated from the parliamentary system. Civic education was needed to strengthen support for democratic processes.
3. The activities of extremist parties, particularly the neo-fascist National Front, seemed to be in danger of influencing the younger generation. Objective teaching was needed to counteract this propaganda.

However, if young people were to be taught to be effective citizens of a healthy democracy, merely learning factual details about constitutional structures and procedures was obviously insufficient. Citizens needed to be 'politically literate'. What did this term mean and how should schools go about the task? A research and development project, called the Programme for Political Education, answered these questions. Its report contains the following summary definition:

> Thus a person who has a fair knowledge of what are the issues of contemporary politics, is equipped to be of some influence, whether in school, factory, voluntary body or party and can understand and respect, while not sharing, the values of others, can reasonably be called 'politically literate'. (Crick and Porter, 1978, p. 7)

A similar viewpoint was expressed by two senior members of Her Majesty's Inspectorate (HMI) (see Box 8.4), though they used the term 'political competence'.

However, by the 1980s the momentum of the political education movement had weakened. This was partly due to suspicions entertained by some members of the Thatcherite governments concerning the desirability of such teaching. For example, the Education Act (No. 2) of 1986 forbade the promotion of partisan political views in schools. The catch was in the word 'promotion': could it be used to discipline any teacher handling controversial issues? (As we saw in Chapter 4 uncertainty in the law is dangerous: it can undermine the rule of law.) The loss of momentum was also partly due to the new emphasis by all political parties on the concept of citizenship. Now, while citizenship is undoubtedly a political concept, the citizenship role involves more than politics. Consequently, citizenship education must contain a few additional ingredients. Most importantly, multicultural education and law-related studies were being actively promoted.

From the time of the immigrations from the West Indies, Africa and the Indian subcontinents in the 1960s onwards, Britain has become increasingly obviously a multicultural society. Physical appearance, cultural and social habits, even often religion and language distinguish the families of recent arrivals from the long-established Celtic and Anglo-Saxon inhabitants. The educational question has been how to complement the legal status of citizenship,

Box 8.4

Two HMIs explained in an article why they believed that schools needed to improve the kind of political education they were providing. Here is a short extract.

there is an increasingly democratic temper in our society. This recognises that inevitably in human society there will be diversity of objectives, and considerable disagreement as how best to achieve them. A democratic society seeks to involve in this process of resolution all points of view in such a way that they will all survive. However, since . . . the rapidly increasing complexity of political decisions, often involving technical, scientific and economic considerations, the ability of individual citizens to understand, much less actively to influence the decisions of central government appears to be diminishing. Thus there has been a rapidly increasing pressure for participation in smaller, often local units of decision-making: trade unions, factories, schools, and pressure groups. People are seeking, and claiming, their right to discuss and to choose. The school curriculum would be wise to recognise this and to increase the likelihood of responsible participation by supporting it with knowledge and an informed understanding of the potential, and the limitations, of the contribution of individuals to their own government. (J. Slater and R.A.S. Hennessey, 'Political Competence', 22 February 1977, reprinted in Crick and Porter, 1978, pp. 252–3)

which the minority ethnic groups enjoy, with a sense of civic cohesion.

Educational policies have shifted over time. At first, the idea was *assimilation*. This meant teaching the ethnic minority pupils how to be the 'same' as the majority inhabitants of Britain – to iron out as far as possible any differences. The second phase was *integration*. This recognized the impossibility, at least in the short term, of complete assimilation. The emphasis was therefore on tolerant acceptance by both majority and minority groups of each other's differences. Thirdly, we have *multiculturalism* – based on the recognition that cultural diversity can positively add to the country's cultural richness. Finally, some educationists advocate *anti-racist* education, actively to combat prejudice and discrimination.

Each of these policies represents a slightly different concept of citizenship education. All accept that every citizen, of whatever origin, should participate in community and civic life. However, there is a difference of emphasis between stress on homogeneity or on tolerance. Citizenship involves treating all people equally (originally especially to cut across class differences); it also involves treating all people with respect. At the assimilation end of the spectrum of policies the emphasis is on homogeneity, sameness, equality. At the multicultural/anti-racist end, it is on tolerance and respect.

The riots in a number of inner-city areas in the early 1980s, most significantly in Brixton in 1981, showed that many ethnic minorities felt themselves to be second-class citizens. The Swann Report of 1985 urged a multicultural style of education to counteract such a feeling. It was quite adamant that 'all schools and all teachers have a professional responsibility to prepare their pupils for life in a pluralist society and the wider world' (DES, 1985, p. 560).

Part of the egalitarian element in citizenship is, of course, equality before the law. Similarly, part of education for citizenship should be the fostering of an understanding of the law. Yet in Britain this subject has rarely featured in school curricula in any systematic way. Concerned about this gap in school work, the Law Society has funded, with the help of the National Curriculum Council, two Law in Education Projects. These have led to the production of two sets of classroom materials for the 11–14 and 14–16 age ranges. In 1989 this initiative was incorporated into a broader educational body called the Citizenship Foundation. By this time the new National Curriculum was being planned.

THE NATIONAL CURRICULUM

The Conservative governments which held office from 1979 introduced many bills affecting the education systems of England and Wales. Among a number of far-reaching provisions, the Education Reform Act of 1988 required the establishment of a National Curriculum as a framework for teaching all pupils of compulsory school age in state schools. A National Curriculum Council (NCC) was established to guide this work. The original intention was that all pupils should be taught a range of 'core' and 'foundation' subjects (e.g. mathematics, history), while some minority time could be allocated for additional subjects if so desired (e.g. Latin, economics). In addition, provision was made for 'cross-curricular themes'. Eventually five were identified, including citizenship (see Box 8.5). The idea was that elements from each of these topics should be taught through the relevant core and foundation subjects.

Box 8.5

The National Curriculum Council has explained its belief in the importance of citizenship education and its place in the school curriculum.

NCC has identified education for citizenship as one of five cross-curricular themes. . . . The others are education for economic and industrial understanding, health education, careers education and guidance, and environmental education. The themes are inter-related and share common features, eg the capacity to promote discussion of values and beliefs, to extend knowledge and understanding, to encourage practical activities and decision making and to strengthen the bond between the individual and the community.

Education should and must develop pupils' potential to the full and prepare them for the world in which they live. . . .

No school in England would deny its responsibility for educating pupils for citizenship, but the task may be approached in different ways. (National Curriculum Council, 1990, p. 1)

True, the curriculum could not be overloaded by the constant adding of new subjects. Nevertheless, critics of the tactic of cross-curricular themes expressed several misgivings. With particular reference to citizenship these included:

1. Fragmentation and incoherence. Pieces of the theme will have to slot into the subject syllabuses. The relationship of these pieces to the theme of citizenship as a whole will not be very explicit for the pupil.
2. Separation of theory and practice. The essence of citizenship education should be preparation for behaving and acting as a citizen. If theory and practice are dealt with by different teachers in different lessons and are not reflected in the school's organization, the connections may not be obvious.
3. Was citizenship chosen as a 'safe' alternative to political education? If citizenship is interpreted as the Conservative concept of active citizenship (see pp. 123–6), then an education biased towards an emphasis on non-political voluntary work and civic duties will be the result.

4. Because cross-curricular teaching is always extremely difficult to plan and execute; and because, unlike the core and foundation subjects, the themes are not mandatory, they may in practice be excluded from or given only marginal attention in school curricula.

1990 was the year when citizenship education was particularly highlighted in England. It seems almost as if the task of encouraging citizenship was passed in that year from the Home Office (see Chapter 6) to the Department of Education and Science. The background was twofold: the appointment by the Speaker of the House of Commons of a Commission on Citizenship (see p. 45); and the identification, as we have just seen, of the topic as a cross-curricular theme.

As part of the work of the Speaker's Commission, a national conference on citizenship education was held at Northampton in February. The Secretary of State spoke of the need for the home and the school to share the responsibility for 'equipping . . . the citizens of tomorrow'. In July, one of his junior ministers, in describing the work of the Politics Association, called politics and citizenship 'these very important subjects' (Howarth, 1992, p. 326).

In October the Report of the Speaker's Commission was published. Although the Commission did not primarily deal with schools, 'concern about whether we offer enough encouragement to our young people to learn how to be good citizens' (Commission on Citizenship, 1990, pp. v–vi) was a significant subsidiary consideration. Three of the eight appendices relate to work in schools. One of these was a report of a national survey undertaken at Leicester University of the current state of education for citizenship in secondary schools in England and Wales. The problem that has plagued so much of the discussion on the topic since the late 1980s – namely, a lack of precise definition – is immediately evident from the items listed by the schools, which we have already cited (p. 156).

Another appendix is a note of evidence by the Commission to the NCC. This also ducked the problem of definition. Instead, it relied heavily on the Recommendation of the Council of Europe's Committee of Ministers on Human Rights Education. True, this document is broadly drafted and education for citizenship and for human rights have significant areas of overlap. However, they are not synonymous. Whatever its precise meaning, the Commission, as might be expected, gave wholehearted support to the teaching of citizenship, both theoretically and practically, in all schools; and, indeed, in further and higher education and the youth service.

Finally in 1990, the NCC produced its Curriculum Guidance booklet on citizenship education. The general purpose of the booklet is made clear: to produce ideas for teaching, not definitive syllabuses; and to emphasize the need to involve the whole community in this aspect of the school's work. We are also given a succinct definition and a brief statement of aims:

> Education for citizenship develops the knowledge, skills and attitudes necessary for exploring, making informed decisions about and exercising responsibilities and rights in a democratic society.
> *The aims of education for citizenship are to: establish the importance of positive, participative citizenship and provide the motivation to join in; help pupils acquire and understand essential information on which to base the development of their skills, values and attitudes towards citizenship.*
> (National Curriculum Council, 1990, p. 2)

The lists of objectives and essential content (pp. 3–5) provide more detailed insight into the thinking of the NCC. Knowledge should embrace: the nature of community, roles and relationships in a democratic society, and the nature and basis of duties, responsibilities and rights. Skills include, for example, working with others, arguing a case, detecting bias, making choices. The list of 'positive attitudes' includes independence of thought, concern for human rights, respect for rational argument, respect for different ways of life. Under the heading of moral codes and values is the following statement:

> Pupils should be helped to develop a personal moral code and to explore values and beliefs. Shared values, such as concern for others, industry and effort, self-respect and self-discipline, as well as moral qualities such as honesty and truthfulness, should be promoted.

The list of important syllabus contents gives eight 'essential components'. These are:

The nature of community
Roles and relationships in a pluralist society
The duties, responsibilities and rights of being a citizen

The family
Democracy in action
The citizen and the law
Work, employment and leisure
Public services

It is quite evident that these objectives and essential components must be interpreted very flexibly according to the age and ability levels of the pupils. The National Curriculum provides for four 'Key Stages' (KS), relating to the age brackets 5–7, 7–11, 11–14, 14–16. The following examples from the booklet reveal the approach recommended:

The citizen and the law, KS 1
Pupils listen to a story such as 'The Three Little Pigs' and discuss what makes a home 'safe', making up rules to ensure safety at home and thinking about who is responsible for it. Think about the action of the wolf. Was it right? Was the wolf fairly punished? How are we protected from people who would harm us? Can we talk about times when we are not safe?

The citizen and the law, KS 4
As part of their work-related studies, pupils investigate patterns of part-time employment in the class. By gathering and evaluating data, they obtain a picture of the extent to which existing laws are observed . . . the need for health and safety legislation. Historical examples . . . are used to underline the need for legal controls in this area. (National Curriculum Council, 1990, pp. 21 and 27)

Commitment to the principle of citizenship education in the schools of England and Wales (Scotland has a separate system) would seem firm. The words 'essential' and 'entitlement' appear in official statements. This commitment has been expressed by Government ministers and Opposition spokesmen; it is overtly stated by the prestigious Speaker's Commission; and the means of implementation have been outlined by the NCC.

Even so, all is not entirely well. We have already commented on the weak position of cross-curricular themes in the National Curriculum. The Speaker's Commission voiced that concern too (p. 104), but, more than that, the work of both the Speaker's Commission and the NCC has been subject to critical comment – regrets that they did not make better use of their opportunities to provide a thorough picture of what citizenship education should really mean for schools. The criticisms fall into three main categories.

The first is the failure to learn from, even acknowledge, the work that has already been undertaken. Let us take two examples. The first is a complaint from a distinguished headmaster who has written that:

> Those who taught 'civics' in the fifties and sixties will surely groan at the patronising way so many today deride their work. The Speaker's Commission on Citizenship, with no research evidence to defend the criticism, has declared that the study of citizenship today should not be 'presented as theory without practice, as in civics courses'.... The best of civics courses certainly did not make that division. (Marland, 1991, p. 24)

The other example is the absence of any reference in statements issued in 1990 (except for Alan Howarth's) of the work in political education and political literacy in the 1980s.

The second criticism concerns the lack of precision in defining citizenship. We have already noticed that the Speaker's Commission's evidence to the NCC did not get to grips with this. NCC's *Curriculum Guidance 8* booklet does. However, in trying to hit their target, have they not used a scatter-gun instead of a precision weapon? Dr Porter of the London Institute of Education thinks so. Citing illustrative material from the list of essential components and syllabus suggestions, he concludes:

> Much of this seems to be concerned with a form of personal, social, health and careers education which is both vague and ill-defined as well as being heavily permeated with moral imperatives. (Porter, 1993)

One could conclude, a mite unkindly, that the efforts of the NCC had advanced the cause of defining citizenship education only marginally beyond the confusion discovered by the Leicester University survey (see p. 156).

A colleague of Dr Porter, and a former senior member of HMI, Professor John Slater, has been even unhappier about the outcome of the intense work of the *c.* 1990 period. He believes that '*Curriculum Guidance No. 8* is a pallid, feeble affair' (Slater, 1992, p. 312). He argues (and this is the third criticism) that the emphasis on such values as respect and tolerance is 'a touch cosy, seemly, even smug

... a sight too confident, safe and self-satisfied' (pp. 313 and 314). The booklet, he suggests, avoids the really tricky problems – of conflicting beliefs which cannot be reconciled, of disrespect which is unyielding to reason, of attitudes which should *not* be tolerated. How do young citizens cope with these knotty real-life issues? How are they to be taught to react to and handle these problems in a citizenly manner?

The Director of Education for the London Borough of Hackney also believes that the NCC has not faced up to the tough questions. He believes that the key question is 'who defines what values we should encourage in citizenship education and with what objectives in mind?' He continues:

> The NCC guidelines portray the process as a neutral, uncontentious exercise. Yet far from being timeless, universal principles, the kind of values promoted in schools clearly depends to a large extent on the social structures within which we all operate and the dominant ideology of the day.

He fears that

> Young people soon dismiss many of the values we seek to inculcate in them as hypocritical and oppressive and subscribe to a different code. (John, n.d.)

The extreme difficulty of providing truly effective citizenship education in schools may be highlighted by reminding readers of the context in which schools operate. Political apathy, alienation from the police, ethnic or religious intolerance, sexual prejudice, class divisions may all, in small or large measure, be endemic to the society of which schools are a part. Parents, role-models and the communications media may well reinforce desirable civic attitudes. Equally they may purvey the kinds of attitudes, inimical to citizenship values which we have just listed. Priorities for and styles of teaching about citizenship must therefore take these considerations into account. What is suitable for Bradford is not necessarily apt for Bournemouth, and what is apt for Bournemouth might not be suitable for Belfast.

Teachers still need and indeed deserve much more help and sympathy in performing a task which is so simple to undertake mechanically and so difficult to accomplish in a truly worthwhile manner.

One of the difficulties facing teachers is the confused and uncertain condition of citizenship in Britain. Their task would in this regard be simplified if the status and rights of citizens were to be legally codified – the subject of our next chapter.

FURTHER READING

Citizenship Journal of the Citizenship Foundation.

Fogelman, K. (ed.) (1991) *Citizenship in Schools* (London: David Fulton).

Jones, N. and Baglin Jones, E. (eds) (1992) *Education for Citizenship* (London: Kogan Page).

Lynch, J. (1992) *Education for Citizenship in a Multicultural Society* (London: Cassell).

9

IMPROVING THE LEGAL
FOUNDATIONS OF CITIZENSHIP

SUMMARY

How might the legal foundations of citizenship be strengthened? Elements of subjecthood and institutionalized exclusion from the sense of belonging to the community (for example, some aspects of the monarchy, and the establishment of the Church of England) could be reformed. Popular sovereignty could replace the sovereignty of 'The Queen in Parliament'. Individual autonomy could be strengthened in various ways; but this ought not to take a form that precludes acceptance of the idea that individuals owe obligations and responsibilities to the community.

Citizens' ability to hold government to account and participate in politics could be improved. Civil and political rights could be improved in a range of ways, through detailed legislation, or a Bill of Rights, or a Declaration of Rights – several models of such instruments are available. Social and economic rights could be enhanced by specific statutory provisions, but it is not easy for a Charter of Social Rights to be introduced that would give individually enforceable substantive social and economic rights. Environmental rights are the most difficult of all to protect. A combination of measures including legislation, international cooperation and regulation of pollution would be required.

SUBJECTS AND SOVEREIGNTY

We have seen in previous chapters that citizenship rests in part on legal foundations, in part on educational and cultural foundations. In this chapter we consider the question as to whether the legal foundations need to be strengthened, and if so how this might be achieved. We draw on examples from other constitutions and on drafts that have been produced for the United Kingdom to illustrate the possibilities. One of the themes of previous chapters has been that our legal and social arrangements still treat the individual in some respects as a subject rather than a citizen. Another has been the emphasis on individual autonomy, a liberal approach, in preference to the classical idea of citizenship involving political participation by individuals and a sense of duty to the community. A question that arises is whether the legal system should be altered both so that it does not contain features that inhibit the development of citizenship in this classical sense, and in order to encourage such development.

The term 'subject' is, even today, frequently used in legislation in the field of nationality law and by the courts. Sometimes this term is used unthinkingly, and the lawmaker, if asked, would deny that it was intended to suggest that individuals were not regarded as autonomous individuals or as citizens in the classical sense. However, the notion of a relationship between sovereign and subject, even if used often metaphorically, affects the framework of thinking about the role of the individual and relations with the state. It inhibits the idea that 'the people' are the source of sovereignty by implying instead that 'the Crown in Parliament' is sovereign.

The approach to the relationship between individuals and the state in the United Kingdom has positive and negative aspects. The idea that sovereignty comes from the people (see examples in Box 9.1) can be used to legitimate majoritarian rule: 'the people have the power to do what they want, and what they want to do must be democratic'. Clearly individuals need more protections than that against being discriminated against, excluded from political activity and influence and denied their autonomy. So, unless strong protections for citizenship were built into a constitution, a move to the idea that 'the people' are sovereign could well introduce more problems into the system than the present basic framework: this accepts that 'the Crown in Parliament' has sovereign power, but *tolerates* that position only as long as it is accountable and subject to the rule of law. In a sense, in the United Kingdom conditional consent to government is given by the people: this conceptualization of the relationship could place government under stronger constraints of accountability than the idea that power is 'delegated' to Parliament and government by the people would do.

The importance in the UK legal system of 'the Crown'

Box 9.1 Popular sovereignty in constitutions

The following are examples of how popular sovereignty could find expression in a constitution.

1. Preamble to the Constitution of the United States of America:

   We the People of the United States, in Order to form a more perfect Union, establish Justice, insure domestic Tranquillity, provide for the common defence, promote the general Welfare, and secure the Blessings of Liberty to ourselves and our Posterity, do ordain and establish this Constitution for the United States of America.

2. Articles 2 and 3 of the Constitution of the Union of Soviet Socialist Republics, 1936:

   Article 2: The Soviets (committees) or Working People's Deputies, which arose and developed as a result of the overthrow of the landowners and capitalists and of the attainment of the dictatorship of the proletariat, shall constitute the political foundation of the USSR.
   Article 3: All power in the USSR shall be vested in the working people of town and country as represented by the Soviets of Working People's Deputies.

3. Preamble to the Basic Law of the Federal Republic of Germany, 1949:

   The German People ... have enacted, by virtue of their constituent power, this Basic Law for the Federal Republic of Germany.

4. Article 1 of the Constitution of the Fifth French Republic, 1958:

   The Republic and the peoples of the Overseas Territories who, by an act of free determination, adopt the present Constitution thereby institute a Community.
   The Community shall be based on the equality and the solidarity of the peoples composing it.

perpetuates a narrow idea of the status of the individual, and an exclusivity which is anachronistic in the late twentieth century in a European democracy. For example, Members of Parliament, Privy Councillors, judges and other important public figures swear allegiance to the Crown: this suggests a highly personal relationship and sense of loyalty: loyalty can be an excuse for unquestioning obedience, and this, it is suggested, is a dangerous attitude to encourage among public officials.

It could be said, in reply to this point, that these arrangements are simply a quaint hangover from former times, the sort of tradition to which many subjects are attached. It is impossible to establish conclusively whether this kind of tradition affects the attitudes of individuals and officials to their roles, but it clearly conveys a message that is not consistent with the idea of citizenship. In addition to swearing allegiance, judges promise to do justice to all people according to law – an impersonal promise. It is suggested that it would be more conducive to citizenship if public officials had to give only impersonal undertakings of this kind about their discharge of their functions, and not personal ones (see Box 9.2).

THE MONARCHY AND THE CHRISTIAN RELIGION

We suggested earlier that the monarchy encourages an exclusive notion of 'citizenship'. This flows from the constitutional position of the monarch as head of the Church of England and 'defender of the faith'. This implies that those who are not members of the Church of England are 'outsiders' as opposed to 'insiders'. The monarch may not marry a Roman Catholic, nor, of course, may the monarch adhere to any other religion or profess atheism. In the Coronation Oath the sovereign undertakes to preserve the Protestant religion, the Church of England and the Presbyterian Church in Scotland.

The clear implication of these arrangements is that other Christian denominations, particularly Roman Catholic and Orthodox, are less acceptable than these, and that atheism and adherence to religions other than Christianity are in some way inferior, and their followers 'outsiders', as far as the state is concerned. This approach is echoed in the position that only the Christian religion is protected by the law of blasphemy: would it not be more logical if all or no religions were so protected? For historical reasons a number of Christian schools

---

Box 9.2 A new constitutional oath?

Here are three models of constitutional oaths that do not involve
the idea of personal allegiance.

1. The Presidential Oath under the Constitution of the USA is:

   *I do solemnly swear (or affirm) that I will faithfully execute the
   Office of President of the United States, and will to the best of
   my Ability, preserve, protect and defend the Constitution of
   the United States.*

2. John Macdonald QC of the Liberal Democrats produced a draft
   written Constitution for the United Kingdom in 1991. It
   included the following oath to be taken by ministers:

   *I do solemnly swear (or affirm) that I will faithfully execute my
   Office and will to the best of my ability preserve protect and
   defend the Constitution of the United Kingdom.*

3. Tony Benn MP introduced his Commonwealth of Britain Bill
   into the House of Commons in 1991. One of his proposals was
   a new Constitutional Oath to be taken by persons in authority.
   It reads as follows:

   *I . . . do solemnly declare and affirm that I will be faithful to the
   Constitution of the Commonwealth of Britain, and will respect
   its laws, as enacted by Parliament; will preserve inviolably the
   civil rights and liberties of the people, including the right to
   self-government, through their elected representatives, and
   will faithfully and truly declare my mind and opinion on all
   matters that come before me without favour.*

(and some Jewish schools) are voluntary-aided, whereas this is not
the case with, for example, Muslim schools: would it not be more
logical if no denominational schools were financed by the state, or if
new denominational (and non-denominational) schools were eligible
for funding? Religious education is required in schools, and has to be
of a broadly Christian character. This implies inequality of respect
for those who are not Christians in the community. In some respects,
it is suggested, adherence to the Christian religion plays the role that
nationality (strand four in our discussion of citizenship theory in
Chapter 1) plays in other countries' notions of citizenship.

Here again, the argument may be put that such arrangements
reflect the history, tradition and culture of the country, that they do
no harm. Some would even suggest that society would fall apart if the

Christian religion and its values did not have a special place in our constitutional arrangements. It is difficult to believe this when we consider that most of the other Member States of the European Community, and of the Commonwealth and the United States, do not have established churches, and often have provisions in their constitutions insisting on secularity and separating Church and state.

In a broadly liberal, multicultural system provisions of this kind can cause offence to and alienate non-Christians and members of churches other than the established church from the rest of the community. It also encourages a sense of superiority, prejudice and discriminatory attitudes on the part of Christians and members of the Church of England – attitudes that are not consistent with the idea of universal and equal citizenship. Clearly the question arises as to whether the Church of England should be disestablished, and how else the discrimination in favour of (or against) particular religions or churches may be removed from the legal system.

CITIZENS AS RIGHTS-BEARING INDIVIDUALS?

As we saw in Chapters 3 and 4, individuals have won considerable civil and political freedoms since the seventeenth century. It has been through the development of the rule of law that the status of 'subject' has been cut down, though not eliminated, and that the status of the autonomous individual has taken up some of the space vacated by subjecthood. Yet the step has never been taken by Parliament of granting individuals rights as opposed to freedoms.

In the daily lives of most individuals this has little importance, but all of us are liable to find ourselves in situations where it would be important to us to have legal rights that we could seek to have protected in the courts and which we could call in aid against the state. For example, in 1993 the Government proposed legislation to protect individuals against invasions of their privacy by the press. Possibilities under consideration included the criminalizing of bugging and interception of communications, and the introduction of a right to sue for damages for interference with a person's privacy. Whatever the merits of these proposals, it is remarkable that they did not involve any guarantee of freedom of expression, especially press freedom. They were an example of the state whittling away freedoms without drawing a clear line beyond which freedom of expression should not be cut down, or appreciating that freedom of expression at least needs to be acknowledged to be an important value that should only be limited for good reasons.

The absence of any legal acknowledgement of freedom of expression was illustrated again in the attempts of the Government to obtain court orders preventing the broadcasting of a television programme which included an interview with a convicted mass murderer, Nilson, in January 1993. The Government's reason was that the programmes might upset relatives of the victims. There would be very little freedom left in the media if they could be prevented from broadcasting material that might upset people.

To continue with recent examples of how the absence of strong protections for civil and political rights leaves individuals exposed to arbitrary action by government, during the Gulf War of 1991 Iraqi nationals who had been living peacefully in the United Kingdom were interned for fear that they might support the Iraqi side and bring the conflict to Great Britain. These people had no constitutional right to freedom of the person, and thus no recourse to the courts against the Government. There was no right to have the legality or the grounds of the detentions determined by an independent tribunal, no right to know what evidence there was against them. In fact, at least one of those detained was the victim of mistaken identity.

We have seen in the examples given in Chapter 3, how the absence of clearly defined civil rights can mean that individuals' autonomy in their most intimate and private lives can be interfered with by the courts: a woman may be subjected to a Caesarean section against her will; an anorexic patient may be forcibly transferred to an institution. The problem here is that Parliament has never passed a Bill of Rights or legislated specifically on these matters, and so the courts have no express standards against which to measure the arguments in such cases. If they had, it is of course possible that the same decisions might be made, but at least it would be on the basis of broadly accepted standards which the individual concerned knew about in advance, and which the judge had to apply, rather than unpredictable decisions by a judge.

HOW COULD THE LEGAL FOUNDATIONS OF CITIZENSHIP BE STRENGTHENED?

We have considered already some of the ways in which the concept of 'subject' could be removed from the legal system. We turn now to consider how the autonomy of the individual could be better protected, and at the same time how citizenship in the classical sense could be promoted. First, we need to appreciate the relationship between individual autonomy and citizenship. This has already been referred to in previous chapters, but here we shall bring the strands of the argument together.

Individuals who are subject to personal control by the Government are denied the right and the opportunity to participate in the political process: the very idea that they owe duties of obedience to the state in return for protection is a denial of rights of participation. The establishment of civil and political freedoms since the seventeenth century has been a reaction against the status of subjecthood, and the impetus has been towards emancipation from personal control. This carries with it the view that individual autonomy is the supreme value. However, it is part of our argument that emancipation from control and individual autonomy, even if they were enhanced, are not the same as citizenship, even though in many respects emancipation, autonomy and citizenship complement one another. Let us consider what makes for citizenship.

Citizenship is not simply a legal status: the social and political aspects are important. The legal side would involve the individual having rights to participate in the political processes that take place at many levels of government – local, national and European, even world levels. Participation, of course, means the right to vote in elections, and elections that can have a genuine effect on the conduct of government. As we have seen individuals in the United Kingdom do have such rights in national, local and European elections. Even so, as we saw in Chapters 3 and 7, the qualifications vary so that only British nationals and Commonwealth citizens may vote in local and national elections, and when the Treaty of European Union takes effect, nationals of Member States of the European Community will be entitled to vote in municipal elections and European Parliament elections in any state within the Community where they are resident.

However, the right to vote is only a part of what citizenship can be. The liberal and classical traditions would favour providing opportunities for individual citizens to participate in the decisions made by state bodies in many other ways that require legal protection: the right to join political parties, pressure and campaigning groups; the right to demonstrate, to express critical views and so on, and the right not to be discriminated against for political activity.

Various measures could be taken to promote political participation. A Bill or Declaration of Rights (see below) could ensure that some of these activities could not be interfered with by Government. Provisions giving people legal rights of access to official information, for example, about themselves (medical files, for instance) or about Government actions or policy, public safety, pollution and so on, enable individuals both to hold government to account for what it does or fails to do, and to exercise their own autonomy. If we do not know, for example, that certain foods carry a risk of infection, then we cannot make informed choices about what we eat, nor can we campaign for Government to take steps to improve the state of the products in question.

As we have seen in Chapter 7 (Box 7.2) European Community law allows the individual to bring actions against the Government of a Member State that has infringed the individual's rights, partly for the sake of the rights, and partly because this will put pressure on the state in question to give effect to European law. In such cases the citizen is playing an important public function. The position in English law, where there is no European law dimension to a problem, is uncertain. Until the late 1980s, the courts accepted that interest groups had the right to apply to the court for judicial review if a public body was not acting in accordance with the requirements of public law on a matter in which the group, or even an individual, had an interest. However, in the *Rose Theatre* case (*R. v. Secretary of State, ex parte Rose Theatre Trust* (1990)), the court decided that a group of actors and others who were interested in the theatre and its history, and a company they had formed, did not have the right to challenge a decision by the Secretary of State for the Environment. This decision was that the remains of the ancient Rose Theatre, which had been uncovered on a building site near Southwark Bridge in the City of London, need not be preserved by a listing order. In effect, they were regarded as busy-bodies instead of good citizens. This approach means that in English law, unlike European law, citizens are not regarded as having a function in protecting the public interest in the rule of law through the legal process – a function that would go with the classical ideal.

In order to participate effectively in Government and in holding Government to account, individuals need education, information about the working of the system, and experience of participation and collective activity. This can take place in 'private' activities, institutions of civil society – trade unions, clubs, schools, churches and so on – and it is partly for this reason that citizenship in education and education for citizenship (see Chapter 8) are particularly important. Without opportunities to practise participation individuals are unlikely to be effective citizens. Here again, there is a role for the law in protecting freedom of association and establishing participatory procedures in many institutions of civil society – schools, churches, companies, trade unions, for example.

True citizens also need to feel that they are not excluded from society by discrimination, either personal discrimination on the part of employers and others or institutionalized discrimination in the laws, for example in the matters of religion referred to briefly above.

In order to participate in civil society and 'public' political activity, individuals require freedom not only from destitution but from pressures which preclude their involvement in social and political processes. This is a strong basis for social and economic rights (see Chapter 5) in that it not only gives people the freedom to participate, but also enables them not to feel excluded and alienated from the community at large.

These then are some of the elements of citizenship. We could consider how the law could be reformed in detail to enhance autonomy and citizenship in a wide range of areas, from criminal procedure to anti-discrimination law, from improved entitlements to social security to access to higher education and so on. We could put forward a blueprint for constitutional reform, looking at local government, decentralization and so on. However, as we indicated in our introduction, it is not our purpose here to discuss or recommend specific detailed reforms. Other books have done this. Rather we consider some of the broad approaches that might be taken to enhancing the legal foundations of civil, political, social and economic rights, drawing, for the purposes of comparison and to illustrate the possibilities, on provisions in other constitutions and draft proposals that have been put forward in this country.

THE ENTRENCHMENT OF CIVIL AND POLITICAL RIGHTS

A (perhaps *the*) salient characteristic of English law in relation to civil and political rights is, as we saw in Chapter 4, that people in the

United Kingdom do not enjoy civil and political 'rights' in any strong sense. Broadly, the position we saw is that we are free to do anything that is not contrary to law. Yet there are many laws that restrict what we may do, including the exercise of our civil and political freedoms. We do enjoy some 'rights' in the sense that Acts of Parliament give legally enforceable entitlements, for example, to vote and stand for election to local government, the House of Commons and the European Parliament. However, there are no statutes granting us other important civil and political rights – to free speech, to associate, to demonstrate. Generally, it is unlawful for state officials or private bodies to interfere with our exercise of such freedoms by using or threatening physical coercion; but this generalization is subject to important exceptions: for example, it is not unlawful for employers, whether state employers or private ones, to insert into the contract of employment a term that employees must not 'blow the whistle' on questionable activities by the employer. There is also no statutory provision preventing state bodies from putting various pressures on organizations, journalists and others not to criticize what public bodies do. Of course, there are also occasions when the police can use physical coercion to prevent demonstrations under the Public Order Act 1986, if, for example, they believe that a demonstration will cause disorder or disruption to the life of the community. As we saw in Chapter 7, the United Kingdom is a party to the European Convention on Human Rights (the ECHR), and individuals may petition the European Court of Human Rights if they allege that domestic law does not comply with the requirements of the European Convention; but that convention is not enforceable in our courts directly, and the judgments of the European Court or the decisions of the European Commission on Human Rights are not legally enforceable in the United Kingdom.

So when we say that people do not enjoy civil and political 'rights', we mean that civil and political rights or freedoms do not have any specially protected status in law which prevents government from interfering with them save in exceptional circumstances. Many of the Western democracies do have special constitutional legal protection for civil and political rights – the US Bill of Rights and the French Declaration of the Rights of Man (see below Boxes 9.3, 9.4 and 9.5) are examples. The question that arises, then, is whether civil and

Box 9.3 Extracts from the US Bill of Rights

The US Bill of Rights took the form of ten amendments to the Constitution, and was ratified and became effective in 1791.

First Amendment: Congress shall make no law respecting an establishment of religion, or prohibiting the free exercise thereof; or abridging the freedom of speech, or of the press; or the right of the people peaceably to assemble, and to petition the Government for a redress of grievances.

Fourth Amendment: The right of the people to be secure in their persons, houses, papers, and effects, against unreasonable searches and seizures, shall not be violated, and no Warrants shall issue, but upon probable cause, supported by Oath or affirmation, and particularly describing the place to be searched, and the persons or things to be seized.

Fifth Amendment: No person shall be held to answer for a capital, or otherwise infamous crime, unless on a presentment or indictment of a Grand Jury . . .; nor shall be compelled in any criminal case to be a witness against himself, nor be deprived of life, liberty, or property, without due process of law; nor shall private property be taken for public use without just compensation.

Sixth Amendment: In all criminal prosecutions, the accused shall enjoy the right to a speedy and public trial, by an impartial jury of the State and district wherein the crime shall have been committed, which district shall have been previously ascertained by law, and to be informed of the nature and cause of the accusation; to be confronted with the witness against him; to have compulsory process of obtaining Witnesses in his favour, and to have the assistance of counsel for his defence.

Eighth Amendment: Excessive bail shall not be required, nor excessive fines imposed, nor cruel and unusual punishments inflicted.

In addition the Fourteenth Amendment, added later, provides:

All persons born or naturalized in the United States, and subject to the jurisdiction thereof, are citizens of the United States and the State wherein they reside. No State shall make or enforce any law which shall abridge the privileges or immunities of citizens of the United States; nor shall any State deprive any person of life, liberty, or property, without due process of law; nor deny to any person within its jurisdiction the equal protection of the laws.

Box 9.4 Extracts from the Declaration of the Rights of Man and the Citizen 1789

The National Assembly *recognizes and declares in the presence and under the auspices of the Supreme Being the following rights of man and of the citizen:*

1. *In respect of their rights men are born and remain free and equal. . . .*
2. *The final end of every political institution is the preservation of the natural and imprescriptible rights of man. These rights are those of liberty, property, security and resistance to oppression.*
3. *The basis of all sovereignty lies, essentially, in the Nation. No corporation nor individual may exercise any authority that is not expressly derived therefrom.*
4. *Liberty is the capacity to do anything that does no harm to others. Hence the only limitations on the individual's exercise of his natural rights are those which ensure the enjoyment of these same rights to all other individuals. These limits can be established only by legislation.*
5. *Legislation is entitled to forbid only those actions which are harmful to society. . . .*
6. *Legislation is the expression of the general will. All citizens have a right to participate in shaping it either in person, or through their representatives. It must be the same for all, whether it punishes or it protects. Since all citizens are equal in its eyes, all are equally eligible for all positions, posts and public employments in accordance with their abilities and with no other distinctions than those provided by their virtues and their talents.*
7. *No individual may be accused, arrested or detained except in the cases prescribed by legislation and according to the procedures it has laid down. . . .*
8. *The only punishments established by legislation must be ones that are strictly and obviously necessary, and no individual must be punished except by virtue of a law passed and promulgated prior to the crime and applied in due legal form.*
9. *. . . every individual is presumed innocent until found guilty. . . .*
10. *Nobody must be persecuted on account of his opinions, including religious ones, provided that the manifestation of these does not disturb the public order established by legislation.*
11. *The free communication of thoughts and opinions is one of the most precious rights of man; hence every citizen may speak, write and publish freely, save that he must answer for any abuse of such freedom according to the cases established by legislation.*

15. *Society possesses the right to demand from every public servant an account of his administration.*

17. *Since property is an inviolable and sacred right, no individual may be deprived of it unless some public necessity, legally certified as such, clearly requires it; and subject always to a just and previously determined compensation.*

Box 9.5 The Preamble to the Constitution of the Fourth French Republic, 1946

On the morrow of the victory won by the free peoples over the regime which has sought to enslave and degrade the human personality, the French people, once again, proclaims that all human beings without distinction of race, religion or belief possess inalienable and sacred rights.

It solemnly reaffirms the Rights and Liberties of Man and the Citizen hallowed by the Declaration of Rights of 1789 and the fundamental principles recognized by the laws of the Republic. It proclaims, in addition, as particularly necessary to our time the following political, economic and social principles:

1. *The laws shall guarantee to women, in every sphere, equal rights with men.*
2. *Every individual who is the victim of persecution by reason of his activities in favour of freedom shall possess the right of asylum within the territories of the Republic.*
3. *Every individual has the duty to work and the right to employment. Nobody shall be allowed to suffer injury in respect of his work or occupation by reason of his origins, his opinions or his beliefs.*
4. *Every individual shall have the right to defend his rights and his interests by trade union activities and to join the trade union of his choice.*
5. *The right to strike shall be exercised within the framework of the laws which govern this.*
6. *Every worker shall participate through his delegates in the collective arrangements of work conditions as well as in the running of the firm.*
7. *Every resource or enterprise the working of which has acquired or is in the process of acquiring the characteristics of a public national service or, effectively, a monopoly, must pass into public ownership.*
8. *The Nation shall assure to the individual and the family the conditions necessary for their development.*
9. *It shall guarantee to everybody and notably to children, mothers and elderly workpeople, health care, material security, rest and leisure. Every human being who by reason of age, physical or mental condition, or economic situation is incapable of working shall have the right to obtain the means of subsistence from the community.*
10. *The Nation proclaims the solidarity and the equality of all the members of the French people when faced with the responsibilities arising from a national calamity.*
11. *The Nation guarantees to children and adults equal access to education, professional training culture. The organization of free, public and secular instruction at all levels is a duty incumbent upon the state.*
12. *The French Republic, faithful to its traditions, shall conform to the rules of international public law. It will never engage in wars of conquest nor use force against the freedom of any people.*
13. *Subject to reciprocity, France will consent to such limitations upon her sovereignty as are necessary for the organization and defence of peace.*

political rights should be given additional protection in the legal systems of the United Kingdom.

Additional legal protection for civil and political rights and liberties could be given in a number of ways. There could be piecemeal legislation, which is how the problem has been dealt with in the United Kingdom over the years, protecting civil and political rights as and when a need is perceived. For example, the Equal Pay Act, the Sex Discrimination Act and the Race Relations Act, among others, have sought to prohibit discrimination on grounds of sex and race in important aspects of an individual's life. There is scope for these measures to be broadened and made more effective – they could cover discrimination on grounds of religion, as is the case in Northern Ireland, and on grounds of sexual orientation, age, health and so on. Such measures could reduce irrational prejudice and so enable people who currently feel excluded from full participation in parts of our national life to become more involved members of the community.

There is much to be said for dealing with shortcomings in the legal foundations of citizenship by special, detailed legislation: it can be precise, it can make clear both to possible beneficiaries of the legislation and to those who are bound by it – employers, for example – what their rights and obligations are, and thus reduce the incidence of breaches of the law. It can have an important educative effect, making people realize that it is no longer publicly acceptable to be prejudiced. Detailed legislation leaves relatively little scope for judges to get round the spirit of the law, whereas broad statements of rights are much more flexible and often more vague.

However, there are also shortcomings in relying only on specific detailed legislation to deal with the problems we are concerned with. If the provisions are very specific and detailed there are bound to be cases which fall outside the strict letter of the law, although the situation may be one in which the spirit of the law would be to provide additional protection. The educative effect of detailed legislation may be lost in a welter of words, rules, exceptions and riders.

The main alternative to relying solely on detailed specific legislation is some form of Bill of Rights or Declaration of Rights, such as the United States and France have. These can take a wide variety of forms, and can have a wide range of legal statuses.

In the United States, a Bill of Rights is written into the Constitution (see Box 9.3 for extracts) and is fully 'justiciable': the Supreme Court of the United States has asserted, since the case of

Marbury v. *Madison* (1803), the right to review Acts of government for their constitutionality and to strike down legislation that is incompatible with the Constitution, which includes the Bill of Rights.

The adoption of this sort of approach to the protection of civil and political rights in the United Kingdom would be highly controversial. It can lead to the making of politically motivated appointments to the higher courts; to judges finding themselves very much in the political arena, exposed to accusations that their decisions are politically, religiously or socially partisan, and the complaint that the sort of choices that they make ought to be left to politicians who are democratically accountable rather than to judges who are insulated from political and democratic accountability.

The US Bill of Rights allows for no express exceptions to the freedoms it protects. This is unusual in Bills of Rights, which commonly allow for exceptions where, for instance, this is necessary to protect the rights of others, or where it is necessary in a democratic society for the protection of public order, public health, national security and so on.

France has adopted a different approach to the protection of civil and political rights. There is no Bill of Rights in the Constitution of the Fifth Republic, but there are two documents of constitutional importance which have influenced the legal protection of those rights, the Declaration of the Rights of Man and the Citizen 1789, and the Preamble to the 1946 Constitution of the Fourth Republic (see Boxes 9.4 and 9.5 for extracts).

These two documents were both reaffirmed in the Preamble to the current, 1958, French Constitution. Although they are not directly enforceable in the courts, they are a source of general legal principles in the sense that they influence the courts when interpreting *lois* and *règlements* (statutes), and they provide grounds for review of government action in the Conseil d'État, the administrative court. These principles include the essential liberties of the citizen, equality before the law, the doctrine of the separation of powers, the principle of non-retroactivity of laws, especially penal laws, and access to a court for judicial review.

There is no direct equivalent of these documents in the UK Constitution, but there are certain ancient measures which provide some important principles which the courts often seek to uphold: Magna Carta, the Habeas Corpus Acts, the Bill of Rights 1689, the Act of Settlement 1700 and the Act of Union with Scotland 1707.

However, the English courts are not consistent in drawing on these as sources of fundamental principles, and when they do so they lay themselves open to criticism for manipulating the law to meet their own preferences, sometimes in an artificial or contrived way.

A Bill of Rights for the United Kingdom could take the form of one of the internationally recognized instruments by which the United Kingdom is already bound in international law – the European Convention on Human Rights, for example, or the International Covenant on Civil and Political Rights. Alternatively, it could take the form of an amalgam of the best parts of these instruments. An Act of Parliament could be passed by the Parliament at Westminster 'incorporating' one of these instruments or an amalgam into domestic law, so that it could be applied and enforced by our own courts.

Advantages in using these instruments as the basis for a Bill of Rights are that they are already tried and tested by the international courts which administer them, and to a degree by courts in other countries (France and Germany, for instance) which, unlike the United Kingdom regard them as domestically enforceable. Since the United Kingdom is already a party to such instruments and has been for many years they are more or less uncontroversial. It is often said that it would be better if the United Kingdom could deal with complaints that it is in breach of these instruments in its own domestic courts rather than have them washed, dried, ironed and aired in international courts.

Yet a number of objections may be advanced to using any of these instruments as the text for a Bill of Rights. Generally they are drafted in very general terms, which makes them so vague that it is difficult to predict how the courts would decide a particular case: this line of argument prefers special detailed legislation of the sort briefly discussed above. International instruments also allow quite broad exceptions. Thus, for example, Article 10 of the European Convention on Human Rights starts by reciting that 'Everyone has the right to freedom of expression'. It goes on to include in this freedom the right to receive and impart information and ideas. However, the second part of the Article permits such restrictions on the exercise of these freedoms 'as are prescribed by law and are necessary in a democratic society in the interests of national security, territorial integrity or public safety, for the prevention of disorder or crime, for the protection of health or morals, for the protection of the reputation or rights of others, for preventing the disclosure of information received in confidence or for maintaining the authority and impartiality of the judiciary'. It could well be objected that the need to protect health, to protect the authority of the judiciary, or even to protect confidential information does not necessarily justify restrictions on freedom of speech.

An alternative to the adoption of an international instrument as a Bill of Rights would be a specially drafted Bill to meet the needs of the country. A number of such drafts has been produced in recent years. The Institute of Public Policy Research produced a draft Bill of Rights in 1991, as part of the *Constitution of the United Kingdom*, which borrowed from the European Convention on Human Rights and the International Covenant on Civil and Political Rights. Liberty (the National Council for Civil Liberties) produced a People's Charter in 1991. Both of these would have been enforceable in the courts, as the US Bill of Rights is.

Although there is fairly widespread agreement that certain rights or liberties are in need of some kind of legal protection, and although drafts have been produced, it could well be difficult to obtain cross-party agreement about the precise wording of a Bill of Rights. For example, those who agree in principle that free speech is necessary in a democracy might well disagree among themselves about what sort of exceptions there should be to free speech. Should civil servants be allowed to disclose information received in the course of their work? Is it legitimate to prohibit the publication of hard or soft pornography, should blasphemy be a crime, should it be extended to protect other religions, or should it be abolished as a crime altogether? Should incitement to racial hatred be a crime? What about defamation, invasions of privacy, and so on? Several attempts have been made to have Parliament pass private members' bills legislating for a Bill of Rights, but without success.

Proposals for a British Bill of Rights raise a number of important and difficult issues (see Oliver, 1991, ch. 9), not only about what such a Bill of Rights should say, but how it should be enforced. Should the Bill be enforceable in the courts, like the US one, or only relevant as a source of principles and values, like the French Declaration of the Rights of Man 1789 and the Preamble to the Constitution of the Fourth French Republic? Would it be wrong to give the judges the power to uphold a Bill of Rights against the will of the democratically elected House of Commons, Government, or local authority? If it is to be enforceable, should it also be 'entrenched' in the sense that Parliament could not legislate to interfere with the rights without, say, a referendum, as in Ireland, or a special majority in Parliament? This question raises difficult points about whether the UK Parliament could be bound by entrenching provisions without adopting a new written constitution.

We pose these questions to illustrate the range of difficulties in strengthening the foundations of civil and political rights as part of citizenship. Although, as we have seen from examples taken from other constitutions, these problems are not insuperable.

THE PROTECTION OF SOCIAL AND ECONOMIC RIGHTS

So far we have been concentrating on how civil and political rights could be protected in a Bill of Rights. The question also arises whether a Constitution or a Bill or Charter of Rights could or should protect social, economic and environmental rights (see Chapter 5).

Tony Benn MP produced a draft constitution for 'the Commonwealth of Britain' in the form of a Bill introduced into Parliament in 1991. It included proposals for the protection of first, second and third generation rights (see Box 9.6).

It is clear that most of the 'rights' in this Charter of Rights could not be legally enforceable by an individual without being supplemented by detailed legislation. Even the political and legal rights do not admit of exceptions (for example, to freedom of speech) although any legal system has to make provision for exceptions to many of these 'rights'. In effect, this sort of Charter lays down the broad *policy* or programme the government is to pursue, and the principal sanctions would be exposure to political embarrassment, criticism, loss of electoral support and so on, rather than the legal ones.

The Institute of Public Policy Research's draft of a Constitution for the United Kingdom in 1991 included a Bill of Rights that protected civil and political rights, and provided for social rights, but without making them enforceable in the courts (Box 9.7).

This kind of provision places a strong political and moral duty – but not one that is enforceable in the courts by an individual – on the state to give effect to social and economic rights.

Box 9.6 The Commonwealth of Britain Bill 1991

Schedule I to the Bill was a Charter of Rights. It provided as follows:

1. *All citizens of Britain shall be entitled to enjoy, and to campaign for, universal democratic and enforceable rights, both individual and collective, enshrined in law, adhered to in practice and respected by society, as a precondition of self-government and the achievement of full political, social and economic emancipation within a civilized society;*
2. *Every citizen shall have the following political rights:*
- *to freedom of speech;*
- *to freedom of assembly and of association for the purpose of expressing an opinion, without interference from the State;*
- *to organise for common political, social or economic ends;*
- *to practise, or not to practise, any or all religions;*
- *to vote in all elections, participate in all electoral processes and institutions, and to contest all elections;*
- *to privacy and the protection of personal information and correspondence from surveillance or interference;*
- *to information about public, political, social or economic affairs;*
- *to freedom of movement, unhindered by arbitrary interference, and to be given asylum from political social or economic oppression; and*
- *to conscientious objection to service in the armed forces.*
3. *Every citizen shall have the following legal rights:*
- *to personal freedom from arbitrary arrest, detention or harassment;*
- *to a fair and impartial hearing by a jury of the citizen's peers if accused of any unlawful activity, and to equal treatment before the law and equal access to legal representation;*
- *to be presumed innocent until proved guilty, to be informed of all charges laid and the evidence in support of them, and the right to silence in court;*
- *to freedom from torture or cruel and degrading treatment, and from capital punishment;*
- *to legal advice and services, free at the point of use; and*
- *to equal treatment before the law, and in the community, without discrimination, and regardless of race, sex or sexual preference, colour, religious or political conviction or disability.*
4. *Every citizen shall have the following social rights:*
- *to adequate and warm housing and comfortable living conditions;*
- *to rest, recreation and leisure, to a limitation of working hours and to holidays;*

Box 9.6 The Commonwealth of Britain Bill 1991 (continued)

- *to enjoy access to literature, music, the arts and cultural activities;*
- *to good health care and preventive medicine, free at the moment of need;*
- *to lifelong and free educational provision;*
- *to dignity and care in retirement;*
- *in the case of women, to control of their own fertility and reproduction;*
- *to free and equal access to child care;*
- *to free, effective and equitable means of transportation;*
- *to a healthy, sustainable, accessible and attractive environment and to clean water and air;*
- *to media free from governmental or commercial domination; and*
- *to full access to personal information held by any public authority, subject only to a restriction order signed by a Minister and reported to Parliament.*

5. *Every citizen shall have the following economic rights:*
- *to useful work at a fair wage that provides an income sufficient to maintain a decent standard of living;*
- *to belong to a trade union and to withdraw labour in pursuit of an industrial dispute;*
- *to participate in all decisions, including those relating to health and safety, affecting the workplace and to information, representation and expression of opinion for all employed persons;*
- *to full and equal access to all state or social benefits at a level sufficient to meet basic needs; and*
- *to freedom from taxation in excess of an ability to pay.*

These drafts raise the question 'What do we mean by "rights"?' The term is very ambiguous, but generally, and certainly in the context of civil and political rights, we mean a benefit to which individuals are entitled as individuals and which any one individual may seek to enforce by resort to the courts for his or her benefit. In that sense the 'rights' in Tony Benn's Bill would probably not be treated as rights by the courts, because they are too vague to be judicially enforceable. They are rather duties owed by the state to the

---

Box 9.7 Institute of Public Policy Research draft constitutional provisions for unenforceable social rights (1991)

[Article] 27.1 In making provision for the social and economic welfare of the people of the United Kingdom, Parliament . . . shall be guided by the principles contained in the International Covenants and Charters to which the United Kingdom is signatory, and in particular by –

.1 the right of workers to earn their living in an occupation freely entered upon;

.2 the right of everyone to an adequate standard of living, including adequate food, clothing and housing;

.3 the right of everyone to social security;

.4 the right of everyone to the enjoyment of the highest attainable standard of physical and mental health;

.5 the right of everyone to education;

.6 the right of workers to resort to collective action in the event of a conflict of interests, including the right to strike;

.7 the right of every worker to enjoy satisfactory health and safety conditions in their working environment.

27.3 The provisions of this Article are not enforceable in any court.

---

population of individuals, enforceable only through means other than action in the courts by and for the benefit of an individual.

Another approach to the protection of social and economic rights would be to draft a Social Charter for the United Kingdom, that would be much more detailed than the drafts referred to above. Proposals have been made from time to time that a Bill of Rights, or a written constitution, should give protection to these 'second generation' rights in the United Kingdom. Lewis and Seneviratne produced such a draft in 1992 (see Box 9.8 for extracts; see also Coote, 1992) based on the European Social Charter, which was produced by the Council of Europe. This Charter was adopted in 1961 and came into force as an international instrument in 1965. Although the United Kingdom is a party to it, it has not accepted all of the provisions.

The machinery for international 'enforcement' of the European Social Charter is weak. The parties must report every two years to the Secretary General of the Council of Europe on measures taken to apply those provisions of the Charter that they have accepted. In due course, a report is made to the Parliamentary Assembly of the Council of Europe which in turn reports to the Committee of Ministers which makes recommendations to the parties about their compliance or non-compliance with the Charter.

Lewis and Seneviratne propose that the European Social Charter form the basis for a British Charter of Social Rights. Most of the rights covered in it are already in legislation in the United Kingdom to some extent, and the effect of the Charter would be to provide guidance for officials and courts dealing with cases, rather than itself giving rise to new rights that are not covered in legislation at all at present.

ENVIRONMENTAL RIGHTS

Finally, there is the creation and protection of environmental rights. It is only relatively recently that consideration has been given to incorporating these into constitutional measures, or indeed to including broadly worded general duties of respect for the environment in Acts of Parliament. We have seen the clause in Tony Benn's Bill in Box 9.6, but other drafts produced have not even attempted to include environmental rights and duties. Here, as we saw in our discussion in Chapter 5, it is particularly difficult to identify who is responsible for pollution and to control its production and movement. It is commonly impossible to place liability for transboundary or global pollution on a particular public authority or state: the Chernobyl disaster, caused by the 'melt down' of a nuclear power station in the Ukraine was exceptional in that the source of the pollution could be identified. However, even in such a case it is difficult if not impossible for individuals to obtain redress from those who were responsible, especially if they are overseas or are sovereign foreign states. Hence, in this field of rights an eclectic and mixed set of protections is required, including international cooperation and state and international regulation of pollution. Individual rights of enforcement, which are characteristic of the liberal approach to citizenship, have only a small part to play in this world-scale problem.

Box 9.8 Extracts from a draft Social Charter for the United Kingdom by Lewis and Seneviratne

Section 2 The right to medical care

(1) The Government undertakes to secure the provision of services in respect of a condition requiring medical care, which shall include the following:
(a) general practitioner care, including domiciliary visiting;
(b) specialist care at hospitals for in-patients and out-patients, and such specialist care as may be available outside hospitals;
(c) the essential pharmaceutical supplies as prescribed by medical or other qualified practitioners;
(d) hospitalisation, where necessary.

. . .

Section 3: The right to social security
The Government undertakes to maintain a system of social security at a satisfactory level at least equal to that required for ratification of the European Code of Social Security, and to endeavour to raise progressively the system of social security to a higher level.

. . .

Section 14
(1) All legislative provisions in force before the passing of this Act shall, after the coming into force of this Act, be interpreted so as to give effect, wherever possible, to its provisions.
(2) All publicly exercised discretion affecting any matters which relate to the subject matter of this Act shall be exercised so as to give effect, wherever possible, to its provisions.
(3) All legislative provisions introduced after the passage of this Act shall be interpreted so as to give effect, wherever possible, to its provisions unless an Act of the United Kingdom Parliament expressly provides to the contrary.

CONCLUSIONS

This brings us to the end of the discussion in this book of the legal aspects of citizenship and their relationship with citizenship theories and historical, political and philosophical debates. The next chapter seeks to draw general conclusions. We have seen in Chapters 3, 4, 5 and 7 that citizenship rests, in part, on legal as well as social foundations, and in this chapter we have explored some general approaches to the possible uses of the law in strengthening and building the status. There are a range of ways in which the legal foundations of citizenship, especially civil, political, social, economic and environmental rights, could be strengthened and underpinned, in particular the adoption of some form of Bill of Rights and a Social Charter. Improvement of these legal foundations cannot, of itself, achieve all of the development of citizenship that might be required, but it could form part of an action plan for citizenship in the United Kingdom and beyond.

FURTHER READING

Ewing, K. and Gearty, C. (1990) *Freedom under Thatcher. Civil Liberties in Modern Britain* (Oxford: Clarendon Press).

Liberty (1991) *A People's Charter* (London: Liberty).

Robertson, G. (1989) *Freedom, the Individual and the Law* (Harmondsworth: Penguin).

10

CURRENT PERSPECTIVES

SUMMARY

The old problem of different interpretations of the nature of citizenship has been compounded in recent years by a number of factors. These include the disagreements between liberals and communitarians, the debates surrounding the relationship between citizenship and capitalism, and difficulties in giving precise legal definitions, not least in Britain.

As the established association of citizenship with nationality seems increasingly inappropriate, the idea of multiple citizenship has become an attractive alternative idea. This involves an individual having more than one civic identity, psychologically and in law. In constructing a multiple citizenship, it is important to ensure a healthy civil society as its foundation. Then, at the state level, it is helpful to distinguish between 'nationality citizenship' and 'new citizenship'. The latter recognizes the existence of human rights outside the context of the state.

Although the idea of world citizenship cannot be said to have any firm legal or political reality, it is a concept which many find useful for a spectrum of programmes from reform of the United Nations to federal world government.

Owing to the complexity, even subjectivity of the citizenship idea, no universally accepted definition or description has been produced. However, we conclude by outlining four models which attempt the task in different ways.

THE PROBLEM OF DIVERSE VIEWS

Does citizenship exist in any comprehensible way at all? The word is used in so many different senses, with so many different explanations that it seems almost impossible at times to pin the concept down. The difficulty of arriving at any agreed definition is not new. Aristotle noted that there was considerable disagreement in his own times. The problem is compounded today by a number of issues.

One is the post-modernist determination to challenge all accepted values and definitions as inadequate to the complexity of reality. On the basis of this approach, any definition of citizenship will depend on the point of view of the person who compiled it. The search for unity or coherence is the search for an illusion because citizenship, by its very nature, cannot be captured. It is composed of multifaceted values: a definition can only be a reflection of those faces that the particular viewer finds most congenial.

We saw in Chapters 2 and 6 especially, that the analysis of the nature of citizenship has been subjected to a number of different ideological interpretations. This process has intensified and polarized the differences in the emphases that may be placed upon the concept. In particular, the antagonism between the liberal stress on rights and the communitarian stress on duties has seemed, at times, to render the two interpretations irreconcilable.

Similarly, there is the dichotomy between those who believe that the operation of the capitalist free market is essential for the freedom that citizenship entails, and those who believe that the two principles of capitalism and citizenship cannot comfortably coexist. Consider the following two comments. The first is by Vernon Bogdanor commenting on the differences between the British Conservative and Labour parties.

> [One] aspect of the conflict is whether there remains a public interest over and above that of the market. . . .
>
> The struggle between the ethic of the marketplace and the ethic of citizenship seems to me to represent the true dividing line between the parties; and how it is resolved will determine the kind of society in which we live as we approach the end of the 20th century. (V. Bogdanor in *The Guardian*, 1992a)

Yet, as we saw in Chapters 2 and 6, the Conservatives believe that they have a perfectly valid notion of citizenship in harmony with the operation of the market.

The second quotation on this dilemma is taken from an article by two writers in Poland commenting on post-Communist eastern Europe:

> Democracy requires that the reform process should enjoy broad-based social support [i.e. citizenship]. But vigorous free market conditions have jeopardised the welfare of much of society, and can only be sustained if society is excluded from the policy-making arena. (J. Luxmore and J. Babiuch, *The Guardian*, 1992b)

Yet many other commentators have seen the collapse of Communism as the occasion for a revival of citizenship hitherto stifled by the totalitarian features of the previous regimes: totalitarianism reduces the individual to the position of subject.

Citizenship is not, however, confined to the provinces of political philosophy and party political doctrines. It is also a legal concept. Even so, the precision which we might expect to find in the law is somewhat lacking, especially in the United Kingdom. In Chapters 3 and 4 we have explained that in some legal respects Britons are subjects or autonomous individuals rather than citizens in any true sense; and that, in any case, absolutely clear-cut legal definitions of rights and duties would be inadvisable. Furthermore, when it comes to defining the rights attached to a notional British citizenship in practice, we find that some are enjoyed by individuals who are not British citizens by legal nationality. For example, citizens of the Irish Republic may vote in elections and resident aliens have certain rights of social welfare.

The rigid distinction between citizen and alien has been made increasingly difficult in a number of states in recent times because of the fluidity of populations. The resultant ambiguous and uncertain status of migrants together with the questionable effectiveness of the supposed rights of full citizens, have led to a distinction being drawn between formal and substantive rights. The two by no means coincide. The catalogue of formal rights as delineated, for instance, by Marshall may not be substantively (i.e. in practice) enjoyed by all those individuals who are in an indisputable legal sense citizens of the state, where those rights are claimed to exist. On the other hand, as we have seen in Chapters 4 and 5, some rights are substantively enjoyed by individuals whose claim on them does not rest on legal citizenship or nationality status.

Does not all this uncertainty and dispute surrounding the principle of citizenship ignore the less measurable idea of good citizenship? Is there not some truth in the view that a citizen is someone who behaves as a citizen? If, therefore, we can demonstrate that there is widespread evidence of good citizenly behaviour, then surely citizenship can be said to exist in an easily recognizable form. Here again, we run into difficulties, on three counts.

In the first place, it can be argued, the classical picture of civic virtue (see Chapters 1 and 6) was either a misty-eyed distortion of historical reality or the presentation of an unrealistic ideal. In the second place, in so far as the practice of good citizenship has existed in modern times, it is a form of behaviour which is suffering a rapid decline. Citizenship in the sense of good citizenship is disappearing in a social climate whose predominant features are selfishness, divisiveness and crime. Finally, there is the danger that, in failing to make a clear distinction between citizenship as status and citizenship as behaviour, we are confusingly conflating the two. The French, after all, have two separate words – *citoyenté* for the status; *civisme* for behaviour.

None the less, the very interest that has flowered in recent years in the matter of citizenship is proof enough of a general belief that it is a concept worth preserving, elucidating and implementing. These tasks, it is clear, require a number of activities. First, there must be a search for ways of making different styles of the ideal as compatible as possible with each other. Second, citizenship must incorporate new social developments which may not have been in evidence when citizenship theories and practices evolved in former ages. Third, politicians, pressure groups and individual citizens themselves need to ensure that a pattern of citizenship which might hypothetically, even legally, exist, is in fact practised.

Meanwhile, behind all this detailed work, we must not lose sight of the private individual. No-one, surely, wants even the most assiduous of citizens to live like the proverbial proud and dutiful soldier who slept with his medals pinned to his pyjamas. An acceptable model of citizenship involves citizens 'switching on' their civic consciousness

---

Box 10.1

Are the different conceptions of the good citizen mutually incompatible? A French authority warns of the pitfalls to avoid in constructing a modern concept of citizenship.

Important as it is, recovering some of the concerns of the civic republican tradition, with its richer conception of the political, and recapturing our insertion in a political community and our identities as citizens, should not be done in such a way that the modern recognition of pluralism is made void. The individual is not to be sacrificed to the citizen. . . . On the other hand, we must recognise that the current search for a more active citizenship is a response to the limitations, not only of the liberal conception that has reduced citizenship to a legal status, but also to the bureaucratic and statist conception of politics that has for many years been the principal alternative presented by the Left. (C. Mouffe in Mouffe, 1992, p. 5)

---

on appropriate occasions. A state composed of twenty-four-hour-a-day citizens would exude an intolerable zealotry. What is more, such behaviour would be utterly inappropriate in today's world whose complexity requires a highly flexible notion of citizenship.

MULTIPLE CITIZENSHIP

For most practical purposes citizens practise or enjoy their citizenship in the context of a state and for most legal purposes a citizen is defined by nationality. The reason for this is simply explained: modern citizenship has evolved with the modern nation-state. On the other hand, as we saw in Chapter 1, the idea of multiple citizenship is by no means new. Five aspects of the idea have particular currency today. One, the building of a European Community citizenship alongside the national citizenships of the Member States and the consequent conflicts, have been examined in some detail in Chapter 7. Another, the idea of world citizenship, will be handled in the next section. Here we shall concentrate on the psychological issue of multiple identity; the importance of civil society; and the concept of 'new citizenship'.

A significant component of the principle of citizenship is the

---

Box 10.2

An authority on nationalism argues that people can feel more than one loyalty, although loyalty to the nation is the most powerful.

human beings have multiple collective identifications, whose scope and intensity will vary with time and place. There is nothing to prevent individuals from identifying with Flanders, Belgium and Europe simultaneously, and displaying each allegiance in the appropriate context; or from feeling they are Yoruba, Nigerian and African, in concentric circles of loyalty and belonging. It is, in fact, quite common, and very much what one would expect in a world of multiple ties and identities.

This does not mean that such ties and identities are entirely optional and situational, nor that some among them do not exercise a greater hold and exert a more powerful influence than others . . . national identity does in fact today exert a more potent and durable influence than other collective cultural identities. (Smith, 1991, pp. 175–6)

---

expectation that citizens will identify with and be loyal to their state. This is a matter of heart and conscience, of emotion and duty. For roughly two centuries, from *c.* 1790 to *c.* 1990, citizenship and nationality were tightly bonded together. Increasingly today, the kind of sense of identity and loyalty that has been expected of citizens in relation to their state is also being asked of citizens in relation to their ethnic communities, religion, locality, region, continent (in the case of Europe), and the world even.

The question therefore arises whether it is feasible for an individual to experience feelings of multiple identity. Not only is it feasible, it is a natural corollary of mankind's social life. In the words of Professor Smith (1991, p. 4), 'the self is composed of multiple identities and roles – familial, territorial, class, religious, ethnic and gender'.

In speaking of the idea of multiple citizenship, we are therefore merely adapting an age-old social–psychological habit. The difference is twofold. First, a multiple citizenship identity is a politico-legal identity. It follows that each component in that identity should be given some kind of legal recognition and some means of political expression. These are not usually necessary requirements for family or gender or religious identities, for example. A woman has a female identity, a Roman Catholic has a religious identity irrespective of any laws which may or may not have existed relating to discrimination.

Second, there is a difference between the relationships within the social–psychological range of identities on the one hand and the relationships of the several identities involved in multiple citizenship on the other. Identities related to gender, class, religion, for instance, overlap and intersect like a Venn diagram. Not all women are middle class, not all middle-class people are Presbyterians, for example. Yet some individuals do belong to all these categories. In contrast, multiple citizenship is concentric in pattern. Every citizen of a town is a citizen of the region in which it is contained, is a citizen of the state in which the region is contained, ... and so forth.

Now although there would appear to be no inherent psychological bar to the idea of multiple citizenship, there might well be practical problems. These concern both institutional structures and individual behaviour. Leaving aside, for the moment, the matter of world citizenship, the European Community has been moving towards a multiple citizenship structure. The Maastricht Treaty in particular has confirmed the status of 'citizenship of the Union', the need to create Regional Councils, and the principle of subsidiarity, requiring decision-making at different levels (see Chapter 7). The logical outcome of these proposals must be multiple citizenship at four levels. An individual living in Aberdeen, for instance, would in that case be simultaneously an Aberdonian, a Scot, a Briton and a European – not just in terms of a sense of identity, but also in terms of opportunities to exercise the rights and duties of the citizenly status. However, institutional solutions do not resolve the problems that can well face the individual citizen in practice. Multiple citizenship places a great strain upon individuals to understand the issues at the several levels and to judge where their primary loyalty should lie in the event of a conflict of needs or policies. Is it, for instance, asking too much of our hypothetical Aberdonian to support a Common Market policy which is to the benefit of the Community as a whole but detrimental to his city's economy?

Yet, if citizenship is today in a sad and weak condition, and if our social lives would benefit from its enhancement, is it not precisely at the interest-group and local, functional level that this strengthening is most likely to be both efficient and beneficial? Citizens will be better citizens and the state will be politically healthier if there is a strongly rooted civil society, that is, collectivities of different associations. As

Professor Walzer has reminded us, the reconstruction of such a society has been given high priority in former Communist European states:

> the first task of the new democracies... is to rebuild the networks: unions, churches, political parties and movements, cooperatives, neighbourhoods, schools of thought, societies for promoting or preventing this and that. (Mouffe, 1992, p. 90)

It is within this kind of civil society network that citizens learn collaborative behaviour; and the existence of such a network protects the citizen from being turned into an obedient automaton by an overbearing state.

The traditional equation of citizenship with nationality is, in fact, becoming so difficult to sustain that the idea of a 'new citizenship' to exist alongside 'nationality citizenship' has been devised (see Gardner, 1990). The complexities which have brought this about are evident in several countries. In Germany, for example,

> Declining population, rising immigration, the discontent of third-generation 'German Turks' and the claims to citizenship of the descendants of emigrants whose ancestors left Germany centuries ago, raise the underlying question, 'Who is a German?'. (Wallace, 1992, p. 437)

However, the need for a clear understanding of new citizenship derives more from the current confusion relating to legal rights than from questions of nationality. One of the most important attributes of citizenship historically has been its conferment of rights. An individual is now recognized as having human rights totally unrelated to the status of state citizenship. These are defined for the whole of humanity in the Universal Declaration and subsequent declarations and conventions. For most Europeans they are not only defined by the European Council's Convention, but are protected by the investigations of the European Commission of Human Rights and the judgments of its associated Court.

In the context of the European Community, especially as a result of the Single European Act, labour is becoming increasingly mobile. Rights of residence and social welfare must be enjoyed irrespective of the worker's nationality citizenship: migrant Community workers become *de facto* citizens of the state within which they happen to reside or be employed (see Chapter 7).

International law made by the United Nations, the Council of Europe and the European Community has thus seriously undermined the simple concept of the rights of citizenship defined by nationality. Moreover, the complications are compounded in Britain by the convolutions of British law and practice. British citizens do not have a set of rights clearly delineated by a bill of rights, for example (see Chapter 9); the European Convention on Human Rights has not been incorporated into UK law; and the law regarding Commonwealth citizenship is confused (see Chapter 3). As a consequence, the position of new citizenship in Britain, so necessary in today's fluid world, is decidedly unclear; though it is clear that it is not based on nationality.

WORLD CITIZENSHIP

The idea of world citizenship, as we saw in Chapter 1, is two and a half thousand years old. It has never existed in any tangible political or legal sense; and yet, as an idea, it refuses to die.

Four different kinds of programmes of action currently sustain the notion:

1. Reform of the UN
2. Concern for global environment and poverty
3. Strengthening world law
4. World federal government.

The first would provide citizen representation; the second emphasizes citizenly duties; the third, citizenly rights as well as duties; while the fourth would mirror the whole panoply of state citizenship.

It is often remarked that, for all its failings, the United Nations is the nearest set of institutions we have to a world government. Even so, it provides virtually no opportunities for the individual to act through its structures as a world citizen. Discontent with the United Nations has led to many suggestions for reforms. One is for the creation of a Second Assembly composed of representatives from various international bodies (International Non-Governmental Organisations – INGOs in UN parlance). Through membership of such bodies, private individuals could act in some measure as world citizens by electing the representatives.

Even the main INGOs number several hundreds, and many of these have been founded because of concern about world poverty and/or the degradation of the global environment. Members of these organizations often feel that they think and campaign as world citizens. After all, the issues they work for are not confined by state boundaries – they are planetary in scope. Citizenship involves consideration for one's fellow citizens, concern that they should be treated with justice. No citizen therefore should expect to enjoy excessive privileges in comparison with his or her fellow citizens. World citizenship extends this principle in both space and time. Thus, it is argued, it is a violation of global social citizenship for millions to die of starvation and the diseases of malnutrition while others are supplied with more than adequate quantities of food. Also, it is a violation of the rights of future generations to pollute and plunder the planet beyond reasonable recovery. It is the moral duty of world citizens to try to persuade states and industries to adopt globally responsible policies in these respects.

If the citizen is to enjoy rights as well as perform duties in a global context, then a framework of international law is required to define those rights and, preferably also, ensure that they are honoured. However, whereas municipal (i.e. state) law recognizes the individual as a person (i.e. a unit capable of engaging in legal action), international law has (with some important exceptions) almost entirely recognized only the state as a 'person'.

The concept of human rights has helped to change this situation since the Second World War. Most dramatically Nazi leaders were tried at Nuremberg after the war for 'crimes against humanity'. The guidelines for the trials included the assertion that 'individuals have duties which transcend national obligations'. In other words, international law recognizes that the individual as well as states are subject to its codes of behaviour; citizens have a duty to disobey their state if that state offends the international moral code; and individuals have rights as human beings which international law should attempt to guarantee.

The logical follow-up to this interpretation was the sheaf of UN declarations and conventions relating to human rights. The main thrust of these documents is to persuade states to honour these standards in the treatment of their own citizens. Nevertheless, the

Preamble of the initial Universal Declaration of 1948 interestingly states as one of its aims 'that every individual . . . shall strive . . . to promote respect for these rights and freedoms and . . . to secure their universal and effective recognition and observance. . . .' This is assuredly a basic assertion that individuals should behave as world citizens.

All this is, of course, very tentative, a far cry from the symbiotic relationships which link state and citizen in the strict sense of the term. On the other hand, there are advocates of world government; and if their proposals were put into effect, individuals would have the same kind of civic relationship to that world state as currently citizens have to their nation-states. For example, a World Association of World Federalists was started in 1947. A World Citizens Assembly was held in Paris in 1977. However, the importance of these movements lies more in the spread of universalist attitudes of mind than any immediate prospect of creating a United States of the World.

Box 10.3

Since the Second World War a number of organizations have been created to promote the idea and ideals of world citizenship. One is the International Registry of World Citizens, based in Paris. Here is an extract from its Declaration.

While retaining their own nationality, those who register as World Citizens
Recognise that:

1. *The technical unity of the world, the growing economic interdependence and the clashing political rivalries have awakened the conscience of Man to his right to express his responsibility and his sovereignty on world level.*
2. *Sovereign states, constitutionally limited to the defense of their particular interests, are incapable of protecting and satisfying the interests and needs now common to all men. . . .*
3. *Only a world authority deriving its powers directly from the people of the world can give the necessary priority to these common needs and interests and provide their effective defense and organization. (reprinted in* Mundialist Summa, *1977, p. 18)*

SOME MODELS

Readers who have followed us to this point cannot fail to be struck by the extraordinary complexity of citizenship, the different perspectives from which it is viewed and the interconnections of its component parts. Is it possible to encapsulate the concept in any concise form so as to view it whole without doing violence to its intrinsic complexity? Let us look at four models which attempt this task in different ways.

The first is in Bellah *et al.* (1985, pp. 200–2). Here we find the proposition that there are three quite distinct understandings of modern citizenship. Figure 10.1 provides a brief summary. The politics of community represents the citizen as neighbour. It is closest to the classical city-state ideal of all citizens knowing each other and the resolution of problems by face-to-face discussion. The politics of interest is the pluralist model akin to the thought of Bentham and some of his followers. Participation through interest groups ensures the expression and satisfaction of the multifarious needs of members of the whole community. This form of citizenship has the potential disadvantage of breeding antagonism and the potential advantage of breeding understanding, tolerance and give-and-take. The third

The politics of the community

Involvement for the good of the local community.

The politics of interest

Pressure groups to achieve a particular end.

The politics of the nation

Participation to express loyalty to the state.

Figure 10.1 Modern citizenship.

style, the politics of the nation, cannot involve day-to-day or detailed participation (except by fighting for one's state in war) because of the size of most present-day states. Citizenship in this form is therefore mainly participation in symbolic rituals of loyalty involving, for instance, the national flag and anthem.

There is much in this model to illuminate our understanding of citizenship. It has the virtue of being easily comprehended. Nevertheless, so much has been omitted in the process of simplification that we would need to supplement it with considerations, for example, of the balancing of rights and duties, of the legal status of citizenship, of the operation of citizenship in the national context beyond the merely symbolic.

Our next model has been constructed by Professor Bryan Turner (Mouffe, 1992, pp. 33–60). The tabulations in Figure 10.2 are taken from his paper (Diagram (a) represents the general typology;

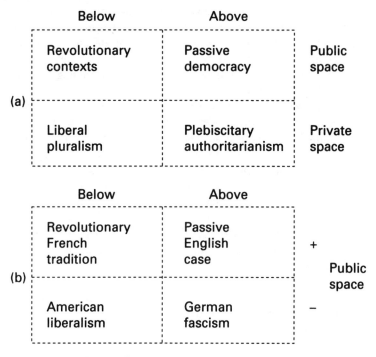

Figure 10.2 Models of citizenship: (a) general typology, (b) examples.

Diagram (b) provides examples). His is an historical explanation of how different styles of citizenship have developed. He distinguishes between citizenship rights handed down from ABOVE by the government, from a situation in which they are extracted from BELOW by the people. He further sees a distinction between a citizenship which expects public duty (where there is an emphasis on PUBLIC SPACE) and citizenship which expects individuals to behave mainly as private persons for most of the time (where there is an emphasis on PRIVATE SPACE).

The analysis of styles of citizenship evolution along these lines gives us four general types:

1. The active form of citizenship with an emphasis on rights extracted from below as benefits by struggle against the government, together with a strong commitment to political activity by the citizenry. The exemplar of this type is the French revolutionary tradition stemming from the events of 1788–94.
2. The active form of citizenship with an emphasis on rights extracted from below as benefits by struggle against the government, but with the expectation of private life (e.g. family, religion) being unaffected by the citizenly status. The exemplar of this type is American individualist liberalism stemming from the War of Independence and the frontier mentality.
3. The passive form of citizenship with an emphasis on privileges handed down by Government from above, together with a strong commitment to political activity by the citizen. The exemplar of this type is the English form of democracy stemming from the post-1688 Settlement and the status of citizen as subject.
4. The passive form of citizenship with an emphasis on privileges handed down by Government from above, but with the expectation that the individual will act as a citizen only in strictly defined circumstances. The exemplar of this type is Nazi Germany with the mobilization of the citizenry for the legitimation and exaltation of the leader.

Clearly this typology is not merely of historical interest. In many cases the traditions have persisted to the present day. On the other hand, although this categorization is extremely useful, it must be treated with caution. The differences are not as clear cut as the simplification of boxed tabulations suggests. For example, historians conscious of the various radical movements in England from the Levellers to the Suffragettes, would be unhappy at labelling the English tradition as entirely passive.

The third model, as presented in Figure 10.3, is a slight development in web form, of material in Heater (1990, pp. 318–36). The basis of this model is the proposition that the concept of citizenship contains five essential elements. These are Marshall's triad of civil, political and social citizenship plus civic virtue and identity. However, it must be further recognized that the word 'citizenship' in English does service for two ideas, namely, a status and a feeling.

The depiction of the essential components of citizenship in web form shows how interconnected they are. The civil, political and social forms flow from citizenship as status. They involve both rights and duties. In contrast, civic virtue, being a good citizen, relates to attitudes and behaviour. It expresses itself to some extent as loyalty to the state and the community and, together with the discharge of duties, expresses itself as a sense of responsibility. Identity is a double-barrelled concept: it is part of citizenship as status in the passport sense of defining one's citizenship legally by nationality; it is also part of citizenship as feeling in the basic social–psychological sense of the need of the human being to belong to social groups. Though, increasingly today, the individual, as well as being a citizen by nationality, also has need of multiple civic identities.

Again, this model is an oversimplification which omits important nuances. In particular, it ignores the significant differences between the various traditions highlighted in the Turner model.

Finally, we come to the model devised by Dr Porter (1993) and represented in a very simplified form in Figure 10.4. He argues that most recent discussions in Britain concerning the nature of citizenship and citizenship education has implicitly divided the concept into status and volition. He further argues that a third component, namely, competence, is essential for a complete analytical picture.

By status, Porter means the relationship of the citizen to the state, often defined, in the form of rights and duties, by law. He accepts that the status is dynamic – it has evolved and continues to evolve as a result of struggle. He also includes legal identity under the heading of status. Volition is an affective category, involving feelings,

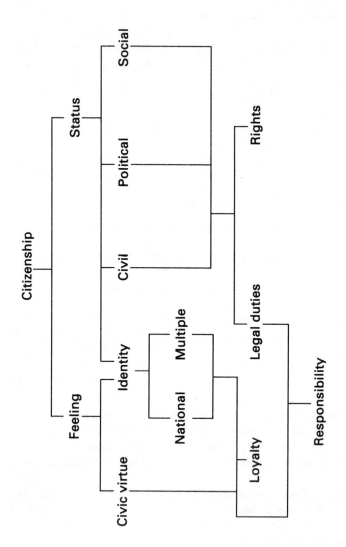

Figure 10.3 The model of citizenship by Heater (1990).

Status	/	
Legal, political and social position in relation to the state.	/ / /	*Tensions*
	/ /	Multiple; Privilege v. right
Volition	/	
Attitudes and behaviour in relation to others in the community.	/ / /	
Competence		
Understanding, skills and dispositions to act as citizens.		

Figure 10.4 Citizenship viewed by Porter.

inclination, attitudes, intentions, resolution. It embraces identity in the sense of fraternity; loyalty in the sense of honour and pride; a sense of responsibility in the sense of willingness to support valid causes. However, status and volition are sterile if the citizen lacks competence to bring them into play. Competence involves understanding of the political, legal and social systems; skills for participation; and a predisposition to respect democratic modes of procedure.

This analysis has the considerable merit of neatness, yet the meanings and implications of status, volition and competence can be filled in to the level of detail and complexity one wishes. Porter himself concedes that the pattern is overly neat and that certain tensions within the concept must be incorporated. One is the tension between traditional national citizenship and modern requirements of multiple citizenship. Another is that between citizenship rights as entitlements and as privileges.

The word 'citizen', usually accompanied by a defining word, is constantly being used. We speak of an American citizen, a European citizen, a world citizen, a good citizen, an active citizen, an ordinary citizen. We do not quite so frequently stop to think what we mean by such terms. We should. The reality of our legal, political and social lives, and the potential for their improvement depends on how near we can reach towards our ideal of citizenship. And it behoves each citizen to decide what that ideal should be.

FURTHER READING

Commission on Citizenship (1990) *Encouraging Citizenship* (London: HMSO).
Heater, D. (1990) *Citizenship: The Civic Ideal in World History, Politics and Education* (London: Longman).
Mouffe, C. (ed.) (1992) *Dimensions of Radical Democracy* (London: Verso).

REFERENCES

Andrews, G. (ed.) (1991) *Citizenship* (London: Lawrence & Wishart).

Aristotle (1948) *Politics* translated by E. Barker (Oxford: Clarendon).

Aristotle (1955) *The Ethics of Aristotle* translated by J. A. K. Thomson (Harmondsworth: Penguin).

Barbalet, J. M. (1988) *Citizenship: Rights, Struggle and Class Equality* (Milton Keynes: Open University Press).

Barker, E. (1956) *From Alexander to Constantine* (Oxford: Clarendon).

Bellah, R., Madsen, F., Sullivan, W. M., Swidler, A. and Tipton, S. M. (1985) *Habits of the Heart: Middle America Observed* (London: Hutchinson).

Benn, A. (1991) *Commonwealth of Britain Bill* (London: HMSO).

Beveridge, W. (1942) *Social Insurance and Allied Services* (London: HMSO).

Blackstone, W. (1803) *Commentaries on the Laws of England* Vol. 1.

Carvel, J. (1988) 'Restrain greed, Tories urged by Hurd' *The Guardian* 6 February.

Citizen's Britain: Liberal Democrat policies for a People's Charter (1991) (London: Liberal Democrats).

Citizen's Charter: Labour's better deal for consumers and citizens (1991) (London: Labour Party).

The Citizen's Charter: raising the standard Cm. 1599 (1991) (London: HMSO).

Cobban, A. (1964) *Rousseau and the Modern State* (London: Allen & Unwin).

Commission on Citizenship (1990) *Encouraging Citizenship* (London: HMSO).

Commission on Social Justice (1993) *The Justice Gap* (London: IPPR).

Condorcet, M. de (1982) *Une Education pour la démocratie* edited and translated by B. Baczko (Paris: Editions Garnier Frères).

Coote, A. (ed.) (1992) *The Welfare of Citizens* (London: IPPR/Rivers Oram Press).

213

Crick, B. and Porter, A. (eds) (1978) *Political Education and Political Literacy* (London: Longman).

DES (1985) *Education for All* (Swann Report) (London: HMSO).

Gardner, J. P. (1990) 'What lawyers mean by citizenship' in Commission on Citizenship (1990) *Encouraging Citizenship* (London: HMSO).

Giddens, A. (1985) *A Contemporary Critique of Historical Materialism* Vol. 2 (Cambridge: Polity Press).

The Guardian (1992a) 29 August.

The Guardian (1992b) 2 November.

Gutmann, A. (1987) *Democratic Education* (Princeton: Princeton University Press).

Heater, D. (1990) *Citizenship: The Civic Ideal in World History, Politics and Education* (London: Longman).

Hindess, B. (1987) *Freedom, Equality and the Market* (London: Tavistock Publications).

Howarth, A. (1992) 'Political education: a government view' in B. Jones and L. Robins (eds) *Two Decades in British Politics* (Manchester: Manchester University Press).

Hurd, D. (1988) 'Citizenship in the Tory Democracy' *New Statesman* 29 April.

Hurd, D. (1989) 'Freedom will flourish where citizens accept responsibility' *The Independent* 13 September.

Institute of Public Policy Research (1991) *The Constitution of the United Kingdom* (London: IPPR).

John, G. (n.d.) *Education for Citizenship* (London: Charter 88).

Macedo, S. (1990) *Liberal Virtues: Citizenship, Virtue and Community in Liberal Constitutionalism* (Oxford: Clarendon).

McGurk, H. (ed.) (1987) *What Next?* (London: ESRC).

Machiavelli, N. (1970) *Discourses* edited by B. Crick (Harmondsworth: Penguin).

Marland, M. (1991) 'Curriculum Counsel' *EG, The Guardian* 10 September.

Marquand, D. (1988) *The Unprincipled Society* (London: Cape).

Marshall, T. H. (1950) *Citizenship and Social Class and other Essays* (Cambridge: Cambridge University Press). Also reprinted in Marshall and Bottomore.

Marshall, T. H. (1981) *The Right to Welfare and Other Essays* (London: Heinemann).

Marshall, T. H. and Bottomore, T. (1992) *Citizenship and Social Class* (London: Pluto Press).

Merriam, C. E. (1931) *The Making of Citizens* edited by G. Z. F. Bereday in 1966 (Columbia University, New York: Teachers College Press).

Mill, J. S. (1910) *Representative Government* edited by H. B. Acton (London: Dent).

Ministry of Education (1949) *Citizens Growing Up* (London: HMSO).

Mouffe, C. (ed.) (1992) *Dimensions of Radical Democracy* (London: Verso).

Mundialist Summa (1977), *One World of Reason* (Paris: Club Humaniste).

National Curriculum Council (1990) *Curriculum Guidance 8: Education for Citizenship* (York: NCC).

Nelson, J. L. and Michaelis, J. V. (1980) *Secondary Social Studies* (Englewood Cliffs, NJ: Prentice Hall).

Oldfield, A. (1990) *Citizenship and Community: Civic Republicanism and the Modern World* (London: Routledge).

Oliver, D. (1991) *Government in the United Kingdom* (Milton Keynes: Open University Press).

Patten, J. (1988) 'Launching the Active Citizen' *The Guardian* 18 September.

Plato (1970) *Laws* translated by T. J. Saunders (Harmondsworth: Penguin).

Porter, A. E. (1993) 'Impoverished concepts of citizenship in the debate on the National Curriculum' in J. Gundara and A. Porter *Diversity, Citizenship and the National Curriculum Debate* (London: Institute of Education).

Reich, C. (1964) 'The New Property' *Yale Law Journal* vol. 73, p. 733.

Rousseau, J.-J. (1911) *Émile* translated by B. Foxley (London: Dent).

Rousseau, J.-J. (1968) *The Social Contract* translated and edited by M. Cranston (Harmondsworth: Penguin).

Slater, J. (1992) 'New curricula, new directions' in B. Jones and L. Robins (eds) *Two Decades in British Politics* (Manchester: Manchester University Press).

Smith, A. D. (1991) *National Identity* (Harmondsworth: Penguin).

Stevens, O. (1982) *Children Talking Politics* (Oxford: Martin Robertson).

Pollard, D. (1992) *The Unseen Treaty: Treaty on European Union, Maastricht 1992* (Oxford: David Pollard), p. 3.

Thompson, J. M. (ed.) (1948) *French Revolution Documents 1789–94* (Oxford: Blackwell), pp. 260–1.

Thucydides (1954) *The Peloponnesian War* translated by R. Warner (Harmondsworth: Penguin).

Turner, B. S. (1986) *Citizenship and Capitalism* (London: Allen & Unwin).

Wallace, W. (1992) 'British foreign policy after the Cold War' *International Affairs* vol. 68, no. 3, pp. 423–42.

INDEX

active citizenship, 1, 6, 11, 45, 48, 114, 116, 123–6, 129–31, 163
allegiance, 58–60, 63, 173
  see also national identity/loyalty
American War of Independence, 10, 15, 28, 208
Aristotle, 11, 12, 19, 28, 36, 114, 116–19, 152–3, 196
Association for Education in Citizenship, 150
Athens, 11, 12, 32
autonomy, 52, 63–9, 82, 90, 103, 106, 111, 176, 178, 197
  duties and, 170
  economic rights, 93
  education and, 107
  empowerment, 92
  environment, 92, 111–12
  health, 101
  medical treatment, 64–5, 67, 68, 102
  protection, 171, 177–9
  women, 64

Barbalet, J.M., 35
Bellah, R., 206–7
bias/indoctrination, 147, 153–5, 157, 160, 163

Bill of Rights, 39, 46, 50, 74, 76, 99, 178, 184–8, 203
British nationality, 4–5, 24, 55–8

capitalism, 20, 31–4, 37–9, 125, 195–7
Charter, 88, 39, 45–6
Chartists, 18, 81
children
  protection, 74
  rights, 64, 65, 66, 67, 68
Christianity, 24, 59, 118, 173
Church of England, 7, 59, 170, 173–5
Cicero, 13, 22
Citizen's Charters, 32, 46–51
  Conservative, 47–9, 104, 108, 109–10, 126
  Labour, 47, 49–50
  Liberal Democrat, 50
civic duties, 67, 69, 81–8, 97–8, 107
  see also police – duty to help; tax, duty to pay
civic republicanism, *see* classical tradition of citizenship/civic republicanism
civic virtue, *see* good citizenship/civic virtue

civil liberties, 75, 179–80
  see also civil rights
civil religion, 118–19, 127
civil rights, 1, 2, 4, 5, 7, 16, 20,
    33–4, 38, 48–61, 62, 68, 71,
    75, 76, 77, 135, 136, 170,
    175–6, 179–88, 190–1, 209
  see also free speech; European
    Convention on Human
    Rights
civil society, 3, 7, 59, 93, 179, 202
class, 20–1, 33–6, 150
classical tradition of citizenship/civic
    republicanism, 3, 5, 11–16,
    27–8, 32, 36, 61, 70, 74,
    80–1, 96, 101, 105, 109,
    114–20, 122, 126–31, 177–8,
    198–9
  economic rights, 93
  European Convention on Human
    Rights, 137
  political rights, 71, 77, 80
Cleveland school case, *see* education
communitarianism, 32, 37, 114–16,
    120, 122, 126, 128–30,
    195–6
community
  benefit to, 96–7, 115, 126, 156,
    206
  duties to, 67–8, 107, 130, 131
  participation in, 5, 94, 96, 124–5,
    130, 161, 178–9, 184
  representation and, 81
  sense of, 1, 2, 6, 7, 67, 107, 125,
    127, 165
Condorcet, Marquis de, 28
consumers, 49–51, 94, 105, 109–10,
    126, 138
Council of Europe, 133, 137
  see also European Convention on
    Human Rights
courts, access to, 77
  see also rule of law

definitions, problems of, 195–212
decentralization/devolution, 19, 50,
    127, 131

  see also subsidiarity
Dewey, J., 29
Dietz, M., 41–2
discrimination, 71, 72, 73, 77, 95,
    140, 179, 184
  see also women; ethnic minorities
dual citizenship, 10, 24–5
duties, 4, 11, 13–14, 25, 114–132,
    165, 198–9, 201, 209–10
  see also police – duty to help; tax,
    duty to pay

economic actors, citizens as, 5, 6,
    108, 138
economic rights, 4, 5, 31, 92, 170
  meanings, 36, 39, 93–4
  protection of, 50, 188–92
  rationales for, 39, 96–8
education, 20, 45, 48, 50, 78, 104,
    124
  Cleveland school case, 106–9
  empowerment, 92, 104
  rationales for, 106–8
  right to, 135
education curriculum
  human rights, 164
  law-related, 148–9, 158, 160, 162,
    166
  moral, 149–50, 156, 158
  multicultural, 147, 151, 159–62
  national identity/loyalty, 29, 148,
    156, 158–9
  personal and social, 149, 158, 167
  political, 147, 149, 159–61, 167
  world citizenship, 151–2, 158
education for citizenship, 3, 7, 8, 11,
    27–30, 45, 118, 127, 147–169,
    178, 179, 209
  arguments against, 147, 152–3
  arguments for, 147–9, 152–6, 168
  objectives/aims, 148, 150–1,
    156–7, 161, 165
elections, *see* vote
emancipation, 5, 52, 63–7, 74, 77,
    90, 177
empire, legacy of, 22–4, 35, 43,
    150–1, 160, 203
employees, 50, 64

employers, 63, 64
empowerment, 5, 19, 39, 92, 104–6
enablement, 95
enforcing citizen, 145, 178
English Civil War, 16, 28, 209
Enlightenment, 14, 15, 26
entitlements, 4, 38, 96, 138
entrenchment of rights, 76, 179–88
see also Bill of Rights
environmental rights, 5, 92, 110–12,
   170, 192–3, 204
ethnic minorities, 70, 74, 184
European citizenship, 6, 55, 108,
   133–46
   civil rights, 134–7
   diplomatic protection and, 134,
      142
   exclusivity, 134, 140, 143
   political rights, 133, 134–7
   right to petition the European
      Parliament, 134, 142
   right to vote, 72, 133
   see also European Community;
      European Convention on
      Human Rights
European Community, 6–7, 41, 55,
   203
   citizens as law enforcers, 144, 145
   citizenship of, 25, 132, 133–4,
      137–46, 199, 201
   civil and political rights, 133, 139,
      140
   constitution of, 137
   Council of Ministers, 133, 139, 140
   elections, 139, 142
   elections to the Parliament, 72
   European Commission, 133, 139,
      140
   European Parliament, 133, 134,
      139, 140
   four freedoms, 137–8
   Maastricht Treat, *see* Treaty of
      Union
   Ombudsman, 142
   Single European Act, 1978, 133,
      139, 144
   Social Charter, 49, 144
   social rights, 144, 202

Treaty of Rome, 137, 139
Treaty of Union, 27, 133, 134,
   137, 138, 140, 141, 201
European Convention on Human
   Rights, 2, 6, 133, 134–7,
   202, 203
   as a Bill of Rights for the United
      Kingdom, 186
   European Community, 141, 142
   free speech, 78–9, 135
   legal status, 134–6
European Court of Human Rights,
   135
   right of individual petition, 135
European Union, 55, 133–4, 137

feminism, 41–2
first generation rights, 5, 70, 71–81,
   98–9
France, 10, 22–3, 29
franchise, *see* vote
fraternity, 118, 128, 211
free speech, 70, 71, 74, 77–80, 135,
   175–6, 186–8
   public officials denied, 74, 79, 80
   public opinion, 78
   'Spycatcher' case, 80
   see also European Convention on
      Human Rights
freedom of association, 71, 77, 136,
   137
French Revolution, 10, 15, 17, 21,
   22, 23, 28, 32, 118, 208

good citizenship/civic virtue, 3, 5, 6,
   10–11, 13, 27–8, 32, 36, 64,
   70, 74, 82, 90, 97, 106,
   114–23, 156, 198–9, 209
   see also police – duty to help; tax,
      duty to pay
Greece, classical, 10–12, 24–8, 40,
   116, 129
Green, T.H., 15, 21

health services, 92, 95
   rights to, 100–4
Heater, D., 209–10

Hennessey, R.A.S., 160–1
'hidden curriculum', 157
human nature, theories of, 60, 64, 66
human rights, 195, 202, 204–5
Hurd, D., 124–6
husbands, 64

information, access to, 1, 46, 48, 49, 105, 136, 178
international law and citizenship, 5, 52–5, 203–4

liberal tradition of citizenship, 3, 4, 5, 6, 10, 16–19, 28, 36, 61, 63, 65, 70, 71, 74, 81, 82, 93, 105, 109, 114–15, 120–3, 126, 128–31, 195–6, 199
  European Convention on Human Rights, 137
  political rights, 71, 80
liberal civic virtue, 120–3
liberty, *see* civil rights

Maastricht, *see* European citizenship
Macedo, S., 120–3
Machiavelli, N., 13–14, 114, 117–20, 130
Marcus Aurelius, 26, 27
Marquand, D., 131
Marshall, T.H., 4, 20–1, 31–6, 40, 49–50, 61, 71, 93, 96, 138, 197, 209
Marx, K./Marxism, 20, 38, 42, 50
medical treatment, 95, 101–4
  doctors' duties, 103
  patients' rights, 103, 68
Merriam, C.E., 149
military service, 118–19, 127
Mill, J.S., 17
minorities, 4, 32, 40, 43–5, 70, 73, 74, 77
monarch, 7, 170, 173
  law-making powers, 60–1
  powers over subjects, 59
  sovereignty, 76
Montesquieu, Baron de, 14, 15

Mouffe, C., 199
multiple citizenship, 3, 6, 7, 24–7, 72, 112, 133, 137, 140, 199–203, 209
  see also European citizenship
Mundialist Summa, 205

National Curriculum (England and Wales), 148, 150, 157, 162–9
national identity/loyalty, 22–4, 29, 147–8, 156, 158–9, 195, 200, 202, 207, 209
nationality, 3, 4, 6, 7, 22–3, 52–8, 71, 134, 135, 197–9, 203, 209
  discrimination, 95, 140, 179
  rights in the UK, 94–5
nation-state, 7, 22, 112, 134, 140–4, 199
need, 96
Nelson, J., 156–7
'new citizenship', 195, 199, 202
New Right, 22, 35–7, 123
Nigeria, 24, 149, 200

Oldfield, A., 116, 127

Parekh, H.B., 145
parent, rights and duties, 63, 64, 65, 66, 105–9
passive citizenship, 18–19, 207–8
Pericles, 12
Plato, 28
police, 82, 83
  duty to help, 82–4
  duty to protect the peace, 82–3
political rights, 2, 4, 5, 7, 11–12, 16–17, 20, 22, 33–4, 36, 38, 49, 61, 68, 71, 75, 76, 135, 170, 175, 179–88, 190–1, 209
popular sovereignty, 7, 171–2
Porter, A.E., 209, 211
poverty, 40, 204
property
  and citizenship, 16, 19, 20, 31, 36–7, 93, 94

public opinion, 78

Renaissance Italy, 10, 13, 32
right of silence, 82, 83
Rome, classical, 10–14, 22, 24, 27, 118, 127
Rousseau, J.-J., 14, 15, 114, 117–20, 122, 127, 129
rule of law, 5, 61, 62, 71, 72, 75, 77, 88–90, 144, 185
  and duties of good citizenship, 70

second class citizenship, 12, 32, 40, 44, 162
second generation rights, 5, 70, 92, 93–104
  legal provision for, 98, 99–100
  resource implications of, 98–9
Skinner, Q., 130, 131
Slater, J., 160, 161, 167–8
Smith, A.D., 200
social citizenship, 3, 19–22, 61
social rights, 4, 20, 34, 37, 38, 61, 92, 104, 170, 188–92, 209
  meaning, 34, 93
  protection of, 48, 50, 188–92
  rationales for, 33, 96–8
sovereign, 5, 76, 171
  law-making powers, 72
  powers over subjects, 58–60
Sparta, 11, 13, 14, 118, 155
Speaker's Commission on Citizenship, 45, 164, 166–7
state's duties to citizens, 70, 88–90, 190–1
Stevens, O., 153
subjecthood, 5, 7, 52, 55, 58–63, 66, 101, 148, 170, 175, 197
  allegiance and, 58–9

subsidiarity, 127, 134, 140, 143
Swann Report (*Education for All*), 151, 162

tax, duty to pay, 36, 47, 84–9, 97
third generation rights, 5, 70, 92, 110–12
Turner, B., 38, 207–9

United Nations, 29, 195, 203–5
USA, 10, 22, 24–5, 29, 33, 127, 148, 149

vote, 16–18, 29, 36, 41, 43, 59–60, 70, 71–2, 76, 142, 150, 151, 177, 197
  proportional representation, 1
  Reform Acts, 17, 151
  value of, 81, 177
  women and, 72
  see also European Community – elections

welfare state, 4, 20–2, 31, 35, 37, 39, 48, 123, 202
wives, 64
women, 32, 40–1, 72–3
  courts' attitude, 73
  discrimination, 40, 70, 73, 140, 184
  excluded from citizenship, 11, 72
  law and, 73–4
  participation in public life, 42, 72–3
  voting rights, 17, 72–3
world citizenship, 10, 26, 29, 195, 199, 203–5
workers/working class, 20, 38, 94, 151